THE

AMERICAN CITIZEN:

HIS RIGHTS AND DUTIES,

ACCORDING TO THE SPIRIT

OF THE

CONSTITUTION OF THE UNITED STATES.

BY

JOHN HENRY HOPKINS, D. D., LL. D.

BISHOP OF THE PROTESTANT EPISCOPAL CHURCH IN THE DIOCESE OF VERMONT.

NEW YORK:

PUDNEY & RUSSELL, 79 JOHN-STREET.

1857.

R. C. VALENTINE,
Stereotyper and Electrotyper,
81, 83, and 85 Centre-street,
New York.

PUDNEY & RUSSELL,
Printers,
No. 79 John-street,
New York.

TABLE OF CONTENTS.

CHAPTER III.

CHAPTER IV.

CHAPTER V.

CHAPTER VI.

CHAPTER VII.

CHAPTER VIII.

CHAPTER IX.

CHAPTER X.

CHAPTER XI.

CHAPTER XII.

CHAPTER XIII.

CHAPTER XXI.

CHAPTER XXII.

CHAPTER XXIII.

CHAPTER XXIV.

CHAPTER XXV.

CHAPTER XXVI.

CHAPTER XXVII.

CHAPTER XXVIII.

CHAPTER XXIX.

CHAPTER XXX.

CHAPTER XXXI.

CHAPTER XXXII.

CHAPTER XXXIII.

INTRODUCTION.

When the subject of the following work was first proposed to me, the objection presented itself, as it has probably occurred already to the reader, that the design was not in harmony with my ministerial office, and that it could be far more acceptably and usefully accomplished by some other individual, whose name and talents were known and approved amongst the statesmen and politicians of the country. And doubtless, in the minds of many, there would be much force in the objection. For the most part, the servants of the sanctuary have little familiarity with the topics suggested by the title of the present volume. The kingdom to which they are mainly devoted is not of this world. The spiritual, rather than the secular interests of mankind, are the objects of their care. And hence, the popular impression of their incapacity to form a right judgment on temporal questions, seems to have a plausible argument in its favor.

But on further reflection, I was unable to discover any good reason for declining the task, on the ground of this supposed professional disqualification. For, although it may be true enough that the clergy, as a class, cannot be expected to give much time or thought to Constitutional, legal, and secular matters, yet it is certainly untrue that the Gospel excludes them from a full and just appreciation of the whole circle of social rights and duties. On the contrary, we know that the Scriptures deal largely with the principles of earthly government. The precepts of religion bear directly upon the obligations of man to man. The apostle Paul declares that "godliness is profitable unto all things, having promise of the life that now is, and of that which is to come."—(1 Tim., iv. 8.) Fairly considered, therefore, the profession of the ministry takes the broadest survey of human nature, contemplates our race in its widest variety of aspects, and ought to qualify the mind and the heart for the most thorough, comprehensive, and impartial examination of all the relations of society.

Being thus satisfied that there was no real propriety in declining the enterprise proposed, on the mere ground of professional objection, the only difficulty which remained was the personal doubt, whether I could hope to execute it acceptably. True, indeed, it was, that it might be better done by others. But this could hardly be admitted as a valid excuse, because it would operate equally against every human undertaking. All that I had a right to assume was the necessity of possessing a competent share of the knowledge, reflection, and experience which the work required. The first thirty years of life passed in the studies, business, and intercourse of the world—seven of those years given to the profession of the law—sixteen years devoted to the task of education—the training of a numerous family—abundant opportunities of intimacy, abroad and at home, with all the classes of society, and the whole united, from my youth up, with the constant love of books, and the peculiar tastes and habits of an author—all this seemed to warrant the hope that I might produce a work of some utility on the rights and duties of the American citizen, without any serious diminution of the labors due to the paramount service of the Gospel. At all events, I could not honestly deny that I ought to be tolerably qualified to make the effort, with a fair promise of success; and therefore I concluded that the attempt would not be justly liable to the charge of inconsistency or presumption.

With these views, I have undertaken to discuss the various

relations of the American citizen, under the general heads of religion, politics, business, the domestic relations, and social life. I have not entered into the peculiarities of any Church or sect, beyond the range suggested by the Constitution. Neither did I propose to examine the character of any party organization. My object was to consider those principles which ought to govern alike all who would be worthy and consistent members of our great Republic, according to the true spirit of our national charter; so as to show how perfectly the precepts of Christianity, the rules of law, the maxims of philosophy, and the dictates of sound common sense, accord in recommending the course which can alone secure the lasting honor, safety, and prosperity of the whole, in just connection with the highest welfare of each individual. In the discussion of those principles, I have freely set forth my own convictions on a variety of questions, under the full belief that they will often be found to conflict, very seriously, with the prevailing prejudices, habits, and notions of the day. But I have too much confidence in the good sense of my readers to doubt their attachment to that FREEDOM OF SPEECH, which is the Constitutional right of every American citizen; and I am quite sure that, if this freedom can be exercised in any case without offence, it ought to be, when it is used by an old man who loves his country, both North and South, who represents no party, and who has as little to fear from popular censure, as he has to hope from popular applause. Such, then, is the general plan on which these pages have been written. The theme is sufficiently extensive, and would be worthy of far higher powers than mine. Yet I may, at least, aver that nothing has been set forth which I have not examined with care and attention, and with perhaps as large a measure of impartiality and candor, as can be expected from human infirmity. With what measure of acceptance, or success my design has been accomplished, my readers must determine for themselves.

PREAMBLE.

It cannot be disputed, by any thoughtful mind, that the title of an American citizen involves many rights and duties of high privilege and responsibility, well worthy of a serious examination. In several particulars of rare and peculiar interest, the history of our independence and the formation of our government are without a parallel in the annals of the world. The beneficial influence which our country is likely to exert throughout the globe, if we be true to our principles, is beyond the power of calculation. And our failure, on the other hand, would cast a dark shade over the hopes of human progress, which the work of centuries might be unable to dispel.

Before I present, however, to the kind attention of my readers, the series of topics which seem to me worthy of careful consideration on the part of every intelligent citizen, it seems necessary to premise a statement of those special points, in which our noble charter of liberty—the Constitution of the United States—stands alone among the nations.

1. In the primary rank of its peculiarities, we find the striking anomaly which unites us as *one people*, notwithstanding the recognition of sovereign power in each separate State. And it is this, which foreign statesmen have found it so hard to comprehend, although to us, it is so familiar. It is this which provides so admirably for all the wants of local administration, while it

is a wholesome check upon the possible encroachments of the central power. It is this which gives scope for an indefinite enlargement of our vast Republic, since every new addition possesses its own Governor, its own Legislature, and its own guardians of social order; while all are in subordination to the supreme Constitution which controls the whole. It is this which secures the right of the people everywhere, to elect their own immediate rulers, and yet effectually guards against the danger that any one State, however rich and able, should usurp authority over another. In a word, it is this which constitutes the most distinctive element of our national greatness and security.

The idea was suggested, doubtless, by the peculiar condition of affairs, when the patriots of the Revolution met together, in solemn and anxious conclave, to consolidate the weak and uncertain confederacy of thirteen independent States, into one great nation. But it was a sublime political discovery, new to the experience, and inspiring to the hopes of men. And if those patriots had effected nothing else, this alone would justly entitle them to the grateful homage of the world.

2. The second great peculiarity of our American Constitution presents itself in the words of the preamble: "We THE PEOPLE of the United States, in order to form a more perfect union, establish justice, insure domestic tranquillity, provide for the common defence, promote the general welfare, and secure the blessings of liberty to ourselves and our posterity, do ordain and establish this Constitution for the United States of America."

Here we have the only example in the history of mankind, of a truly social compact, adopted by the act of the *whole people.* And in the 6th Article, the controlling supremacy of the instrument is distinctly set forth, in this conclusive form:

"This Constitution, and the laws of the United States which shall be made in pursuance thereof; and all treaties made or which shall be made, under the authority of the United States, shall be THE SUPREME LAW OF THE LAND, and the judges in every State shall be bound thereby, anything in the Constitution or laws of any State to the contrary notwithstanding."

Now, it is manifest that the *supreme law of the land* can only be established by the sovereign power. And as the Constitution was so established by the *people* of the United States, it results, of necessity, that the *sovereign power* is here declared to be *the people.* Every citizen, therefore, being one of the people, has his share of the sovereign power. And every officer holds his authority, directly or indirectly, by the will of the people, under the Constitution. This is the great guaranty of our universal suffrage, by which alone the will of the people can be properly ascertained. And it confers a dignity and value on the title of an American citizen, which make it worthy of all high and honorable estimation.

3. The third peculiarity which I would here notice, meets the eye in the 9th Section of the 1st Article, where we read that "No title of nobility shall be granted by the United States." And this follows naturally from the preceding principle. For there can be no title of nobility higher than the sovereign power. But the people are themselves the sovereign power. And each citizen is, in his own right, a sharer in the sovereignty. Hence, there can be no title above the citizen, and any other badge of nobility, conferred by the authority of the people, would therefore involve a manifest incongruity. This provision, however, does not forbid those words of special reverence which our forefathers imported from Europe, and which were in general use before the Constitution was established. For these are terms of office, and not titles of *nobility.* It is not anti-republican to give the epithet of *Excellency* to the President or Governor, whom the people have elected, as the more excellent, to occupy those exalted stations. Neither is it anti-republican to call him *Honorable,* whom the people have honored by putting him into the office of Judge or Legislator. But titles of *nobility,* on the contrary, are personal privileges of superior rank, which have no respect to the choice of the citizens, no necessary connection with the official duty of public service, and no regard to the equal rights of the community. And hence, the Constitution

wisely prohibits them, as inconsistent with its fundamental principle.

4. Having thus shown that the people hold the sovereign power by the express terms of our national charter, and that each citizen possesses an indefeasible right and share in its administration, the way is prepared for the fundamental question of the opening chapter.

THE AMERICAN CITIZEN:

HIS RIGHTS AND DUTIES.

CHAPTER I.

ON THE CONSTITUTIONAL REQUIREMENT OF RELIGION.

THE high dignity and vast importance of religion give it, most justly, the leading place in a work devoted to the rights and duties of the American citizen. For our nation claims a lofty rank amongst the nations of Christendom. Our people are universally acknowledged as a Christian people. And yet, the absence of any distinct averment on the subject, in the Constitution of the United States, has made it a matter of doubt, with many, whether, *in our national character*, we stand pledged to Christianity, by any legal obligations. This, therefore, presents the first inquiry, to which I would invite the reader's attention.

In the discussion of this very serious question, I hold it to be of no importance whether we find our answer in the terms of direct positive enactment, or only in the equivalent form of necessary implication. For it cannot be reasonably denied, that whatever the mode may be in which the will of the people is plainly declared by our great national charter, it is equally imperative. I shall now proceed to prove that religion is absolutely required; inasmuch as the Constitution demands an act from every officer which cannot be lawfully performed without religion, namely, the taking of a solemn oath or affirmation.

For thus we read in the first section of the second article, that "the President, before he enter on the execution of his office, shall take the following oath (or affirmation): I do solemnly swear (or affirm) that I will faithfully execute the office of president of the United States, and will, to the best of my ability, preserve, protect, and defend the Constitution of the United States."

And again, in the sixth article: "The senators and representatives" (of Congress) "and the members of the several State legislatures, and all executive and judicial officers, both of the United States and of the several States, shall be bound by oath or affirmation to support this Constitution."

In order to understand aright the only true meaning of these provisions, we must inquire, 1st, What is an oath, in its established legal acceptation; and, 2d, What is the kind of oath which our Constitution thus requires of every officer.

1. The first of these questions cannot be better answered than by citing the language of the highest judicial standard: "An oath is an affirmation or denial, before one or more persons who have authority to administer the same, CALLING GOD TO WITNESS that the testimony is true: therefore it is termed *sacramentum*, a holy band or tie."* Hence it is undeniable that the oath of office is an act which rests on religion for its whole force and validity. And the necessary result is, that when the Constitution demands this oath, it demands religion; since a lawful oath without religious faith is a mere mockery, repudiated by every rule of justice, whether human or divine.

---

* 3 Instit. 165.

It is for this reason that no court of law will admit as a witness any man who acknowledges himself to be an atheist, or who does not believe in a future state of reward and punishment. For the oath is the religious guardian of truth, and no testimony is allowed without this solemn appeal to the Almighty. And hence we find that there can be no office undertaken, and no justice administered, under the Constitution of the United States, without the implied profession of religious faith. The man who takes this solemn oath, while in his heart he regards it only as a senseless form, commits a fraud upon the supreme law of the land, and cheats the nation. And no act of hypocrisy and deceit can be more atrocious than this, because it destroys the very root of public authority and order, and virtually nullifies the fundamental principle of all official administration.

2. The second question, however, is more open to a variety of sentiment, namely, What kind of oath is intended by the Constitution? There are very few men who will dare to patronize absolute atheism, because it shocks the universal feeling of the community. But there are many ready to acknowledge their belief in God, and in a future state of rewards and punishments, who are far enough from professing any form of Christianity. This inquiry, therefore, is indispensable to every mind which seeks to form a true construction of our supreme constitutional platform.

In answering this all-important question, I should say, without hesitation, that the oath intended by the Constitution is a CHRISTIAN OATH. The God to whom it appeals is the only living and true God—the God of the Bible. I hold this to be the plain and necessary construction, by every rule of consistency, of common sense, and of sound legal interpretation.

First, then, we must remember that the Constitution was adopted by the people of the United States, in A. D. 1789, after it was prepared by a convention, consisting of thirty-eight delegates from twelve States, under the immortal Washington, the presiding officer of the body. It may be well to specify their names, for the reader's satisfaction:

GEORGE WASHINGTON, President and deputy from Virginia.

New Hampshire..John Langdon, Nicholas Gilman.

Massachusetts....Nathaniel Gorham, Rufus King.

Connecticut......Wm. Saml. Johnson, Roger Sherman.

New York......Alexander Hamilton.

New Jersey.....Wm. Livingston, Wm. Patterson, David Brearley, Jonathan Dayton.

Pennsylvania....Benj. Franklin, Robert Morris, Thos. Fitzsimons, James Wilson, Thomas Mifflin, Geo. Clymer, Jared Ingersoll, Gouv. Morris.

Delaware.......Geo. Read, John Dickinson, Jaco. Broom, Gunning Bedford, Jr., Richard Bassett.

Maryland.......James McHenry, Danl. Carroll, Dan. of St. Thos. Jenifer.

Virginia........John Blair, James Madison, Jr.

North Carolina..Wm. Blount, Hu. Williamson, Richd. Dobbs Spaight.

South Carolina...J. Rutledge, Charles Pinckney, Charles Cotesworth Pinckney, Pierce Butler.

Georgia........William Few, Abr. Baldwin.

Of these eminent men, we do not know of one who has ever been named as indifferent to Christianity; and it is impossible to suppose that they designed to expose it to discredit in the eyes of the nation at large. Washington himself, Rufus King, Alexander Hamilton, and James Madison, were avowed adherents of the Episcopal Church. Charles Cotesworth Pinckney was president of the Bible Society in Charleston for fifteen years in succession. But we have the best evidence of their Christian feeling in the well-known fact, that at the first assembling of the convention in 1787, when the spirit of dissension threatened to run high, Benjamin Franklin proposed the introduction of prayer, as the only mode of securing the Divine guidance and blessing on their discussions. The motion was adopted unanimously. The Rev. Dr. Duché, an Episcopal minister of Philadelphia, was invited to attend; and that service of Christian prayer, which has since been so well depicted by the pencil of an American artist, produced the happiest effect on the subsequent proceedings, until they finally closed in the adoption of the Constitution.

Now, here is the surest test of the reverence which these admirable men cherished for the Christian religion. Franklin himself, who was the mover of the resolution, made no open profession by uniting in communion with any religious society; but he was educated by parents of the strictest piety, and knew the benefits of Christian devotion. Many other members were doubtless like himself—believers in the truth of the Gospel, but withheld by scruples of conscience, as not sufficiently strict in their personal consistency, from a complete conformity with its claims. Yet they must be supposed to have been Christians in conviction at least; since, otherwise, their unanimous adoption of public Christian prayer, and the excellent effects which followed it, would be entirely unaccountable.

I ask, then, whether it is consistent with their official course to believe, that when they made a solemn oath or affirmation essential to the holding of every office under the government of the whole United States, they could have intended such oath to be any other than a Christian obligation? Did they mean that an infidel, or a deistical philosopher, or a naturalized Turk, or a pagan, might be admitted to the administration of the laws and government of the country, for whose liberty they had labored so nobly and so long? On the contrary, must we not suppose that they designed this very oath of office as a guard upon the religious faith of every public functionary, so that no man should ever be elevated to honor in the land, who did not accord with themselves, in reverence for the Gospel?

But this was only the preparatory work of the convention. It became the constitution by the act of *the people*, who exercised the sovereign power. And what were the people in the year 1789? I answer that they were a Christian people, in whose eyes the oath of office could only have been regarded as a Christian oath, since no other would have been accordant with their principles, their feelings, or their accustomed modes of action. This was the oath which they had constantly seen administered in all their courts of justice. They knew nothing of heathen, infidel, or Turkish forms of appeal to the Deity; and, therefore, in their minds, the oath of office could not have had any other meaning than that with which they had always been familiar.

I ask then, again, whether it accords with common sense to suppose that *the people of the United States* could have intended this oath to bear a different sense from its Christian acceptation? Is it reasonable to believe that they even contemplated the possibility of having Jews, Turks, pagans, or infidels invested with the future government of their country? Yet there was nothing in the Constitution to prevent it, but this very oath of office. And if there could have been any doubt in the minds of Christian men that this was a sufficient protection to the Gospel faith, can it be questioned for a moment that there would have been an indignant opposition raised against the proposed scheme of national union, from one end of the land to the other?

For it should be remembered that this great measure was adopted at a time of strong and universal excitement, soon after the terrible struggle of the Revolutionary war, in which the clergy had borne an active part, by public as well as private exhortation. Even if the people had not been roused to the keenest examination of the plan proposed, their ministers would have taken immediate alarm at the form of a constitution which threatened them with a government of infidelity. What could have quieted their fears, unless they trusted to the oath of office for protection? What could have prevented their loud and earnest remonstrance, but the confidence which they felt in the Christian force of that solemn obligation? Hence, in the very fact that the people adopted the Constitution, with the acquiescence of the clergy, at a period when their voice was listened to with far more respect than now, we have another demonstration obvious to common sense, in favor of its accepted meaning.

Such being the only character of this official oath which can be justified by ordinary reason and consistency, I proceed, in the third place, to consider the accordance of the result with the rules of legal interpretation. And these I shall set forth from the standard authority of Blackstone's Commentaries.

"The fairest and most rational method," saith this learned Judge, "to interpret the will of the legislator is by exploring his *intentions* at the time when the law was made, by *signs* the most natural and probable. And these signs are either the words, the context, the subject-matter, the effects and consequences, or the spirit and reason of the law.

1. "Words are generally to be understood in their usual and most known signification, not so much regard-

ing the propriety of grammar, as their general and popular use.

2. "If words happen to be still dubious, we may establish their meaning from the context—thus the proëme, or preamble, is often called in to help the construction of an Act of Parliament. Of the same nature and use is the comparison of the law with other laws, that are made by the same legislator, that have some affinity with the subject, or that expressly relate to the same point.

3. "As to the *subject-matter*, words are always to be understood as having a regard thereto, for that is always supposed to be in the eye of the legislator, and all his expressions directed to that end.

4. "As to the *effects and consequence*, the rule is, that where words bear either none, or a very absurd signification, if literally understood, we must a little deviate from the received sense of them.

5. "But lastly, the most universal and effectual way of discovering the true meaning of a law, when the words are dubious, is by considering the *reason and spirit* of it; or the cause which moved the legislator to enact it."*

Now let these rules be applied to the question, and I think the result will be perfectly satisfactory.

1. The first rule directs us to understand the words of the law *in their usual and most known signification, not so much regarding the propriety of grammar, as their general and popular use.*

This is precisely what I have done, by appealing to the well-known sense in which an official oath must have been understood by a Christian people. In propriety of *gram-*

* Commentaries, B. I. p. 59, 60.

mar, the term Oath might be taken in a heathen sense, or in a Jewish sense, or in a Turkish sense, or in a deistical infidel's sense, because all of these are in use by certain classes of men and people. Oaths have been in existence amongst all nations from the earliest antiquity, and employed for the same purpose, namely, to be a guard upon the conscience in the service of fidelity and truth. But the *usual and most known signification*—the *general and popular use among the people of the United States who adopted the Constitution*, must be our rule, according to the learned commentator. And what these were, is too plain for dispute or prevarication.

2. His second rule, when words are dubious, is to *consult the context*, and he particularly specifies *the preamble*. Now the preamble to the Constitution is in these words:

"We, the people of the United States, in order to form a more perfect union, establish justice, insure domestic tranquillity, provide for the common defence, promote the general welfare, and secure the blessings of liberty to ourselves and our posterity, do ordain and establish this Constitution." Could the people, who knew and acknowledged no other religion but the Gospel, have intended to attain those objects without a Christian government? Could they have promised these blessings to themselves and their posterity, without the favor of the only living and true God? And with a full knowledge of the awful calamities which befell the ancient Israelites, in consequence of the impiety of their rulers, could they have been willing to expose the nation to the divine malediction, by the total absence of any protection against infidel presidents, and infidel governors, and infidel legislators? Such a supposition is absurd. And therefore, as the oath of office is the only guard provided in the Constitution, it results from the very objects which they had in view, that this oath must receive a Christian interpretation.

But there is an important part of this second rule which aids not a little to strengthen my argument. For the learned commentator directs us to consult the other laws "which have affinity with the subject, or that expressly relate to the same point." And here we have the 6th and 7th Articles of the Amendments to the Constitution, providing that "the right of *trial by jury* shall be preserved, and no fact tried by a jury shall be otherwise re-examined in any court of the United States, than *according to the rules of the common law*."

These provisions, of themselves, establish the Christian character of the Constitution, and of the oath of office, because the *common law* was the birthright which the colonies brought with them from England, and in all its oaths, principles, and sanctions, it is inseparably connected with the Christian faith.

Thus Blackstone saith: "Blasphemy against the Almighty, by denying his being or providence, or by contumelious reproaches of our Saviour Christ, as well as all profane scoffing at the holy Scripture, or exposing it to contempt and ridicule, are offences *punishable at common law* by fine and imprisonment, or other infamous corporal punishment; for CHRISTIANITY IS PART OF THE LAWS OF ENGLAND."*

And again, the same standard authority lays down the following principle: "Doubtless the preservation of Christianity as a national religion is, abstracted from its own intrinsic truth, of the utmost consequence to the civil state.

---

* Commentaries, B. IV. p. 59.

The belief of a future state of rewards and punishments, the entertaining just ideas of the moral attributes of the Supreme Being, and a firm persuasion that he superintends and will finally compensate every action in human life (all which are clearly revealed in the doctrines, and forcibly inculcated by the precepts of our Saviour Christ), these are the *grand foundations of all judicial oaths;* which call God to witness the truth of those facts which perhaps may be only known to him and the party attesting. All moral evidence, therefore, all confidence in human veracity, must be *weakened by apostasy, and overthrown by total infidelity.* Wherefore all affronts to Christianity, or endeavors to depreciate its efficacy in those who have once professed it, are highly deserving of censure."*

The crime of apostasy was formerly punished by death, in England, and the writ *de hæretico comburendo* was "thought by some," saith Blackstone, "to be as ancient as the common law itself."† But this severity was done away by the Reformation, and the nation was afterwards afflicted by a great irruption of licentiousness in the time of Charles II. The account of this, given by the learned commentator, is instructive and valuable. "About the close of the 17th century," saith he, "the civil liberties to which we were then restored being used as a cloak of maliciousness, and the most horrid doctrines, subversive of all religion, being publicly avowed, both in discourse and writings, it was thought necessary again for the civil power to interpose, by not admitting those miscreants to the privileges of society, who maintained such principles as destroyed all moral obligation. To this end, it was enacted by statutes 9

* Commentaries, B. IV. p. 43. † Ib. p. 46.

and 10, W. III., c. 32, that "if any person educated in, or having made profession of, the Christian religion, shall, by writing, printing, teaching, or advised speaking, deny the Christian religion to be true, or the holy Scriptures to be of divine authority, he shall, upon the first offence, *be rendered incapable to hold any office or place of trust;* and, for the second, be rendered incapable of bringing any action, being guardian, executor, legatee, or purchaser of lands, and shall suffer three years' imprisonment without bail. To give room, however, for repentance, if, within four months after the first conviction, the delinquent will, in open court, publicly renounce his error, he is discharged for that once from all disabilities."*

This salutary statute was adopted in principle by many of the colonial legislatures, and became the general guide of public sentiment throughout the whole; thus affording another strong legal ground for the fact which I have asserted, viz., that the people of the United States, at the time when they adopted our great American Constitution, could never have intended infidels to occupy any public office, and therefore must have understood the oath which they required, according to its established and customary sense, as importing a belief in Christianity.

But to recur to the common law, which is distinctly recognized in the Amendments to the Constitution, I claim it, under the second rule of legal construction, as perfectly conclusive upon the character of the oath of office, because there can be no such thing, in legal interpretation, as the separation of our common law from the Christian religion. It was under Christianity that this law assumed its English

* Commentaries, B. IV. p. 44.

form. The very name of *jury* (*juratores*) is derived from the oath, as they swear to give a true verdict, and this oath, by which they are qualified, has never been, and can never be, dissociated from the sense of Christian obligation. So true is this, that a conviction for blasphemy or a sentence of excommunication, would be, at common law, a fatal objection to a juror; and on challenge, *propter delictum*, in legal parlance, he must be set aside.* Indeed the very idea of a jury of Turks, Jews, or infidels, would be regarded, in law, as a pure absurdity. Thus, the oath demanded by one part of our Constitution as an essential qualification for every office in the United States, is virtually defined by the *common law and trial by jury*, which are demanded in the other. For it is not possible to find any reason why the character of that solemn appeal should bear a different interpretation, in the several clauses of the same instrument.

3. I pass on, accordingly, to the 3d rule of construction, which is, that words are always to be understood as having a regard to the *subject-matter*, for *that is always supposed to be in the eye of the legislator, and all his impressions directed to that end.*

This is precisely the ground which I have taken. The *subject-matter* of the oath of office can only be understood as a *qualification* for office, since, if it be not this, it is manifestly good for nothing. But I have just shown, on the authority of Blackstone, that a belief in the essential truths of Christianity is the *grand foundation of all judicial oaths*, and that *all moral evidence, and all confidence in human veracity, must be weakened by apostasy, and overthrown by total infidelity.* Hence, when the foundation of Christian

* Co. Lit. 158, B.

belief is taken away, the oath is stripped of all validity in the eye of the English common law, from which we have derived our own. The intended qualification for official character becomes an idle form, and the whole *subject-matter* of this Constitutional requirement is perfectly annihilated.

4. And this brings me to the 4th rule of construction, which is equally applicable to my conclusion, namely, the *effects and consequence*—a rule of so much importance that *when the words of a law, literally understood, bear either none, or a very absurd signification, we must a little deviate from the received sense of them.*

Happily, in the present case, there is no such difficulty, because the word Oath, in its proper legal sense, and in its established popular meaning, bears the right interpretation. But the practical abuse of our political liberty, on account of which I have considered it necessary to treat the subject so much at large, has debauched the public mind to a fearful extent in our day. And therefore I proceed to show that this 4th rule is worthy of an important place in the argument.

What then would be the *effects and consequence* of the construction for which I contend? Simply these: that no man could take the oath of office in its true Constitutional sense, unless he were a believer in the essential truths of the Christian religion, as revealed in the Holy Scriptures, and thus all infidels would be excluded, in accordance with the statute of William III., not from their social intercourse, not from the free exercise of their business or profession, not from the unmolested indulgence of their individual opinions, but from those high and public functions which invest men with authority and influence, and render their principles and conduct practically operative, to a wide extent, on the whole character and destiny of the nation.

What, on the other hand, are the probable *effects and consequence* of the opposite construction? That the popular mind will learn, more and more, to discard the religious basis of oaths, and of all other moral obligations—that the most solemn appeal to the only living and true God will be considered as a mere form, signifying nothing—that the favor of the Almighty towards these United States will be exploded, as being no real element of national prosperity or success—that every thing will be held to depend on human talents and human energy, without regard to religious truth or conscience—that public honor and respect will be considered as having no connection with individual private character—that the most abandoned profligate will often be preferred as the best and worthiest representative and legislator—that the highest temporal good will be confidently expected from an evil instrumentality—that the man who chooses a reckless and unprincipled course for himself, will be thought as likely as any other to pursue a pure and patriotic career for his country—that, in fine, the Constitution will be regarded as if it were constructed for the express accommodation of the infidel—as if the voice of the people were the only voice of God, and he who could secure this, in the awards of the present life, need give himself no concern about the judgment of eternity.

Surely the *effects and consequences* of these opposite constructions give vast importance to the right decision of the question. No reflecting mind can doubt that the exaltation of men to offices of public honor and profit, who are known to be irreligious and profane, must work increasing evil to the faith and morals of the nation. While, on the contrary, a just respect to the truth and majesty of God, exacted, by general consent, from every candidate for popular distinction, must tend most powerfully to guard and preserve the best and highest principles of real patriotism, and elevate our noble republic more and more, by the divine favor, in the esteem and confidence of the whole civilized world.

The 5th and last rule of the learned commentator, which he calls "the most universal and effectual way of discovering the meaning of the law," is "to consider the *reason and spirit* of it, or the *cause* which moved the legislator to enact it." And this I hold to be perfectly conclusive on the point. For the *reason and spirit* of a law demanding an official oath, can only be found in the obligation which it is believed to impose on the *religious conscience* of the officer who takes that solemn form upon his lips. And it is impossible to assign any *cause which moved* the convention who prepared, or the people who adopted the Constitution, in requiring such an oath, except the *determination* to *exclude* from public office every man utterly destitute of Christian principle.

I have thus gone over the whole of the tests to which this grave and important question should be subjected, because I am perfectly aware that my conclusions are likely to meet with little favor, in the reckless liberality of the present day. Yet I may safely challenge a refutation of the argument, on any ground of law or reason. And I pass on to some other aspects of the subject, with a consoling reliance on the familiar maxim, that "truth is mighty, and will prevail." Perhaps not now—perhaps not soon—but certainly hereafter.

CHAPTER II.

THE OBJECTIONS TO THE CHRISTIAN CONSTRUCTION.

Fully persuaded, in my own mind, that the religious aspect of the oath of office is of the highest value to the character and the best interests of our beloved country, and desirous to have the argument in its favor perfectly understood, I shall devote the present chapter to a candid examination of the reasons usually assigned in support of the contrary notion; which is doubtless the popular one, and therefore the more dangerous, as it is the more difficult to overcome.

The most plausible argument on the side of the prevailing opinion, is derived from the 3d Section of the 6th Article of the Constitution, where it is provided that "no religious test shall ever be required as a qualification to any office or public trust under the United States." In addition to which, the 1st Article of the Amendments expressly directs that "Congress shall make no law respecting an establishment of religion, or prohibiting the free exercise thereof." These enactments are apt to be misunderstood by the ordinary reader, as quite conclusive against the Christian character of the oath of office. Let us consider their true import, under the acknowledged rule of legal interpretation, that every clause must be so explained as to harmonize with the rest, in order that the whole may stand together.

To this end, we have only to ascertain the real meaning of the phrase, "religious *test*." And that, as every lawyer knows, must be settled by a reference to the familiar history and current phraseology of the mother country. Now England had then, as she still has, a Church establishment. She had also a variety of laws, commonly called *test*-laws, by which every man was excluded from holding office who could not conform his religious opinions to the standard fixed by the authority of Parliament. Those test-laws were, of course, exceedingly obnoxious to all, except the members of the established Church; since, under their provisions, not only the Roman Catholic dissenters, but the numerous Protestant sects, were effectually debarred from every civil office in the public service. Thus, they were tolerated *religiously*, while they were not tolerated *politically;* and the disadvantages of their position doubtless operated powerfully in drawing them away to the colonies of America, where perfect toleration and equality, both religious and political, were secured to them. Hence, when those colonies had succeeded in casting off their former allegiance, and the new republic was about to adopt the grand constitutional principles of rational liberty, which were to define its future character among the nations of the earth, it was justly regarded as an essential point that there should be no infringement of the rights of conscience, no test-laws to confine the honors of public office to any privileged religious class, no Church establishment to claim superiority over the other Christian societies, and no restriction to discourage the free exercise of every known and admitted variety of the Gospel system.

That such is the historical, natural, and legal sense of the clauses in question must be obvious, on reflection, to every candid reasoner. And, therefore, the attempt to construe them so as to tolerate infidelity, seems to me exceedingly wild and preposterous. The Constitution does not say that no religious *faith* should be required, but that no religious *test* should be required, which, when we remember the well-known *test-laws* of England, conveys a totally different meaning. If we abandon this construction, we fall at once into the most absurd inconsistency; for the Constitution demands the official oath, and the oath of jury trial according to the common law. And I have already proved that these oaths are *religious obligations*, involving, of necessity, amongst professed Christians, a certain amount of *Christian faith*. But it is impossible to suppose that the Constitution would require the oath, and yet prohibit the requisition of the religious faith which gives that oath its whole validity. An official or judicial oath, without religion, is a contradiction in terms. And no American citizen can be justified in fixing such a mockery as this, upon the Constitution of his country.

The obvious design of these provisions, therefore, was to guard the Christian rights and liberties which were then enjoyed, from all future danger. The Congregationalists, the Dutch Reformed, the Scotch and English Presbyterians, the German Lutherans, the Friends or Quakers, the Baptists, the Methodists, the Roman Catholics, the Episcopalians—all had an equal interest in the public offices of the government—all professed some mode of the same Christian faith—all were alike anxious to be protected from invasion, and, since none amongst them could pretend to any legalized supremacy above the rest, all were determined to guard their own rights against the possibility of encroachment. With this view, they wisely provided against the attempt, by making it a part of the Constitution that there should be no religious *test* required as a qualification for office, in order that all the various denominations should have free and equal access to the honors of the republic. With this same view, they forbade Congress to pass any law for the establishment of religion, or to prohibit the free exercise thereof, because it was their object to protect Christianity, as it was recognized in their own day, on the fair and equitable ground of enlightened toleration. On this construction, every clause of the Constitution is right, harmonious, and consistent. But if we suppose, on the contrary, that they united to patronize infidelity, to nullify the very oath which they were so careful to require, and to give the same political confidence to those who vilified, as to those who reverenced the common religion of the land, we involve at once the Convention by whom that solemn compact was prepared, and the people by whose vote it was adopted, in an act either of thoughtless absurdity, or of deliberate profanation.

The only remaining argument in favor of the infidel hypothesis rests upon a set of popular fallacies, which may be fairly stated as follows. It is said that the officers and rulers of the nation are required to discharge secular functions, with which religion has nothing to do; that, in fact, the least religious men are often the best qualified, by their superior energy and talents, to perform their allotted duties; that the great leaders amongst our revolutionary patriots were not professors of Christianity in any form; that some of our most successful presidents were even known to entertain infidel sentiments; that the only effect of a rule which should require a religious profession in our public officers, even if it were possible to adopt it, would be to make them hypocrites; and, finally, that such a rule, in the liberal and enlightened temper of our day, is absurd and ridiculous, because it is perfectly impracticable.

Here, assuredly, is a very plausible arrangement of objections, to which candor and reason require me to reply. Let me invoke the same candor and reason on the part of my readers, that they may form a just and fair conclusion.

1. The first branch of the argument consists in the assumption that religion has nothing to do with the discharge of secular offices, and that, in fact, the least religious men are often the best qualified, by their superior energy and talents, to fill them acceptably.

To this I reply, that the successful discharge of every office demands a principle of far higher efficacy than mere human learning, energy, or talent can bestow, namely, the conscientious devotion to our duty, as in the sight of an almighty and unerring Judge, who will not fail to bring us before His supreme tribunal. Let the public functionary be endowed with all the energy and talent in the world, but destitute of a religious conscience, and what security can we have against the claims of his personal interest, his covetousness, his ambition, his neglect, his love of licentious indulgence, and the pestiferous influence of his example? It may be supposed that his pride of character, and his regard for popular opinion, will furnish motives strong enough to keep him in the track of official propriety; but all experience proves that these are weak restraints in the hour of temptation. The chosen servant of the public must have *conscience*, or he is not worthy of our confidence. And it is impossible to have this conscience, without a religious sense of accountability to God. The official oath is required of all our functionaries for that very reason, because it binds the conscience by the religious principle. In demanding this, as the necessary qualification for every office in the United States, there is no risk incurred on the score of energy or talent, because Christians can always be found who have more than enough of these for the public service, and no man can deny the proposition who has the slightest acquaintance with the facts of history.

2. The second head of this objection presents the statement, that the great leaders amongst our revolutionary patriots were not professors of Christianity *in any form*, and that some of our most successful presidents were even known to entertain infidel sentiments. And this is an assertion which is apt to have so much practical influence with the common mind—although, in strictness, it is entirely irrelevant—that I must ask the reader's patient attention to the answer.

I admit, with sorrow, that the great leaders amongst our revolutionary patriots were not professors of Christianity in the *full and complete form* which was required by a just sense of religious duty. But I utterly deny that they were not professors of it *in any form at all*. On the contrary, I assert that they were its friends, its adherents, and its supporters in their public acts, and that there was not one amongst them who could have been induced to ignore its sacred claims, by any distinct and open manifestation. That their public declarations and their private course were not in all respects consistent, must be granted. That the lack of this consistency has deprived their example of a vast amount of moral influence, which they would otherwise have been enabled to secure, must be granted likewise. But, however, as a Christian man and a true lover of my country, I am obliged to lament the fact—however I may be compelled to ascribe to this fact a large share of the official degeneracy which is so generally complained of at the present day—yet, in justice to those distinguished men, I must set forth some unquestionable proofs that the greatest of the class were Christians in belief—Christians in *conscience*—who would have resisted, with all their power, the official claims of infidelity.

To begin, then, with the eminent Washington. His inaugural address, delivered April 30, 1789, contains the following passage, which bears an affecting testimony of his strong desire to do honor to religion:

"It would be peculiarly improper to omit, in this first official act, my fervent supplication to that Almighty Being who rules over the universe—who presides in the councils of nations—and whose providential aid can supply every human defect, that *his benediction may consecrate* to the liberties and happiness of the people of the United States, a government instituted by themselves for these essential purposes; and may enable every instrument employed in its administration to execute with success the functions allotted to his charge. In tendering this homage to the great Author of every public and private good, I assure myself that it expresses your sentiments not less than my own, nor those of my fellow-citizens at large, less than either. No people can be bound to acknowledge and adore the invisible hand which conducts the affairs of men, more than the people of the United States. Every step by which they have advanced to the character of an independent nation, seems to have been distinguished *by some token of providential agency;* and in the important revolution just accomplished in the system of their united government, the tranquil deliberations and voluntary consent of so many distinct communities, from which the event has resulted, cannot be compared with the means by which most governments have been established, without some return of *pious gratitude*, along with an humble anticipation of the future blessings which the past seems to presage. These reflections, arising out of the present crisis, have forced themselves too strongly on my mind to be suppressed. You will join with me, I trust, in thinking that there are none under the influence of which the proceedings of a new and free government can more auspiciously commence."

To this long and interesting expression of religious reverence, I may add another sentence from the same document, which strongly expresses a great fact too often forgotten in our day:

"There is no truth," saith Washington, "more thoroughly established, than that there exists in the economy and course of nature an indissoluble bond between virtue and happiness—between duty and advantage—since we ought to be no less persuaded that *the propitious smiles of Heaven* can never be expected on a nation that disregards the eternal rules of order and right, *which Heaven itself has ordained.*"*

But we have a still more clear and admirable proof of Christian sentiment in his invaluable Farewell Address, published at the age of sixty-five, on his retirement from the presidential chair, where he speaks as follows:

"Of all the dispositions and habits which lead to political prosperity, *religion and morality are indispensable supports.* In vain would that man claim the tribute of patriotism, who should labor to subvert these great pillars of

---

Congressional Edition of the Constitution, p. 212–3.

human happiness—these firmest props of the duties of men and citizens. *The mere politician, equally with the pious man*, ought to respect and cherish them. A volume could not trace all their connections with private and public felicity. Let it simply be asked, where is the security for property, for reputation, for life, if the sense of *religious obligation desert the oaths* which are the instruments of investigation in courts of justice? And let us with caution indulge the supposition, that morality can be maintained without religion. Whatever may be conceded to the influence of refined education on minds of peculiar structure, *reason and experience both forbid us to expect that national morality can prevail in exclusion of religious principles.*"*

"Observe good faith and justice towards all nations; cultivate peace and harmony with all: *religion and morality* enjoin this conduct; and can it be that good policy does not equally enjoin it? *Can it be that Providence has not connected the permanent felicity of a nation with its virtue?*"†

And, once more, in his letter to President Adams, in relation to his appointment, by Congress, as lieutenant-general and commander-in-chief of all the armies raised, or to be raised, under the Federal government, on account of the imminent danger of a war with France, Washington employs this language:

"Satisfied, therefore, that you have sincerely wished and endeavored to avert war, and exhausted to the last drop the cup of reconciliation, we can with pure hearts *appeal to Heaven* for the justice of our cause, and may confidently trust the final result *to that kind Providence which has*

---

* Congressional Edition of the Constitution, p. 224. † Ibid. 226.

heretofore and so often signally favored the people of these United States."*

These extracts are abundantly sufficient to prove that the admirable man who earned the title of "Father of his Country," was not only a Christian in sentiment, but was ready, on the most important and public occasions, to proclaim and enforce his religious principles, and to maintain the all-important truth that religion was the only sure basis of the national prosperity and welfare.

And this was in full accordance with other facts which marked his life. He was known to be in the habit of private prayer. He rebuked, in the army, the common practice of swearing and profanity. He offered thanks to God at his table, in the absence of a clergyman; and he never failed to be punctual in his attendance at the morning service of the Church, where his serious deportment was an example of propriety. With perfect truth, therefore, did General Henry Lee, in the funeral oration which he was appointed to deliver before Congress, December 26th, 1799, characterize the lamented Washington as "*pious*, just, humane, temperate, sincere, uniform, dignified, and commanding, *whose example was edifying to all around him.*"† With perfect consistency did the orator conceive the departed spirit of the patriot sage as uttering from heaven the counsel, "*Reverence religion*,"‡ for such was the counsel which he had always delivered on earth.

I proceed next, however, to show that the model thus exhibited by the first President of the United States was faithfully followed by his successors. Thus the eminent John Adams, in his inaugural address, March 4, 1797, concludes

---

* Congressional Edition of the Constitution, p. 238.

† Ibid. 256. ‡ Ibid. 257.

with the following words: "And with humble reverence, I feel it to be my duty to add, *if a veneration for the religion of a people who profess and call themselves Christians*, and a fixed resolution to consider a *decent respect for Christianity* among the *best recommendations for the public service*, can enable me in any degree to comply with your wishes, it shall be my strenuous endeavor that this sagacious injunction of the two Houses" (to imitate the example of Washington) "shall not be without effect. And may that Being who is supreme over all, the Patron of order, the Fountain of justice, and the Protector, in all ages of the world, of virtuous liberty, *continue his blessing upon this nation and its government*, and give it all possible success and duration, consistent with the ends of his Providence!"*

The inaugural address of the distinguished Thomas Jefferson came afterwards, in March, 1801. And here we find the same distinct acknowledgment. "Kindly separated by nature and a wide ocean from the exterminating havoc of one quarter of the globe; too high-minded to endure the degradations of the others; possessing a chosen country, with room enough for our descendants to the thousandth generation; entertaining a due sense of our equal right to the use of our own faculties, to the acquisitions of our own industry, to honor and confidence from our fellow-citizens, resulting, not from birth, but from our actions and their sense of them; *enlightened by a benign religion, professed, indeed, and practised, in various forms, yet all of them inculcating honesty, truth, temperance, gratitude, and the love of man; acknowledging and adoring an overruling Providence, which, by all its dispensations, proves that it*

---

* Congressional Edition of the Constitution, p. 274–5.

delights in the happiness of man here, and his greater happiness hereafter—with all these blessings, what more is necessary to make us a happy and prosperous people?"*—"Relying, then, on the patronage of your good will, I advance with obedience to the work, ready to retire from it whenever you become sensible how much better choices you can make. *And may that Infinite Power which rules the destinies of the universe lead our councils to what is best, and give them a favorable issue for your peace and prosperity.*"†

In the second inaugural address of President Jefferson, delivered March 4, 1805, he placed on record a still stronger testimony of religious feeling. For thus, at the eloquent close, he saith: "I shall need, therefore, all the indulgence which I have heretofore experienced from my constituents. The want of it will certainly not lessen with increasing years. *I shall need, too, the favor of that Being, in whose hands we are; who led our fathers, as Israel of old, from their native land, and planted them in a country flowing with all the necessaries and comforts of life; who has covered our infancy with his Providence, and our riper years with his wisdom and power; and to whose goodness I ask you* TO JOIN IN YOUR SUPPLICATIONS WITH ME, *that He will so enlighten the minds of your servants, guide their councils, and prosper their measures, that whatsoever they do shall result in your good, and shall secure to you the peace, friendship, and approbation of all nations.*"‡

The venerable James Madison, who succeeded to the presidential chair, March 4, 1809, furnishes the last example which I shall cite on this branch of my subject.

* Congressional Edition of the Constitution, p. 276–7.

† Ib. p. 278.

‡ Ib. p. 283.

For thus he speaks, at the end of his inaugural address: "The source to which I look for the aids which alone can supply my deficiencies, is in the well-tried intelligence and virtue of my fellow-citizens, and in the councils of those representing them in the other departments associated in the care of the national interests. In these my confidence will, under every difficulty, be best placed; *next to that which we have all been encouraged to feel in the guardianship and guidance of that Almighty Being, whose power regulates the destiny of nations, whose blessings have been so conspicuously dispensed to this rising republic, and to whom we are bound to address our devout gratitude for the past, as well as our* FERVENT SUPPLICATIONS AND BEST HOPES FOR THE FUTURE."*

In harmony with these, I shall only notice the testimony of the Congress of the United States, in the ordinance set forth for the Northwestern Territory, July 13, 1787, where the 3d article declares that "*Religion*, morality, and knowledge are necessary to good government and the happiness of mankind."†

A volume might be filled with similar proofs of the care and diligence which the founders and presidents of the republic employed, in *publicly professing* their belief in the religion of the country. The assertion of the objector, therefore, stands in opposition to the evidence. It is true enough that they did not, in many instances, profess Christianity as they should have done, by joining in communion with the Church; but *they did profess it notwithstanding, on the most important occasions, in the eyes of the whole nation and of the world.* Is any one authorized to assume

---

* Congres. Ed. of the Constitution, p. 287–8. † Ib. p. 419.

that they acted hypocritically? Has any one a right to say that they were infidels at heart? Can we, with any reason or justice, impute to such men the baseness of publishing a solemn lie, intended merely to gull the popular ear, and soothe, by a miserable deceit, the Christian feeling of the community? Let those who will, thus slander the departed patriots of the Revolution. Infinitely more reasonable, more consistent, and more just is it to believe, that they wore no political mask, and practised no mean and contemptible chicanery. And therefore I contend that they were what they professed—*Christians in general belief*, able to take the oath of the Constitution with sincerity, and in all good faith; and therefore not simulated, but real friends to the religion of their country.

But the objector may turn to a single case—that of the distinguished Jefferson—whose name is commonly assumed to adorn the cause of infidelity, and whose biography unfortunately includes some passages quite irreconcilable with the Christian faith. I do not consider myself called upon to settle the actual amount, or to judge the precise character of his religion. He was not a member of the Convention which prepared the Constitution, nor, even if he had been, am I aware of any rule which can make the consistency of a single individual, however eminent, a proper test of any Constitutional principle. Some reflection, however, is due to the case of this and other distinguished men, before we adopt our conclusion, as to their personal consistency.

The doctrine for which I contend is, that the Constitution demands the oath of office—that this oath, by necessary implication, is a Christian oath, and therefore that every man who takes it is legally presumed to be a Christian, on the general ground of a conscientious belief in the Gospel system.

But it does not follow, as a logical result, that the Christian faith required to take this oath must be manifested in its most complete form, by a union with the Church. We have all known persons who gave satisfactory evidence of sincere belief, and read the Scriptures with devotion, and lived in the habit of prayer, and did much, in various ways, to support religion, while yet they could not be persuaded to approach the sacramental table. Were they, therefore, infidels? God forbid! On the contrary, they should rather be classed with Christians, although, in some respects, they were inconsistent and erroneous. And to this judgment of charity we are the more obliged, when we contemplate the difficulties presented by the religious dissensions of our day; together with the doubts, scruples, and inward conflicts of opinion to which the human mind is liable.

It should, moreover, be considered, that the class of persons who are marked out, by their prominent talent and energy, as candidates for the official honors of the country, are usually men of superior knowledge and education, accustomed to take a peculiar survey of this very question. They read more, they think more, they are brought into contact with a far wider circle of clashing sentiments; and often, for this very reason, they find it more difficult to come to a fixed decision. In the sadly divided state of Christendom, they see obstacles to their adopting any Church or sect, until they can make time to examine, fairly and impartially, the arguments which each produces. That time they rarely find, in the press and turmoil of their other duties; and therefore they put off, from year to year, the task of comparison, to a more convenient season.

Meanwhile they are surrounded by temptation. The habits of the world into which they are thrown, seem to demand concessions which are hardly reconcilable with the strictness of any Christian profession. In the sphere of public life, they are exposed, more than others, to fluctuations of thought, to irregular indulgence, to the false pride of honor, to the strong excitement of passion, to the snare of popular ambition, to the being "all things to all men," in the natural, though dangerous, wish to avoid offence, and gain a larger measure of general approbation. And yet, throughout the whole, they frequently retain a strong confidence in the truth of the Gospel. They know that all the Churches and sects in Christendom unite in acknowledging the same Bible, and hold the most essential doctrines of that divine revelation, substantially, in the same way. And thus far, they are believers, because there can hardly be error where all Christians agree, although there must be error where they differ. Hence, although these politicians live, and too often die, without the peace, the comfort, and consistency of a settled faith—without the privileges of Christian communion—without the solid approbation of their own secret conscience, or the divine succors of spiritual grace, which are pledged only to the earnest and persevering seeker, yet they are not destitute of a real religious belief, sufficient, at times, to produce the most solemn impressions; and always sufficient to give force to the obligation of a legal oath, and to insure their honest and sincere support to the general interests of Christianity.

How much of this description—of which I have known many examples—would be fairly applicable to Mr. Jefferson, it is not in my power to decide. But one thing is certain. He had the best right to speak for himself, and no man is authorized to question his sincerity, when he chose, on two of the most solemn occasions, to present himself before the whole people of the United States, in the guise of a Christian believer. If there be any discrepancy between his public and his private statements, it is but fair to remember that the exhibition of this discrepancy was not intended by him; and that we have, strictly, no right to violate the implied trust of personal correspondence and individual intercourse, without the knowledge or approbation of the party. Before his biographer resolved to publish those letters and conversations, which have brought upon this eminent man the reproach of infidelity, it would have been but simple justice to ask himself whether Mr. Jefferson had ever sanctioned such an exposure. And if he had not, it needs no argument to prove that the writer took a liberty with the character of the dead, which would have been utterly unwarrantable with that of the living.

But, after all, what do these opposite testimonies establish, beyond the fact so familiar to the experienced observer of human inconsistency? Mr. Jefferson had been long accustomed to the infidel intercourse of Paris, at the time when downright atheism was most rampant, and ranged upon its side the wit and eloquence of the highest society. Is it strange if his mind sometimes fluctuated? Is it strange if, through the common weakness of men who love the praise of authors and philosophers, he accommodated himself to the tone of those whose talents and genius he admired? And if he carried this melancholy complaisance too far, so that he sometimes conversed and wrote, in private, with the tone of an unbeliever, does this prove that he was always in the same mood, and never afterwards felt constrained to do honor, in his serious hours, to the truth of Christianity?

On the contrary, it is by no means improbable that his convictions were actually of the most opposite kinds, at various seasons—driven, like a pendulum, from side to side; so that he may have been sincere when he uttered the words of religious reverence, at one period, although he talked in quite a different strain, at another.

For this we know to have been the fact, in many cases, much more strongly marked than his. Thus, the notorious Thomas Paine, during his last sufferings, was often heard to pray to Jesus Christ for mercy, when he thought himself alone; notwithstanding the pride of consistency prevented his giving any open acknowledgment of his convictions. A far more celebrated instance, however, was that of Voltaire, the unrivalled and supreme dictator of the literary world in France, whose writings did more for infidelity than those of any other author. Yet it is admitted by his biographer, who was himself an infidel, and who, therefore, makes the acknowledgment with the utmost reluctance, that Voltaire actually sent for the Abbé Gauthier, some time before his death, confessed to him, and gave him a profession of faith, in which he declared that "he died in the Catholic religion, in which he was born." He was buried, accordingly, with the usual rites of the papal communion; and even the king of Prussia ordered a solemn service on his behalf, in the Roman cathedral of Berlin.*

This confession of Voltaire's faith, of course, threw the admirers of his infidelity into confusion. But they have never pretended to cast any doubt upon its genuineness. It was made about six weeks before his decease, when he

* See the Life of Voltaire, in the 1st volume of the 12th edition of his works, "Œuvres complètes de Voltaire, Paris, Baudouin Frères, Editeurs," pp. 184–5, 188.

was in full enjoyment of his mental faculties, as is clearly manifest from a very elegant letter addressed by him to the curate of Saint Sulpice, about the time, viz., 4th March, 1778.* Moreover, this confession was in writing, executed in the presence of a priest and two witnesses, the one being the Abbé Mignot, Voltaire's nephew, and the other the Marquis of Villevielle. The prior of Scellières, where he was buried, gave him the usual "spiritual succors due to every Christian," the "Vespers of the dead" were chanted, the solemn mass was performed, and prayers were offered for the repose of his soul.† In a word, the parties concerned gave full credit to his Christian profession, as if they believed it to have been sincere. It is not my duty to pronounce a definitive opinion upon its real character. But I hold it to be most manifest that there is no rule of reason or of justice, which authorizes any one to call it, as this French writer has done, an act of dissimulation. For it is the well-established maxim of law that the declarations of a man, who believes himself dying, are entitled to the highest credit, and therefore they are admitted as testimony, even in capital trials, without an oath. And what worldly power could have persuaded Voltaire, to affect a faith in his last hours, which all his previous efforts had been spent in vilifying? Proud of his surpassing literary fame, surrounded by the satellites of his infidel genius, with all the appliances of taste, opulence, and luxury to give confidence to his position, and stimulated by every possible motive of earthly influence, to make his final act confirmatory of his established reputation, what but the force of his secret convictions could account for his deliberate resolution to disap-

* Ib. p. 571. † Ib. p. 577-8.

point the immense circle of his admirers, and cast the darkest stain, in their opinion, upon the labors of a lifetime, by professing, with his parting breath, the doctrines of Christianity?

No, no! The infidel mode of accounting for such an act, under such circumstances, is altogether absurd and incredible. The conduct of Voltaire can only be understood by a recurrence to the well-known fact, that the heart of man is never truly fixed in any hypothesis which ignores the religion of the Gospel. In the days of bodily health and vigor, tempted by appetite, dazzled by ambition, and applauded by the voice of those who claim pre-eminence for science and liberality, it is not difficult to silence the inward monitor so far as to take a bold stand against the word of God. But *the heart* can find no resting-place in infidelity. And, therefore, when the time approaches for the solemn change—when the soul is forced to turn in upon itself, in the anticipation of a far different tribunal—when wealth, and fame, and human praise, all fade away like the mirage of the desert, leaving nothing but the barren sand behind—it is no dissimulation to turn towards that Christian truth which holds forth the only hope of safety, the only refuge of the self-condemned transgressor, the only promise of any possible escape from the wrath to come. The faith of childhood will then rise up, and assert its simple power; and the perverted logic of the intellect will yield its false and wretched triumph to the stronger instinct of the heart.

I claim this unquestionable case of Voltaire, therefore, as decisive of the view which I have taken of the distinguished Jefferson. For, on a fair comparison, the advantage is altogether in favor of the American patriot. Amongst the works published by himself, there is no attack on religion, no bold and hostile assault upon the Church, nor any indication of an infidel temper. While, on two marked and solemn occasions, he introduced into his inaugural addresses language of a decided Christian character, going far beyond what the mere act of cold conventional propriety required. Voltaire, on the contrary, devoted his extraordinary genius, throughout a long literary life, to the cause of infidelity, and waged a constant warfare against religion, with every weapon in his power. In the guise of philosophy, in poetry, in novels, by serious argument, by flippant wit, by humorous sarcasm, by amusing ridicule, he conducted his skilful and persevering siege of the Church, until his world-wide fame became identified with scoffing derision and profanity. If such a man is entitled to the credit of sincerity, when, in his last hours, he professed himself a Christian, shall Jefferson be denied the same credit of sincerity, when he twice publicly proclaimed his reverence for the religion of his country in the ears of the whole nation? Must a few private letters and conversations, the product most probably of those fluctuations of opinion to which his circumstances made him particularly liable, be allowed to shake our confidence in his most open and deliberate acts, while the closing confession of Voltaire is not to be contradicted by the literary labors of a lifetime?

Hence, on every fair ground of construction, I feel justified in denying the assertion that some or any of our Presidents were known to entertain infidel sentiments. The only one amongst them who has ever been suspected of such a charge, gave to it, himself, a public and sufficient refutation. And the fact, even if it be admitted, that there were times and occasions on which he privately expressed a leaning towards infidelity, although it may prove that he was not always consistent with himself, has yet no weight of sufficient value to overthrow the force of his solemn and official declarations. As to the rest of our presidents, it is well known that their professions have always been distinctly on the side of Christianity. Some of them were even in full communion with the Church. But in discussing the true sense of the Constitution, it should be carefully remembered that we have to do with the public acts of official men, rather than with their personal character. This is the reason why I have already said that such inquiries are irrelevant. No man of common intelligence would attempt to settle the interpretation of the law, by adverting to the private conversations or letters of the judges. And just as irrelevant is the reference to the individual and domestic life of our public officers, when we are discussing the real spirit and meaning of the Constitution.

The remaining objections will be disposed of more readily, because they rest on mere assumption, viz., that "the only effect of a rule which should require a religious profession in our public officers, even if it were possible to adopt it, would be to make them hypocrites; and finally, that such a rule, in the liberal and enlightened temper of our day, is absurd and ridiculous, because it is perfectly impracticable."

The first of these allegations proves too much, and therefore proves nothing. For it is evident that if the requisition of reverence for religion, on the part of our public officers, would make them hypocrites, the requisition of temperance, honesty, truth, or any other moral quality, would be equally objectionable on the same ground; and so we should be reduced to the necessity of discarding morals altogether, as being entitled to no weight in the selecting of the governors, legislators, and rulers of the nation. But such a theory can never be made consistent with the Constitution, so long as that supreme law of the land demands the oath of office. That oath is a *religious obligation*, and no sophistry can change its character. Every man who takes it, professes his belief in the great truths of religion by the very act; and if he be an infidel, the act becomes at once an act of hypocrisy. The objection, therefore, properly stated, is rather an objection to any oath at all. And since the question before us concerns the meaning of the Constitution as it stands, it is evident that the requisition of religious faith is so far from producing hypocrisy, that it is, on the contrary, the only way by which it is possible to prevent it.

The second assumption, viz., that "such a rule, in the liberal and enlightened temper of our day, is absurd, because it is perfectly impracticable," is equally directed against the Constitution, for the very simple reason that it virtually nullifies the force and effect of its plain provisions, and presumes to call that absurd and impracticable, which our supreme law pronounces to be an indispensable qualification. It is evidently taken for granted, by the terms of the objection, that the religious character of the oath is supposed to be generally disregarded. But if so, what is the result? Must we admit that this solemn obligation is actually treated, year after year, by the officers, judges, and legislators of the land, as a worthless and unmeaning form? Do they really appeal to God, without any belief in their religious accountability? Do they perform an act which absolutely demands a religious conscience, without any conscience at all? Supposing that the charge is true, what fouler blot could be cast upon the moral character of our nation? What hypocrisy can be more base than the pretence to acknowledge the judgment of the Almighty by an infidel, who believes nothing of the matter? And if it be the fact that the public sentiment of the United States is so fatally debauched—if an honest attempt to establish the only legal and consistent sense of the Constitution is to be denounced as absurd and impracticable—what is to save our country from the curse of infidelity? What lasting advantage can we gain from the labors of the Christian patriots of the Revolution, when the national heart proves recreant to the law and judgment of that Omnipotent Ruler of the world, who has said, "Righteousness exalteth a nation"—"Those that honor ME I will honor, but those who despise ME shall be lightly esteemed?"

But I am not willing to believe the horrible charge which lies at the basis of this assumption. It cannot be that in less than sixty years from the publication of that admirable "Farewell Address" of Washington, in which religion and morality are so strongly set forth as the only foundations of our national prosperity—it cannot be that we have so fatally degenerated as to have no veneration for the oath of office remaining. I doubt not that there may be a serious amount of careless and thoughtless levity in its administration. I doubt not that the true importance of this constitutional qualification is rarely regarded as it deserves. And this, indeed, is my only apology for giving the subject so large and careful an examination. But I am persuaded that there is quite too much genuine Christian principle and feeling existing in our republic, to allow of any indifference to its claims, when it is made a matter of earnest reflection. And therefore I repel the assumption that the legal meaning of the Constitution is absurd, or that the attempt to establish it is impracticable. No patriot can be justified in thinking it impracticable to fix the true sense of the Constitution of his country. It is only necessary to arouse the attention of the people to any abuse, and we have a right to assume that it will be eventually corrected. And it is the manifest duty of every intelligent citizen to encourage such an effort, instead of yielding to the destructive progress of official profanation, in the tame and cowardly spirit of helpless despondency, or in the still more reprehensible temper of blind and reckless presumption, which dares to calculate on our national progress and prosperity, in defiance of the government of God, and expects to realize the benefits of the Constitution by a practical abolition of its best conservative principle.

CHAPTER III.

ON THE RELIGIOUS DUTIES OF THE CITIZEN, ACCORDING TO THE PHILOSOPHERS.

It is a favorite notion of our modern infidels, that they are acting like philosophers, when they seek to destroy the reverence due to the religion of their country. They fancy that they are thus furnishing the best proof of their superior intellectual powers, when they show how much they stand aloof from the prejudices of the vulgar. And while, for the most part, they are profoundly ignorant of the real object of philosophy, they flatter themselves that they belong to the genuine aristocracy of wisdom, and are pre-eminently qualified to be the guides, the reformers, and the governors of the world.

In the hope of affording, to the candid and sincere mind, the means of resisting this sort of foolish arrogance, I shall devote the present chapter to a statement of the doctrines maintained by the old philosophers, who all saw, clearly enough, the absurdity of the heathen religion which prevailed in their day, and yet universally held that every good citizen must do honor to it, because it was the established system, and the worst religion was better than none at all.

To understand their position aright, however, we must remember that they had no divine revelation, as we have, to instruct them. The knowledge of the true God, which Noah possessed, and which was once universal amongst his posterity, had become sadly weakened and obscured, through the prevailing tendency of the corrupt human heart towards idolatry. Revived and established by the mercy of heaven, through the instrumentality of Moses, the law of the Most High was committed to the nation of Israel; and that chosen people were victoriously planted in Palestine,—the best possible locality, during all the ancient ages, to be the central guide to the world, because it lay at the head of the Mediterranean Sea, and was surrounded by the most active agencies of political and commercial greatness. For a while, the influence produced by this arrangement was salutary and extensive, so that the kings of the earth sought to learn the wisdom of Solomon.* But Israel itself became unfaithful. The favor of God was forfeited. Instead of continuing to be the most prosperous and the most honored of all the nations, it was the subject of the divine

* 1 Kings, iv. 34.

judgments, all of which the prophets had most accurately foretold. With the calamities of Israel, its religion fell into disrepute. Idolatry spread more and more, and sunk deeper and deeper into pollution, amongst the distinguished empires of Greece and Rome; until at length, the appointed time arrived for the last great interposition of divine love, and the altars of heathenism were universally overthrown, by the truth and miracles of the Gospel.

It was during the six centuries of increasing darkness which preceded the advent of the great Redeemer, that philosophy arose and flourished. But this philosophy was the product of human reason, groping after the relics of celestial wisdom, and destitute of any sure and unerring guide, through the rebellion and unfaithfulness of Israel. Hence it presented itself under the names of its several teachers, none of whom could speak with inspired authority. And these became the masters of many different and discordant systems.

Thales, the Milesian, was the first who was reverenced among the Greeks as a superior model of wisdom, about six hundred years before the Gospel era. But we do not find that he founded any school of philosophy, though his sayings were repeated by his successors with great respect. The father of philosophy was Pythagoras, who flourished a century later, and his sect was numerous and influential. He taught that God is the soul of the world, a pure and spiritual ether, expanded through the universe, the cause and fountain of life to all things. That the sun, the moon, and the stars are filled with this ether, and should therefore be adored as gods. That the human soul is a portion of this celestial ether, and is therefore immortal. That this soul is transmigrated after death, from one body to another, being committed to the forms of birds, fishes, and brutes, as a discipline and punishment for sin. And therefore, as all the inferior creatures were likely to be animated by a human soul, their use as food should be strictly forbidden.

A name of far wider renown, however, was that of Plato, the favorite scholar of Socrates, and the instructor of Aristotle. He flourished about four hundred years before Christ, and his doctrines approached so near to the truth of Scripture, that he was commonly believed to have had access to the Books of the Old Testament, during his extensive travels in the East. But he, too, held that the heavenly bodies are deities, and are proper objects of worship; while, in many other respects, his system was open to grave exceptions, although greatly in advance of any other in its general scope and character.

Aristotle, the favorite master of Alexander the Great, was the founder of the school of the Peripatetic philosophy, so called either because their teacher was accustomed to give his instructions while walking about, or because the place where he taught was a walk, shaded with trees. His doctrine was, that all direct knowledge rests on experience: and he opposed the two systems then most in vogue, that of emanation, which maintained that all things were a part of Deity, and the atomic, which supposed that the universe was formed by the fortuitous concourse of atoms. He did not question the being of God, as a most perfect Intelligence, the First Mover and Unchangeable. But he held that the Supreme Being only acted on the heavens, all the inferior spheres being governed by other eternal substances, which were entitled to be worshipped and adored. And virtue, according to his views, consisted in acting according to nature.

The famous Epicurus founded his school about 342 years before the Christian era. He revived and gave acceptance to the doctrine of Democritus, namely, that every thing was produced by the fortuitous concourse of atoms, without the act of any intelligent Creator; that as the world had a beginning, it would also have an end, and that out of its ruins would be formed a new one. He denied that there was any essential difference between men and brutes, since the soul had the same material organization as the body. He admitted the existence of the gods, but taught that they lived in eternal tranquillity, and did not concern themselves with the affairs of mortals. The principle of moral life he maintained to be pleasure or happiness, although he was careful to define this pleasure as being inseparable from the practice of virtue. Yet, as virtue with him, as well as with Aristotle, consisted in living according to nature, it is evident that his system had no element of restraint upon the passions or the appetites: and therefore, notwithstanding many moralists condemned it as nothing better than Atheism, its accommodating principles made it highly acceptable to the educated youth, not only amongst the Greeks, but subsequently, in the corrupt ages of the old Roman empire.

Within the same century, about 380 years before Christ, the school of the Cynics arose under Antisthenes, who had also been a pupil of Socrates. This philosopher chose practical morals as his chief object, and Diogenes was the most famous of his disciples. But his sect was neither lasting nor successful, because, instead of professing to raise mankind to a higher level, they made themselves contemptible and disgusting, by striving to inculcate the simplicity of the brutes. They soon became merged, therefore, in the loftier school of the Stoics, to whose principles of hardy and self-reliant independence their maxims were most closely allied.

The Pyrrhonists or Sceptics had their origin from Pyrrho, a philosopher of Elis, contemporary with the founder of the Cynics, whose aim was said to be uprightness of life, with a perfect indifference, or rather a positive hostility, to all dogmatism of opinion. The doctrine which distinguished his school was, that there could be no settled judgment about any thing, since the arguments on both sides of every question were so equally balanced as to render an absolute decision impossible. And hence it resulted that he alone was to be esteemed wise who avoided all fixed sentiments—who was content with saying that things *seemed* to be so and so, but declined saying that they *were* so, and preserved his own tranquillity of mind undisturbed, amongst the various conflicts of contending systems.

The Stoics derived their name from the Greek word στοα, signifying *the porch*, where Zeno, their founder, taught his doctrines, about 300 years before the advent of the Saviour. This school of philosophers held that the whole universe, being penetrated by the divine intelligence, is God. They also maintained that the heavenly bodies and the powers of nature were deities, which ought to be worshipped, and therefore this system was a complete example of Pantheism. The perfection of virtue, as they taught, consisted in the true harmony of man with himself, independent of reward or punishment, so as to maintain the highest elevation above the pleasures and the pains of sense. They also taught the right of suicide whenever the individual conceived that death was preferable to life. Zeno, their founder, strangled himself at the age of ninety-eight, and Cleanthes, his celebrated successor, destroyed himself by intentional starvation.

The New Academy was formed at a later day, by Arcesilaus, who died at the age of 75, about 240 years before the Gospel era. It was afterwards improved by Carneades, and supported by the celebrated Cicero. Its main object was to effect a more ingenious arrangement of the Pyrrhonian philosophy; and hence, as this system was indulgent to every other, while it favored an easy and courteous indifference towards all, and did not trouble the mind with any positive opinions, it was quite in harmony with the spirit of the age which immediately preceded the rise of the Gospel, and divided with the doctrines of Epicurus the suffrages of the best educated minds in every civilized community.

Lastly, came the Eclectic school, which arose in Alexandria, and was frequently called the Alexandrian school, for that reason. This system had several phases, but its general design was to unite, in one harmonious whole, the Oriental, the Platonic and the Aristotelian philosophy. In its earlier form it seems to have been adopted by Philo Judæus. In its subsequent shape, it was matured by Ammonius Saccas, towards the end of the 2d century. It never succeeded, however, in attaining any considerable degree of credit or importance. For just as the stars in the firmament vanish from the sight, at sunrise, even so did all the heathen systems gradually die away before the triumphant glory of the Christian faith.

But while these ancient philosophers were thus divided, maintaining, with admirable ingenuity and skill, their contending systems, they all agreed in inculcating, with one voice, the duty and necessity of supporting the established religion of their country.

Thus, in the golden verses of Pythagoras, which, though not written by himself, are acknowledged to be a true expression of his doctrines, it is commanded that "men shall always worship the immortal gods, *as they are appointed by the law.*"

So Plato, in his 10th book, *De Legibus*, regards those persons as atheists who do not acknowledge *the gods appointed by law;* and again he saith, that "a wise legislator will not attempt to innovate in any thing relating to the sacrifices *prescribed by the laws of the country.*"*

So Socrates, the instructor of Plato, advised men to honor the public religion by following the established oracles.† And he acted on the principle himself, by openly using divination. The accusation brought against him by Anytus and Melitus was, that "he did not believe those to be gods whom the city acknowledged, and that he introduced other new gods." But against this charge his pupil, Xenophon, zealously defended him, saying, that "Socrates sacrificed to the gods frequently, not only at home, but at the public altars." And Socrates himself, in the apology addressed to his judges, declares that he "wonders how Melitus came to know that he did not esteem those to be gods whom the city regarded as such, since many had seen him sacrificing at the common festivals, and Melitus might have seen him also, if he pleased." He further spake with veneration of the Delphic oracle, and he is stated to have even composed a hymn to Apollo, while he was in prison.‡

So Aristotle, after laying down the principle that "the citizens are *partners in the republic*, since otherwise, strictly

* Plat. Op. p. 702. † Xenophon, Memor. Soc. L. i. c. 1.
‡ Plat. Phædo. Op. p. 876.

speaking, *they are not citizens at all*,"* expressly requires that "*every citizen must worship the gods*, and therefore must *reverence the priesthood*."†

So Epictetus, the chief ornament of the Stoic school, asserts it to be a duty *incumbent on every one*, to offer up libations, sacrifices, and first-fruits, *according to the customs and rites of his country*."‡ Plutarch has several passages to the same effect, and Marcus Antoninus, the eminent emperor and Stoic philosopher, was remarkably strict in the public worship of the gods, and the observance of all the sacred ceremonies.§

So Cicero, in his book *De Legibus*, gives no precept concerning the worship of One Supreme God, although he did not deny the doctrine of Plato, but he expressly prescribes the worship of the *established deities*, and binds it on the people, as a positive obligation, "*to follow the religion of their ancestors*."‖

Much more of the same character might be added, but these citations are abundantly sufficient to prove the strong and united sentiment of the masters of philosophy, as to this great rule of civic duty. Yet while they all decided thus, there were not a few who censured, in many respects, the established and popular religion. Of course, therefore, they rendered their public homage to it, not so much on the ground of personal faith, as on the principle of indispensable necessity. They respected its claims, because it was the only basis for the public security. Without religion of some sort, they all knew that there could be no foundation for law, justice, or moral virtue, in the ordinary

* Aristot. De Repub. L. iii. c. 2, p. 205.
† Ib. L. vii. p. 262—269.
‡ Epictet. Enchirid. c. 31.
§ Ammian. Marcell. L. xxv.
‖ Cicero De Legibus, L. 2, c. viii.

4

conscience of mankind. And, therefore, being well persuaded that philosophy was not religion, and could not supply its place, and being ignorant of the true revelation which God had sent, to be at once the guardian of the government, and the light and comfort of each individual soul, they required it imperatively of every citizen to give the benefit of his example to the established worship of the land, because they had nothing better to offer as its substitute.

Such was the spirit of the real philosophers, and they well deserved the honor which was bestowed on them so freely. Even we cannot refuse to reverence those admirable men, who employed their finest powers in the search after truth, and toiled in the midst of moral and spiritual darkness, without any safe guide to direct them. They did not reject the word of God, because they had it not. They did not despise or neglect the religion of the Saviour, because it was not known to them. But while they felt, sensibly, the gross defects and positive corruptions of the heathen idolatry, and yearned after some higher rule of faith and knowledge, they were conscious that nothing which they were able to attain could claim the authority of a divine religion; and they had too much *love for wisdom* to pull down even the false piety of pagan superstition, until they could present a true celestial revelation in its place.

But what if those genuine philosophers had flourished in our day, in the full light and perfect moral purity of the Gospel system? What would they have said when they saw the citizens of our great republic declining to take part in a really divine worship, turning their backs upon the altars of the only living God, and carefully avoiding every thing which might bring upon them even the suspicion of piety? What would they have said when they found the title of *philosopher* usurped by men who recklessly assailed the established religion of the land, not in order to set up a better one, but merely for the liberty of having no religion at all? What, more especially, would they have said, when they were told that the very oath of office was commonly regarded as an idle form, and that a character for Christian faith and virtue was an obstacle, rather than a recommendation to the public favor?

When we reflect upon the marked contrast between the ancient sages, and our modern leaders in the work of imaginary progress, it seems impossible to justify the application of the term philosopher to the infidels of our age and country. A man may be distinguished for his attainments in the natural sciences—a master in Physiology, Geology, Astronomy, Magnetism, Entomology, and all the rest—he may even be learned in Archæology, and write profoundly about the buried monuments of antiquity—and yet not have the slightest mark of a philosopher, in its true sense and meaning. Every scholar knows that this word, first introduced by Pythagoras, signifies a *lover of wisdom.* Hence, it was never used by the ancients, except to designate that class of thoughtful and exalted intellects, which were occupied in the search after wisdom, as the product of religion and morality. For it is the proper province of wisdom to understand the higher laws of spiritual being; the moral government of God; the religious duties of His intelligent subject, man; the maxims of human legislation, as respects the body politic; and the individual relations to society, by which the virtue, peace, prosperity, and advancement of the whole community and of each private member can be best secured. These were the main studies of the old philosophers. True, they labored under every disadvantage, in the absence of the only unerring guide, divine revelation. True, they differed widely, and erred egregiously, in many of their conclusions. But they never forgot the proper objects of philosophy. They never lost sight of its true design, in the effort to place the best and loftiest interests of our race upon their real foundations. Surely, then, such men as Socrates, Plato, Aristotle, Zeno, Cicero, and Epictetus, would have laughed with bitter derision at the arrogance of our infidel naturalists, whom the good-natured public indulge with the respectable title of philosophers, as if they could be called, *lovers of wisdom!* Alas! what lovers of wisdom are they who assail the highest source of wisdom; who take an insane pleasure in undermining the national religion; and strive to prostrate the sublimest hopes of human destiny, and the only principle of law, government, and morals, which can sustain the good order of the republic, or secure the most sacred rights and privileges of mankind!

CHAPTER IV.

THE RELIGIOUS RIGHTS AND DUTIES OF THE AMERICAN CITIZEN.

Having said enough, I trust, to vindicate the Christian character of our national Constitution, and to prove that on every ground of common sense, reason, legal interpretation, historical fact, and true philosophy, we are obliged to consider it in this religious aspect; I proceed to examine the "rights and duties of the American citizen," which necessarily arise from this fundamental principle. And in order to secure the better method in these subjects, I shall place the *rights* in the first rank, and the *duties* in the second. For such is the proper order in the nature of the case. The Constitution first confers the rights of the citizen, and then claims the performance of his duties.

1. The religious rights of the citizen of the United States consist in the enjoyment of his own conscientious choice, amongst all the forms of our common Christianity which were in existence at the time when the Constitution was established. This must be taken as the full limit of fair and legal presumption, as the two first chapters have sufficiently proved. Therefore I hold it preposterous to suppose that a band of Hindoos could settle in any part of our territories, and claim a *right*, under the Constitution, to set up the public worship of Brahma, Vishnu, or Juggernaut. Equally unconstitutional would it be for the Chinese to introduce the worship of Fo or Buddha, in California. Neither could a company of Turks assert a right to establish a Mosque for the religion of Mahomet. But there is one case, namely, that of the Jews, which forms an apparent exception, although it is in fact supported by the same legal principle. For, the meaning of the Constitution can only be derived from the *reasonable intention of the people of the United States.* Their language, religion, customs, laws, and modes of thought were all transplanted from the mother country; and we are bound to believe that whatever was tolerated publicly in England, was doubtless meant to be protected here. On this ground, there is no question about the constitutional right of our Jewish fellow-citizens, whose synagogues had long before been established in London. But with this single exception, I can find *no right* for the public exercise of any religious faith, under our great Federal

Charter, which does not acknowledge the divine authority of the Christian Bible.

2. And here, I take the opportunity to express my own deep veneration towards the posterity of Israel. I cannot forget their high privileges, as the chosen people of God—that to them the oracles of divine truth were committed—that they were appointed to hold the light of heaven, while all the rest were in heathen darkness—that to them were the inspired prophets sent—that "salvation" in the words of Christ "is of the Jews," since the divine Redeemer Himself was a Jew according to the flesh, and the Apostles were Jews, and the first Church was gathered in Jerusalem, from which the Gospel was sounded forth, through all the earth—that their history is a series of the most wonderful and sublime manifestations of celestial power which the world has ever witnessed—that their present state, scattered for seventeen centuries over the habitable globe, without home, or country, or government, and yet preserved in their marvellous individuality by the mighty hand of God, is not only an invincible proof of the prophecies, but is a continual miracle—that the highest examples of genius, talent, energy, indomitable perseverance and moral purity have been exhibited amongst them; and that the time is rapidly approaching when, as I trust, their long period of bitter calamity will cease, and they shall shine forth in more than their ancient glory—when they shall acknowledge the divine Messiah whom their fathers pierced, and be gathered into His fold, and Zion shall "rejoice and be glad," and shall "reign as a queen among the nations."

The honor in which I hold the Jews, therefore, is most genuine and sincere, for it is a part of my religion. Yet I cannot, for all that, change my views of the constitutional *oath of office*, which I have proved at large to be a Christian oath, and therefore an oath which cannot be consistently taken by any who deny the Christian faith. I have shown why the practice of England is the safest general guide to the great rule of construction, which must determine our interpretation; namely, *the intention of the people*. The Jews had never been admitted to office in the mother country, and we have no ground for supposing that they were intended to be admitted here. They were allowed to give evidence, however, and so, on the principle of necessity, were the Turks and heathen.* They were also allowed to establish their synagogues in England, and a few were even existing in the United States, before the Constitution was adopted, whose rights were questioned by no one. Thus far, then, the point may be settled, without difficulty, on the legal basis, so as to bear the test of thorough examination.

3. But under this aspect of constitutional construction, there is no allowance for any *new invention* of religion, unknown to the sovereign people, and which they could not possibly have anticipated. And, therefore, I hold that Mormonism is entirely excluded from any *right* to the free exercise of its religion, which, though it call itself Christian, rests upon the assumed authority of another Bible, and arrogates to itself the power of opposing the universal sense of all the Churches in the world, by the debasing and monstrous claims of its polygamy. The rise and rapid growth of this alarming evil show clearly the absolute necessity of adopting some definite and legal rule of sound constitutional interpretation; and that rule, according to the fixed and

* See Omichund vs. Barker, Atkyn's Rep.

established maxim which *seeks for the true meaning of every law in the reasonable intent of the authority enacting it*, protects the country at once from all the invasions of reckless infidelity, of revolting heathenism, and of every foul and disgusting innovation.

4. There is still, however, a limitation, necessarily involved in the constitutional right to the free exercise of religion, even with respect to those Christian Churches which were most evidently intended to be protected and sustained; and this will be manifest when we consider the positions of the Church of England and the Church of Rome, at the period when our great national charter was established.

The Church of England, as is well known, stands connected with the State, and the sovereign is invested with a royal supremacy which confers the right of nomination to the sees of the bishops, and of controlling, to a certain extent, the sessions of her House of Convocation. All this, however, being purely a matter of temporal and secular arrangement, was justly regarded as having no necessary connection with the doctrines of faith, or the ecclesiastical system of government and discipline, which she inherited from the apostles, and defended on the authority of the word of God; and hence, when the separation of the colonies from the mother country was consummated, and the independence of the United States was acknowledged and confirmed by the treaty of peace with England, it was immediately seen that the independence of the American Church must follow. Without delay, therefore, an application was made, through our minister at the Court of St. James, by the Episcopalians concerned, for the consecration of three bishops, in order to organize the Protestant Episcopal Church in the United States, without any further connection with the British government. The request was freely granted, with the consent of Parliament. The individuals elected by the joint act of the clergy and the laity, in the three States of Pennsylvania, New York, and Virginia, were consecrated accordingly: and from that time, the Church in this country commenced its independent course, as a strictly American Church, having no further relation to her English mother than the respect involved in the recollection of her descent, and the mutual affection of Christian fraternity.

The Church of Rome was not so favorably situated. The pope was as much a sovereign, and a foreign sovereign, as the monarch of Great Britain. But he was also believed to be the sole vicar upon earth of our Lord Jesus Christ, and as such, he claimed to be the head over all the Churches, and, for religious purposes, over all the nations in the world. This stupendous claim was not allowed by any out of his own communion. It had been proved, over and over again, to be a modern usurpation, perfectly unknown to the primitive Church, for many ages. But, unhappily, it became a fixed article of faith in the Roman Catholic creed, and their priesthood are obliged to pronounce an ecclesiastical anathema or curse, at least once in every year, against the heretics who presume to deny it. Moreover, by the fixed principles of the papal Church, her doctrines are to be received as infallible, while all Churches which do not submit to her, are cut off, as heretical, and pronounced accursed. Their hope of salvation is believed to be entirely forfeited for that sole reason; and therefore, without subjection to the pope, the Romanist holds it impossible to be saved through Christ at all.

Of course it could not be expected that with these principles, maintained as the essential laws of an infallible faith, the position of the Romanists in the United States should be changed by any act of their own, when the Constitution was established. Yet it is quite as impossible to suppose that the people who adopted that Constitution could ever have consented to give their approbation, directly or indirectly, to a set of dogmas which nullified the rights and privileges of every other Christian body, and demanded an unconditional submission of the whole to the supremacy of the pope, on pain of certain damnation. It was desirable, on the one hand, to give the adherents of Rome all the toleration they had previously enjoyed, and necessary, on the other, that their claims to universal dominion should in no way be prejudicial to the conscientious liberty of the rest. And thus we may perceive another use of the important article, "That Congress shall make no law respecting an establishment of religion, or prohibiting the free exercise thereof:" a rule which I have already shown to be applicable to the Establishment of England, but which is obviously quite as applicable to the case of Rome.

Here, then, a safeguard is provided against all danger of Roman supremacy. For the papal system can never prevail, unless it be through an *establishment of their religion*, and a *prohibition of the free exercise of any other*. The history of the middle ages fully proves that the secular power, bearing on the rights of conscience with the strong hand of persecution, was always the most effectual instrument of papal aggrandizement. And therefore, when the Constitution proclaims and guaranties an equal support to all, and forbids the establishment of any, it not only condemns, by necessary inference, the sweeping claims of that single Church, which demands universal submission at the peril of salvation, but further, by a fair implication, condemns the curses so formally pronounced upon those who refuse to obey her.

The result is, that the position of our Roman Catholic fellow-citizens, under the American Constitution, is a perfect anomaly; and several important questions are suggested, to which it is by no means easy for a consistent Romanist to give a satisfactory reply.

1. Every naturalized foreigner swears to support the Constitution, and every native-born citizen is of course under the same obligation. How does the Roman Catholic reconcile this oath of allegiance with his religious creed? By the first, he is sworn to sustain and protect religious toleration. By the second, he is bound to detest it, and pursue the heretic with curses. No opposition can be more complete—none more irreconcilable. Which is the stronger obligation? Which is the more likely to prevail?

2. Is it possible that both can stand together? Can the same man, at the same moment, be expected to curse what he cherishes, and support what he detests?

3. The constitutional oath is required by the human government, and its breach may be said to involve no more than a human obligation. The religious creed, on the contrary, is supposed to be required by the authority of God, and its violation is believed to insure the ruin of the soul. Can the conscientious Romanist hesitate a moment, if a conflict should arise between them?

4. If either one or the other of those obligations must be broken, on which side lies the remedy for the crime? The government has no power to absolve the perjurer from the guilt of irreligion; but the pope can absolve him, as he believes, from the oath of his allegiance, and even make a

merit of the sin. Where is the equality in the influence of the two?

5. Is any government safe, which intrusts its powers to its enemies? And can an intelligent and sincere Romanist be any thing but an enemy to a Constitution which favors heresy, which refuses to establish that Church which is alone governed by the vicar of Jesus Christ, and out of whose pale he believes that there is no salvation? Can he be any thing but an enemy to the success of heretics, or to the extension of those principles of religious liberty, which he holds to be the instigation of the devil?

6. Certain it is, however, that the Roman Catholic population of the United States do not choose to examine such questions very thoroughly. I am by no means sure that even the framers of our excellent Constitution took them into consideration; or, if they did, they probably dismissed them as quite unnecessary, trusting to the happy ignorance and inconsistency of the mass, and believing that it could never be the interest of the Roman laity, nor even of their priests, to seek any undue share of power, so long as they were surrounded by so large a majority of watchful Protestants. And in this they may have been right. But is there any certainty that this Protestant majority will always be found in every State? Is there no danger that in some of them there will be a strong papal ascendency? Is it at all unlikely that the increasing loss of papal influence in many parts of Europe will bring to our shores a vast accession of foreign Romanists, which may give a decided preponderance to their religion in the great western valley, and finally enable them to set up their exclusive claims, in all their old intolerance? For it must be remembered that the Constitution only forbids "*Congress* to make any law

for an establishment of religion, or to prohibit the free exercise thereof." The States are perfectly free to do as each may deem proper; and no State, once admitted, can be prevented from altering its own constitution, whenever the majority of its citizens are prepared to approve the change. Can any one wonder if the priesthood of Rome should combine together in a well-organized effort to secure those rights, which they believe to have been conferred by the Almighty, and even to be absolutely necessary for the salvation of mankind? Can any one undertake to condemn them, if they are now laboring for this very purpose? Certainly I cannot; because, if I held their principles, I should consider myself bound to do the same. The danger is not in the men, but in the system.

7. Repudiating popery, therefore, with all my heart, as a scheme of perilous errors, while, nevertheless, I cherish none but the kindliest feelings towards the vast mass of well-meaning persons who are deluded to maintain it, I am compelled to conclude that, *under the Constitution*, no Romanist can have *a right* to the free enjoyment of his religion, without a serious inconsistency; for the papal system demands intolerance and exclusion, and is the declared enemy to the free exercise of religion, which the Constitution has made one of the supreme laws of the land. These two opposing principles cannot possibly stand together. The Roman Catholic must be inconsistent either with his Church or with the Constitution. If his Church prevail, he cannot be true to the religious freedom of the United States, nor to the political freedom of his heretical fellow-citizens. If his allegiance to the government prevail, he cannot be true to the faith of popery. It is a very painful and troublesome dilemma. But there it stands, and I see no way in

which it can be avoided. For how can he acquire his constitutional right except on the condition of being faithful to the principles of the Constitution? And how can he be faithful to those principles, except by ignoring, doubting, or positively discarding that part of his religious creed, which curses all heretics, and makes the pope of Rome, as the sole vicar of Jesus Christ, the supreme governor of the world? And how can he dare to discard, or even to doubt, any part of that creed, when he holds his Church to be infallible, and is assured that the least departure from her doctrine exposes him to be cursed himself, if not here, yet certainly hereafter?

8. Happily, however, for the peace of mankind, and for the comfort and security of Roman Catholics themselves, especially in a Protestant country like our own, there is a large amount of political expediency allowed, for the sake of which the most odious and unpopular principles of popery are kept as much as possible in the dark, and even boldly denied when it is found to be necessary. The majority of their own most intelligent laity are profoundly ignorant of much that is familiar to the priests. Their very bishops are permitted to take different sides, on all embarrassing and troublesome questions. The masses of their people are not even aware of the formal curses pronounced yearly against all heretics, because the bull *In cœna Domini* (which is a part of the service on Maunday Thursday) is repeated in a low voice, and in Latin. Their popular treatises for the public eye are ingeniously prepared, so as to mystify, and sometimes positively repudiate, all their obnoxious doctrines. The oath which every bishop is obliged to take not only binds him to obey the pope, but also to *oppose and persecute the heretics to the utmost of his*

power. But that oath is also in Latin, and belongs to a book of forms to which the laity seldom have access. And the restraints of the confessional are a very effective instrument to keep them from learning any thing about such matters, because they are constantly warned to avoid the assemblies of heretics, or to read their writings, or to believe one word which they may utter or publish, upon the Church of Rome; every thing coming from such a quarter being "Protestant lies" of course, and therefore to be shunned, as the work of Satan. Hence it is undoubtedly true that Romanism, as it is *practically* given out to the great majority in the United States, is diluted, spiced, and flavored with consummate skill and prudence, so as to accommodate the republican palate, and effectually disguise the pungent and bitter ingredients in the cup. And therefore we are able to rejoice in the fact, which I, for one, most cheerfully acknowledge, that there are many professed Romanists who are perfectly unconscious of the conflict between their Constitutional and their religious principles—many who are innocently persuaded that heretics were never cursed nor persecuted by the authority of their Church—many who, if they knew her true history, would regard it with the spirit of a reformer—many, in a word, who honestly prefer their country to the pope, and who are, with regard to all political intents and purposes, and all social rights and feelings, *much better than their system.*

That the religious principles of such persons are inconsistent with popery, *properly understood*, I cannot doubt for a moment. But this inconsistency is the work of their teachers. The only danger to be apprehended from that quarter lies in the possibility of the fact, that their increasing numbers may give them such preponderance, at a future day, as to call for a more thorough and very different mode of instruction. And if that day should ever arrive, it will soon be made mournfully manifest that there is no real harmony between the claims of the pope, and the Christian liberty of the Constitution.

Meanwhile, however, I have no wish to speak of Romanism, further than to notice the discrepancies between it and the law of the land, because I have stated in the preface, that I should not discuss any point of theological controversy. My obligations to religious truth I have endeavored to discharge on other occasions;* but my present work is confined to those questions which properly belong to the sphere of Constitutional rights and duties, and beyond these I have no desire to travel.

9. I shall only add, therefore, in concluding my statement of the religious rights of the American citizen, that he has an unquestionable right to enjoy his own free choice, amongst the various Churches and sects which existed at the time when the Constitution was adopted, *without being anathematized by any priest or people.* The Roman Catholic has the same right with every other Christian, to prefer his own religion and follow his own creed. But he can have no legal right to curse all those who may be conscientiously obliged to differ. His right, like theirs, must be confined within the bounds of fair and equal toleration, which gives the same measure of protection to the whole Christian community. It is true, indeed, that ecclesiastical censures, suspensions, and excommunications belong of necessity to every Church and sect, and all are obliged, in

* In the "End of Controversy controverted," "The History of the Confessional," "The Church of Rome," and "Lectures on the British Reformation." The first is the most extensive.

some shape, to employ them. The pronouncing of a solemn curse or anathema, however, according to the papal system, is a very different matter, because it assumes the apostolic prerogative of delivering the denounced party to Satan; and, wherever the priests of Rome have established their power, it is followed by a large amount of temporal suffering, through the personal hatred which it excites, and the actual prohibition of intercourse or charity. This severity is in direct contrariety to the Gospel. St. Paul gives us the precept, "Bless and curse not," and again he directs us "not to count the rebellious Christian as an enemy, but to admonish him as a brother." But, besides this Scriptural rule, it is certainly in plain opposition to the religious freedom which the Constitution secures to every citizen, sect, and Church, without exception, that any public minister should be allowed to pronounce a solemn curse on men who are in the line of permitted discretion. When the priest utters such a curse, therefore, and holds up the party to the odium and persecution of the congregation, by which he sustains an injury in person, property, or character, it is a grave and important question whether the law of the land would not sustain an action for the wrong, or whether the practice of Rome would be held a legal justification.

II. Having thus surveyed the religious rights of the American citizen, I now proceed to consider his duties. And these will suggest themselves naturally, as the reasonable results of the foregoing.

1. It has been proved that the Constitution of the United States, in requiring the oath of office and the retention of the common law, has actually based the whole administration of government and justice upon the Christian religion.

Without a belief in that religion, neither the oath of allegiance to the government, nor the oath of office, can be rightly and legally taken. The first religious duty of the citizen, therefore, must be to understand and reverence the Christian faith, to support its claims to respect and confidence, and to discourage, by every proper means within his power, the assaults of infidelity, and the acts of profanation, which tend to expose it to contempt, and destroy its all-important influence.

Of course, as a minister of the Gospel, I hold that this duty rests on a far more high and solemn ground than any earthly obligation, because a sincere and devout faith in the Redeemer of the world is the only way of acceptance with the Deity, including the forgiveness of sin, the peace of God which passeth understanding, the spiritual influence which converts and purifies the heart, and elevates and sanctifies the whole moral nature; the kind and gracious government of Providence in all the events of life; the glorious hope which sustains the soul in the hour of dissolution; and the future inheritance of immortality and happiness eternal beyond the grave. But the object of the present work is rather to display the vast importance of the Christian element to the welfare of all our earthly interests, and the impossibility and philosophical absurdity of any effectual effort to preserve them, without its aid. And therefore I have discussed the question thus far, and shall continue to discuss it to the end, mainly with a view to the secular, legal, and moral aspects of the question.

2. The second religious duty of the American citizen, is to survey the subject of Christianity in the large and comprehensive spirit of the Constitution; remembering that amongst all the divisions of religious sentiment existing at

the time of its adoption, there was only one authority which the whole Christian world reverenced alike as the Word of God, namely, the Bible. In the serious and careful study of that sacred volume, and in no other way so well, can he hope to learn the sublime attributes of the Almighty: His wondrous acts of creation, of preservation, and of personal providence; His laws of spiritual purity, and truth, and moral benevolence, and equity; His judgments upon the guilty, whether nations or individuals; His miraculous displays in connection with each new revelation of His will; and His divine foreknowledge in the predictions of the prophets, the destruction of Nineveh, Babylon, Tyre, and Jerusalem, the coming of Christ, His character, doctrines, and sacrifice for the sins of the world, the establishment of His Church, the exile and calamities of the chosen people, the corruptions and tyranny of the great antichristian power, the final overthrow of wickedness and rebellion at the second advent of the Redeemer to judge the earth, and the establishment of His celestial kingdom in perfect bliss and glory. Nor will the reader of the Bible find it difficult to become familiar with its contents, if he will spend a small portion of each day, together with his leisure on the Sabbaths, in its perusal. And from its pages he will assuredly learn incomparably more of the true principles of life, of virtue, and of happiness, than he can learn from all the world besides.

3. The third religious duty of the American citizen is to compare with the Bible, which all Christians acknowledge, the distinctive systems of the various Churches and sects, until he is satisfied with some one, as being, on the whole, in the best accordance with the Scriptures. The greater truths of Christianity he will find to be professed by all,

with little substantial difference. The Church of Rome he will see to be the only one which confines salvation to her own pale. And the claims which Popery advances upon his homage he will soon discover to be not only destitute of all authority in the word of God, but in actual hostility to its testimony.

4. The fourth duty which will readily suggest itself, will be to attend with punctual regularity on the service of the Church which he has selected, since this is the only mode in which he can openly testify the respect which each citizen owes to the religion of his country, and obey the laws of the State, as all men are bound to do, and keep himself aloof from those temptations which are most numerous and seductive on the Sabbath-day, and thus preserve his health of mind and body, and establish his character for prudence and sobriety.

5. True, all this will not make him a Christian, because, thus far, it will only regulate his intellect and his outward habits, and may fail to make a serious impression upon his heart. But it is manifest that he should do thus much, at least, as a duty to his country, if only in the character of a true and faithful citizen. By any other course, he opposes the spirit of the Constitution. For the basis of the government and the laws is religion. That religion is Christianity. The qualification for every public office is the Christian oath. The morality which obtains for him the esteem and confidence of society is Christian morality. And the great repository of the whole is in the Bible, while the ministers, and the Churches, and the Sabbath-day, are the essential means of keeping the all-controlling truth, on which every civilized community depends, constantly before the people. Can he be worthy of the name of American citizen who

refuses to study, to examine, or to respect the very foundation of the government and order of his country? Is he, in any true sense, a citizen, who habitually acts as an enemy to her most essential and established institutions? Does he, in any way, deserve the honor of a citizen, who lives as if he wished to overthrow the very pillars of public and private principle?

For let the supposition be made, for a moment, that the Bible were lost, and the Sabbath abolished, and the ministry expelled, and the Churches pulled down, and all sense of religion utterly done away by universal atheism, and what would be the inevitable consequence but a scene of anarchy, and bloody violence, and utter destruction of all the rights of man in honor, liberty, property, or even life? A slight specimen of such a result was exhibited, to the horror and amazement of Europe, when the French Directory, through the madness of their first revolution, in 1793, tried the experiment upon the materials which Voltaire, Rousseau, and other infidels of talent had unconsciously prepared for the melancholy catastrophe. Every reader of modern history knows that the Sabbath was changed for a tenth day of public festivity, and the priests were silenced, and the temples of religion closed, and atheism was proclaimed, while a celebrated courtezan was adopted instead of the Deity, and set upon a throne, and adored by the name of the Goddess of Reason. And during the period when this terrible insanity prevailed, what was the condition of the most refined metropolis of Europe? It was a constant scene of the most intense suffering and wretchedness. Robbery, murders, and lust prevailed. The foundations of society were overturned. The prisons were crowded by innocent victims charged with *incivism* by the lowest ruffians. The river Seine was filled with dead bodies, often tied together. The guillotine was kept streaming with blood, for the passage of which it became necessary to make an immense aqueduct in the Place St. Antoine. Every rule of law and justice was laughed to scorn, while the revolutionary tribunals, day by day, sent multitudes to instant death, on the mere presentment of lists handed in by their satellites! Well was this awful period of atheistic madness and ferocity called THE REIGN OF TERROR! The details of the horrid butcheries, given by Prudhomme, occupy six volumes, though far from complete. Amongst them we find, at Paris, 1,278 noblemen, 750 noble women, 1,467 females of the middle ranks, 350 nuns, and 1,135 priests. In La Vendée, 15,000 women, 22,000 children, and 860,000 men of various classes. At Nantes, under the proconsulate of Carrier, 32,000, including 500 children shot, 1,500 children drowned, 264 women shot, 500 women drowned, 300 priests shot, 460 priests drowned, 1,400 noblemen drowned, 5,300 mechanics drowned; and to these the historian adds 31,000 victims in Lyons! This is a mere indication of the misery which reigned throughout France, and brought that mighty nation to the verge of destruction, until at length Napoleon Bonaparte, having seized the reins of power, restored the public service of religion; and law, security, and order returned once more.

It needs but small reflection on the very nature of things, to convince the most thoughtless mind how absolutely every blessing of the present life depends on the religious principle. Even the most corrupt religion is better than none. Such, as I have fully shown, was the universal sense of all the great philosophers of antiquity, who prescribed it to every citizen, in the strongest terms, that he must tender all due and public reverence to the gods, notwithstanding those gods were the idols of heathenism. How much more must it be the duty of the American citizen to honor that pure Christianity which is alone authoritative, because it is alone divine!

Hence it follows, undeniably, that the citizen who refuses to pay open and consistent respect to religion, is acting as the worst enemy of the public good. He is the willing patron of a course which, if it be suffered to prevail, must bring the nation and himself to ruin. He is a breaker of the law of the Sabbath-day, which every State in the Union has established. He is doing his utmost, by his encouragement and example, to destroy the only principle on which the government and justice of the land can possibly be administered. He is casting mockery upon the friends of conscience and of duty. In a word, he is undermining the very foundation of all order and morality, and laying a train which may ultimately scatter to the winds the honor, welfare, and prosperity of his country.

True, it may be said that he does not mean it so. He does not consider that he is bound to look beyond his individual choice and gratification. He thinks that he has a right to please himself, and cannot see that the public interest has any concern with the question. But in this he errs egregiously. I have already quoted the admirable maxim of Aristotle, that "the citizens are *partners in the republic*, since otherwise, strictly speaking, *they are not citizens at all.*"* No citizen, therefore, can separate himself from the rest, or follow a course which is hostile to the general welfare, without sinning against his country. The

---

* P. 72.

interest which he holds in the community is the correlative of the interest which the community hold in him. As a *partner*, he is bound to act for the benefit of the whole, and if he pursues his personal will in a way which is calculated to bring them into peril, he violates the implied compact which holds society together, and forfeits his right to be considered a member of the commonwealth.

6. But he may do all that I have specified—he may render all outward honor to the religion of the land, study the Scriptures with serious attention, select his Church with reference to their inspired authority, and keep the Sabbath-day with punctual reverence, and yet not be a Christian in the spiritual sense. In other words, he may be a Christian *intellectually and conscientiously*, yet not be a Christian *in his heart*. And therefore, if he would be perfectly consistent, he should apply the religion of the Bible to his own soul, pray earnestly and perseveringly for the influence of the Holy Spirit, and never cease, until he is a personal partaker of the inward light and peace which can only be found in a thorough, earnest, and entire adoption of the Gospel system. For however highly he may estimate the rights and duties of the American citizen, yet the time must come when he will feel that they are of little worth, in comparison with those which he should have realized and appropriated, as the citizen of heaven.

CHAPTER V.

MORALITY, AS THE FOUNDATION OF POLITICS.

IT is of the very nature of a republic that the science of politics belongs alike to every citizen, because there it is especially true that "all citizens," in the words of Aristotle, "obey and govern by turns, and are therefore participators in the republic, each in his own lot."* And it is the noblest and most extensive of all human sciences, because it embraces the whole scope of government, law, and moral action.

In its lower sense, however, politics may be considered as an art; and here it is unavoidably open to great abuses, since it is always liable to be degraded from its high and comprehensive function, to the maintenance of individual ambition or cupidity, of factious and disorganizing schemes, and of a narrow party spirit.

But, just as the true basis of morality is religion, so the true basis of politics, considered as a science, is morality. Therefore Aristotle laid down the maxim, that "a treatise on morals is a principal part of politics."† And here, it may be both useful and interesting to trace the principles of morality, as they were exhibited by the better class of the ancient philosophers; in which there is no surer guide than the celebrated Cicero's work *De Officiis*, addressed to his own son, while he was completing his education at Athens. I say "the better class" of the old philosophers, because Cicero himself admits that there were only three of the ancient schools which had a right to lay down any

* Aristot. De Repub. l. vii. c. xiv. p. 266, &c.

† Aristot. Ethic. c. i. t. 2, p. 85.

rules on the subject of morality, namely, the Stoics, who followed Zeno; the Academics, whose founder was Plato; and the Peripatetics, whose oracle was Aristotle. All the rest he repudiates, taking Panætius, the Stoic, for his principal director, but supplying the defects of that philosopher from his own superior stores of wisdom and reflection. It is not my object, however, to translate this author, for that has been already done by others; and neither the limits nor the design of my present work would justify the labor. The substance only of his order and his statements will be given, as equally useful and less tedious to my readers, while a brief title will indicate the special topic of each section.

1. *Cicero, on the Basis of Social Duty.*

First stands the rule, that we must consider what is good, and what is for our greatest good. For this is the main principle which determines our duty. And all the moral philosophers have written most largely about offices or duties, because the whole virtue and credit of our lives depend on these, and all the baseness or turpitude of mankind arises from their violation.

Every action may be regarded with respect to this fundamental rule, and we are obliged to determine, accordingly, 1. Whether it be right, or the contrary; 2. Whether it will obtain for us pleasures, riches, honors, or power, which may be used for the benefit of others, as well as of ourselves; 3. Whether what is right stands opposed to what is profitable, and which we should prefer.

2. *Cicero, on Virtue, as the highest Good.*

The primary law of all creatures is shown in their instinct

of self-preservation, the avoidance of what hurts them, the securing what is necessary for their comfortable subsistence, the desire to propagate their species, and the care and affection which they exhibit towards their young. But man, in addition to these, has the faculty of reason, by which he can extend his thoughts to the consequences of his actions. Moreover, he is formed for society, and can feel for all his fellow-creatures. He is, further, impelled to seek for knowledge and for truth. He is also led to a longing for pre-eminence. He discerns the beauty of order and harmony. He is impressed by grace and symmetry in the objects of sight. In fine, he is endowed with a moral conscience. Hence he possesses a sense of *right* or *virtue*, as the highest good; and this is not only, in its own nature, commendable above all things, but is, in effect, acknowledged and praised by all mankind.

3. *Cicero, on the Subdivisions of Virtue.*

But this virtue may be subdivided into many distinct heads or subjects of examination. First, we may consider the duty of seeking the truth, which is called *Prudence.* Next comes the duty of maintaining the interests of society, of rendering to every man his due, and of fidelity to our word in all engagements, which is called *Justice.* Thirdly, the duty of a brave and invincible mind in the defence of right, which is embraced by the terms *Fortitude* and *Courage.* And lastly, the duty of keeping our words and actions within the proper limits of order and decency, which is commonly termed *Temperance*, or *Moderation.* All these duties are of such high esteem that they are called *virtues;* and the ideal of perfect virtue includes the whole. Let us consider each distinctly.

4. *Cicero, on Prudence, as a Cardinal Virtue.*

The first-named virtue, PRUDENCE, is wholly occupied with the knowledge of truth, and belongs peculiarly to our reasonable nature. For we are all influenced by the desire of knowledge. We account it reproachful and degrading to be subject to imposition, or to be detected in ignorance or error. We look up with respect and reverence to those who are qualified to teach us. We look down with pity or contempt on those who are less intelligent than ourselves, and regard them as children in comparison. But in our efforts to attain knowledge, we must guard ourselves against a great and common cause of failure: namely, a credulous haste and rashness in giving our assent, presuming that we really know, before we have sufficiently examined. To avoid this, we must employ a fair amount of time and labor, and carefully look at both sides of every question, before we decide. And there is yet another frequent error, when we devote an unwise amount of pains and study to subjects which are of very small importance in themselves, to the neglect of the more serious duties of life. For no man can attain an equal knowledge in every department. Prudence requires, therefore, that he should carefully consider the relation of each to his own position in society, remembering always that it is *action* alone which gives true value to virtue.

5. *Cicero, on Justice.*

The next topic, according to our order, is JUSTICE. And it is this which is mainly concerned in upholding society, and regulating the intercourse amongst mankind on which society depends. Hence it is accounted the most glorious of all the virtues, and that which chiefly entitles us to the

appellation of good men. In connection with it, however, we may class liberality and benevolence, without which, the proper ornament of justice is wanting. It is true, indeed, that every one has a right to enjoy his own, and he cannot be deprived of it, by force or fraud, unless justice be violated. But nevertheless, as Plato saith, "We are not born for ourselves alone, since our country, our relatives, and our friends, have a just claim upon us." According to the Stoics, too, it is unquestionable that "whatever exists on earth was designed for the service of men, and men themselves were intended for the service, the good, and the assistance of each other." Therefore we must follow nature, and second her intentions by supporting the general interest of all, by mutually giving and receiving benefits, and by such applications of our knowledge, industry, riches, and influence, as may best maintain the loving and affectionate temper of society. The great foundation of justice, however, is fidelity—a firm adherence to our engagements, and a conscientious performance of all compacts and agreements. The opposite of this is injustice, which may be either positive or negative. The first, or positive injustice, consists in doing some actual injury to another. The second, or negative injustice, lies in our tamely suffering injustice to be done, without any effort to prevent it, even though it may be in our power. Both of these may arise from a selfish fear of evil consequences to ourselves. The latter may also arise from an equally selfish apathy. But generally, the first sort of injustice is the product of some irregular or exorbitant appetite, as the ambition of power, or the covetous desire of riches; while the other proceeds from the dread of giving offence, and so creating enmity: though it is likewise true that some men are chargeable with it merely because they are indolent, or mean-spirited, or so much absorbed in their own affairs that they will not take time to interfere for the protection of their neighbor. It is, indeed, the sentiment of Plato that philosophers are just, even when they neglect those things for which others are contending; since they are wholly occupied in searching after truth, and disdain the ordinary disputes of those around them. But this conclusion is not to be approved, since philosophers ought not to be so engaged in their learning and studies, as to abandon their friends when they need their succor. And still less can those persons be defended who refuse to aid the oppressed from a morose and unsympathizing disposition, on the plea that they meddle with nobody's business but their own. For although such men do no injustice, in one respect, yet they are guilty of it in another, because they desert the common good of society, and give neither time, nor pains, nor money for its preservation.

Here, however, the limits of justice are not so fixed that they cannot be altered by circumstances. There may be a contract or promise, for example, which ought to be broken, because the keeping of it would be more hurtful than the breach, either to both the parties or to the public, or because it was made under the influence of fraud or force, without any real right to exact the obligation. On this principle, the promise or oath given to robbers, that if their victim be allowed to depart he will not accuse them, is not binding—inasmuch as they could not justly claim the fulfilment of a pledge which their own injustice had demanded. But the just rules of morality approve the conduct of Regulus, when he refused to violate his oath to surrender himself to the Carthaginians, if the Romans should decide on rejecting the proposals of peace; because the Carthaginians had already a right to kill him, as a public enemy, by the laws of war; and therefore they had a right to place their own conditions on his embassy when they sent him as their envoy to the Romans: and still further, because his heroic example of conscientious integrity, in the face of a horrid death, was the noblest sacrifice which he could possibly make to the honor of his country.

And there is also a limit dictated by justice, to bounty or liberality. For it must not be exercised to the injury of others, nor beyond the bound of our estates, nor without observing a judicious discrimination between the various merits of its objects. And these are not the only rules. Thus gifts made by princes, when they plunder from one what they bestow upon another—gifts which are the mere product of pride and ostentation—gifts presented in the expectation of an ample return—gifts lavished upon those who do not need them—these are all likewise to be condemned, as no true examples of a just liberality.

6. *Cicero, on Fortitude.*

We come next to FORTITUDE, a virtue which includes constancy of mind, bravery, and courage. Of these, the last-named has always been a special favorite amongst the multitude. But courage is only praiseworthy, when it is employed for the safety and good of our country. The really brave man must always be the friend of truth, benevolence, and justice. And courage is often as necessary in peace as in war, and requires besides, when it is used in the administration of government, far more study, pains, and application.

True *fortitude*, therefore, demands, on the part of those who are concerned in government, a resolute and unyielding adherence to the precepts of Plato; 1st, To make the safety and interest of the citizens the great aim of all their thoughts and efforts, without regard to their own personal advantage; and, 2d, so to take care of the whole republic as not to serve the interest of any party, to the neglect or prejudice of the rest. There should be no contention for office or for honor; no calumnies nor false accusations; no heat nor resentment against adversaries. In States which are free, and where all men enjoy the same privileges, they should especially cultivate courtesy, affability, and serenity of mind. And governors should be like the laws themselves, which punish offenders according to justice, without anger, prejudice, or partiality.

Another duty of Fortitude is, not to be haughty or arrogant when fortune favors us, nor to be cast down by the reverse. The more highly we are raised, the more watchful we should be to keep our words and actions within the bounds of meekness and humility. True fortitude consists in constancy of mind, which does not veer about with the wind of circumstances. Men are often praised for this quality, because they bear hardship well, and struggle bravely with their difficulties. But if the same men become afterwards intoxicated by success, they prove that their former endurance was the work of necessity, rather than the result of principle. Hence the accession of wealth is a sure test, as to the reality of this virtue. He that truly possesses it will first secure his possessions by honest and laudable means, and will then distribute them, without vanity or pride, in acts of just munificence and liberality.

7. *Cicero, on Temperance.*

The last of these eminent virtues is TEMPERANCE, or moderation, which includes modesty, continence, and the strict government of the passions. On the one hand, every action should be guarded against precipitancy and rashness; and on the other, it should be preserved from carelessness and neglect. The appetites must be brought under the strict control of reason, and nothing should be said or done, for which reason cannot give a just account. Jestings and diversions are allowable, provided they do not trespass on the feelings or comfort of others, but be agreeable to the laws of decency and good manners. Those which are vulgar, abusive, scandalous, or obscene, should never be tolerated; but only such as are pure, ingenious, and acceptable to well-regulated minds. In our food, clothing, furniture, and all sensual indulgences, respect must always be paid to health, strength, and propriety, rather than to pleasure. Luxury, softness, and effeminacy should be altogether despised; and we should prefer a life of frugality, strict sobriety, and wholesome moderation.

In all this, however, there is room enough allowed for every one to follow his own peculiar character, provided there be nothing vicious in it. In the choice of business, for example, we should consult nature as to what we are best adapted to pursue. And in manners, we should not imitate those of other people, but be easy, simple, and unaffected, in the style which suits ourselves; for nothing sits so well upon a man as that which agrees with his own disposition. Even actors by profession are not able to succeed alike in all parts, but are obliged to confine themselves to such as best accord with their natural powers. Much more impossible is it that we should succeed for life in a vocation to which we are not adapted. Yet the rules of morality and virtue are the same in every variety of condition. All men cannot plead at the bar, or play the orator before the people, or lead an army, or guide the State. But all may practise justice, fidelity, modesty, temperance, and liberality, and thus contribute their share to the general good.

8. *Cicero, on various maxims of Social Duty and Propriety.*

The young should reverence the aged, and be guided by their counsels; they should also be inured to labor of mind and body, so as to bear the toils of business, and serve their country either in peace or war; while their pleasures should never exceed the bounds of propriety and moderation. The aged should lessen the labors of the body, and give themselves chiefly to those of the mind; advising the young, aiding the republic, and avoiding unprofitable idleness. Luxury and riot are unbecoming at every period of life, but in old age, they are scandalous. Magistrates, in their persons, represent the commonwealth, and are bound to maintain its dignity and credit, as men in public trust. But strangers and sojourners should confine themselves to their own affairs, and not intermeddle with the business of the State, in which they have no allotted duty. In a word, propriety and decorum should govern in every thing. All that may offend the eye or the ear should be avoided. Whether standing, or walking, or sitting, or leaning—nay, in our very countenances, in the cast of our eyes, and the motions of our hands, we should be careful to observe what is becoming; avoiding too much niceness and effeminacy on the one hand, and awkwardness or vulgarity on the other. Men should be especially careful not to use what is appropriate to women, and women should shun what properly belongs to men. And in ordinary discourse we should never abuse those who are absent, nor invade the rights or feelings of the company, but always be content with our own share of attention, and say only what is likely to be entertaining and acceptable.

Our dwellings, furniture, and tables should be, in like manner, suited to our station and our means, but always in moderation, so that men may have no occasion to find fault either with our needless display, or with our parsimony. We should observe the mistakes of others for the purpose of correcting ourselves. And when we are in doubt, we should ask the advice of those who have learning and experience, just as artists and sculptors are ready to improve their work by the taste and judgment of their friends.

9. *Cicero, on Piety, as first in the order of Duty.*

Society is the proper condition of man, who can never be long satisfied with perfect solitude. But our duties in society have a certain order. Reverence for religion stands in the first rank. Next comes our duty to our country; thirdly, our duty to our parents; and so on, to all the rest.

Some persons make a wide distinction between profit and virtue. But this is a great error, because nothing that is not virtuous can be truly profitable. The means to procure the favor of heaven is to lead a holy and religious life. And, next to heaven, men contribute most to the happiness of each other. In like manner, all the calamities produced by famines, pestilences, earthquakes, inundations, and the other natural troubles of mortality, are as nothing in comparison with the miseries produced by men themselves, in wars, seditions, and strifes, through the indulgence of cupidity.

10. *Cicero, on Love, as the strongest Principle of Influence.*

Of all the methods which advance our interest, there is none so effective as love, and none so improper as fear. The most successful tyrants live in perpetual apprehension. Thus Dionysius of Syracuse chose to singe off his beard with coals, sooner than trust his throat to the barber. And Alexander the Pheræan dreaded even to visit the chamber of his wife, without an armed Thracian, holding a drawn sword, to go before him. The Roman republic has sunk into ruin, since her rulers have endeavored to govern by fear, rather than by affection. For, true glory consists in these three ingredients: 1st. The love and good-will of the people; 2d. Their trust and confidence in the man; and 3d. Their estimate and admiration of his character as being worthy of his honors. The means of acquiring these from the public are the same which must be used to secure them from individuals, because the opinions of individuals make up, sooner or later, the judgment of the nation. Hence, the love of the people is chiefly to be gained by bounty and kindness. They are pleased with every word and act which prove the desire to do them good, even when a man may not have the means to effect it. And the very name of liberality, beneficence, fidelity, and justice, united with those qualities which give a pleasing smoothness to our conversation, is of great efficacy. For all men love those in whom they suppose these virtues to reside; while, without them, no wisdom, talents, or energy can secure their confidence and affection.

But those persons are quite in error who think that these virtues can be assumed, so as to pass current. On the contrary, the multitude can never be long deceived; and therefore the man must actually *be* what he would *appear*, or he cannot be successful.

Of those who give largely, some are prodigal, and others are liberal. The prodigal consume vast sums in public feasts, in building theatres, and in getting up other sports and recreations for the people. But such things are soon forgotten. The liberal are those who do good, redeeming poor prisoners, helping men out of debt, and assisting them, in various ways, to make or increase their fortunes. To these, also, may be added works of public utility, such as repairing the defences of the city, constructing public aqueducts, docks, or havens, the memory of which will last and go down to posterity. And as it is laudable to be generous in giving, so we ought not to be too rigorous in demanding, but in every transaction of buying, selling, leasing, and hiring, we should conduct ourselves with fairness and kindness, and be willing even to yield our just rights, on certain occasions, in order to avoid contention. Hospitality, too, is another form of the same virtue, which goes far, when it is practised without pride or ostentation. And in all our acts of liberality, we should remember that it is better to serve the deserving than the great—the poor and honest man, rather than the rich or noble.

11. *Cicero, on the Dangers of Avarice.*

In every variety of business, however, especially if it be of a public nature, nothing is more necessary than to keep ourselves untainted by the suspicion of avarice. It was a well-known saying of Caius the Samnite, that "when the Romans begin to take bribes, there will soon be an end of their flourishing empire." The old Romans were perfectly free from this shameful imputation. Of all the vices, there is none more detestable than avarice, but it is emphatically so in those who bear rule in the government of the State, since it is not only mean and abominable, but even impious, to make a prey of the commonwealth, which has advanced us to honor under the express obligation to labor for the public good. The famous oracle of the Pythian Apollo which declared that "nothing but avarice could be the ruin of Sparta," seems to have been intended not merely for the Lacedæmonians, but for every wealthy and prosperous nation. No accusation, therefore, should be more carefully avoided, since none can be more fatal to the love and confidence of the people.

12. *Cicero, on National Character.*

The virtue of justice, which is so essential to the character of the individual, is yet more essential to the character of a nation. Hence no government should ever allow debts to be repudiated; for faith or credit holds all society together, and this can never be sustained unless men are under some necessity of paying what they owe.

Every man should believe that what is right is always profitable, and that his own interest in particular is the same as that of the community in general; since otherwise, he violates the order of that society which heaven has established. If it were possible, therefore, to hide our actions from the eyes of all others, and even from the divine inspection itself, yet we should be careful to abstain from the vices of covetousness and injustice, of lasciviousness and incontinency.

13. *Cicero, on the True Unity of Interest and Virtue.*

It is a good saying of Chrysippus, that "he who is running a race ought to strive as much as he can to get before his competitor, but he must not trip up his heels, nor thrust him aside with his hands. So, in life, it is allowable that every one should gain what is useful and convenient for his comfortable subsistence, but it is not allowable to take it from other people." There is one short and easy rule which may be applicable in most cases: viz., never to prefer what seems to be profitable, such as honor, riches, or pleasure, before a kindness to a friend; but never to do any thing, even for the sake of a friend, which is an injury to the public, or a breach of our oath, or other solemn engagement; since it is impossible that he who acts thus can ever be a good man.

Those who violate the rules of justice and honesty in the pursuit of political power, are altogether reprehensible. Euripides, indeed, in his tragedy of Phœnissæ, saith,

> "If ever we do break the rules of right,
> 'Tis when a kingdom is the glorious prize.
> In all things else be just."

But this is wicked and detestable, for nothing can be worse than to obtain the responsible dignity of government, by the use of unworthy and unlawful means.

In fine, can any thing be profitable which is inconsistent with justice, continence, temperance, and moderation? Certain philosophers, indeed, and chiefly Epicurus, reduce all good to pleasure. But pleasure is usually contrary to virtue, and virtue disdains the conjunction with pleasure; for although we should allow that pleasure may serve for a kind of sauce to give a relish to duty, yet it has no true profit or advantage in itself.

I have now given to my readers the substance of Cicero's

famous treatise, in which we have the results of the wisdom of the ancients, aided by his personal experience, and combining the philosophy of the Stoics with his own. And here it may be well to mark his peculiar claims, to be considered a standard of authority.

1. In the first place, Cicero possessed the largest qualifications of talents, education, official eminence, and extensive knowledge of mankind, which were ever recognized in any writer on the subject. He was consul in the last period of the old Roman republic, and beheld its liberties expire. His own administration, both civil and military, was conducted with great ability and vigor, united to unquestionable integrity. And when, in the intervals of public duty, he devoted himself to his favorite philosophical studies, he brought to the task the whole wealth of practical familiarity with government, law, popular eloquence, and human character in all its phases; which enabled his extraordinary intellectual powers to form the soundest judgment, and entitled him to the honor which he has received, from eighteen centuries of universal applause.

In Cicero, therefore, we have a remarkable combination. For he was at once the prince of Roman orators, the consistent republican, the practical politician, the brave general, the incorruptible patriot, the successful governor, the acknowledged savior of his country from the conspiracy of Catiline, the profound moral philosopher, and at last, the martyr of expiring liberty. His work *De Officiis*, from which I have culled all the more important principles, is perhaps the most valuable of his numerous writings, and has earned the praise of being, "to this day, the finest treatise on virtue inspired by pure human wisdom."*

* See Art. Cicero, Encyc. Americana.

For these reasons, I have attached so much importance to the sentiments of this distinguished Roman. His death, at the age of sixty-four, took place forty-three years before the Christian era; and it is certainly wonderful to find the general accordance of his principles with the morality of the Gospel, and its singular adaptation to our own times; when we remember that he lived nineteen centuries ago, and in the religious darkness of heathenism.

2. We may observe, in the second place, that this admirable philosopher rested the whole science of politics on religion, morality, and intelligence; without which he held it impossible that any citizen could be worthy of public honor, or could long retain his hold upon the respect or confidence of the people. Prudence, justice, fortitude, and temperance, accompanied by courtesy, liberality, and disinterestedness, were in his view the only qualities which could acquire a genuine and enduring hold upon the popular esteem; and without these, no conceivable amount of address, energy, or talent, could establish a truly desirable and lasting reputation.

3. In the third place, we must look at the principle which Cicero lays down so plainly, that these virtues could not be successfully assumed as a mask to deceive the public penetration. The true character of every man was sure to be generally understood at last, and no art could long deceive the watchful eye of the people. Hence the politician must actually *be* what he would *appear*, since otherwise his efforts to obtain the credit of a patriot must be ultimately abortive.

4. For, this experienced and philosophic statesman utterly abjures the popular fallacy that the private character of a man may be immoral and degrading, while his public

character shall be pure and exemplary. It may seem so for a little while, during the first novelty of his official position. But custom soon destroys the feeble restraint, and nature and habit prove too strong for any disguise of outward expediency.

5. And fifthly, we may remark, that Cicero ascribes the ruin of the Roman republic to the moral degeneracy of the citizens, and particularly specifies avarice, producing bribery and corruption, as the vice which most of all brought the commonwealth to destruction.

Now in all of this, it would be easy to show that the Christian Scriptures abound in similar lessons of political wisdom. But the authority on which they are placed is infinitely more exalted, because every act, word, and even thought, is there shown to be brought under the cognizance of the Almighty; and the argument for virtue is raised from earth to heaven, from the doubtful reward of popular praise to the unerring judgment of eternity. And I know of nothing which tends more strongly to shame the irreligious recklessness of our own age, than to see how wonderfully the Bible is vindicated by the maxims of true philosophy, enjoining the same virtues of piety, prudence, justice, fortitude, temperance, chastity, liberality, and benevolence, as essential to the true patriot and politician; and condemning the same vices of impiety, licentiousness, deceit, falsehood, covetousness, venality, bribery, and corruption, as fatal to the individual man, and no less fatal to the public welfare. For thus we are obliged to acknowledge that the morality of the Gospel is approved by the brightest intellects amongst the heathen themselves; and that he who refuses to adopt it is condemned not only by the law of faith, but by the plain maxims of right reason.

But let us now proceed to examine the *rights and duties* of the American citizen, which are thus directly suggested by the principles both of religion and philosophy.

It is his right, as "a partner in the republic," to express his honest convictions, in word or writing, concerning every candidate for office, and every political measure contemplated or adopted by those who are in possession of the legislative or executive function. And this liberty of speech and of the press, guarantied in express terms by the Constitution, should never be discouraged nor put down by the fear of party, the threats of violence, or the clamor of public prejudice; because it is vitally essential to the maintenance of political integrity, and, therefore, the man who assails its just and proper exercise should be universally regarded as a traitor in his heart to the freedom of his country.

It is a further right of the American citizen to form or join a party of his fellow-citizens, who judge alike of the public interest, and to consult with them in any lawful manner, as to the best modes of giving full effect to what they honestly believe most advantageous to the general welfare. For no man, in matters of a political character, can do any thing alone. Parties, indeed, are the necessary incidents of freedom. The desired results can only be accomplished by numbers, and numbers must be allowed to unite, in order that they may think, deliberate, and act together.

But the exercise of this right must not be suffered to invade the other. For, as every citizen has a right to think and speak his sentiments with the honest sincerity which becomes a freeman, and has also a right to form or join a party consisting of such as are like-minded with himself, so likewise he has a third right, arising directly from these two, namely, the right to leave his party, when he thinks that they are going wrong, or to form a new one, if none of the existing parties accord with his honest convictions of public duty. And all these rights he should be allowed to exercise, without the slightest attempt to intimidate or coerce him. For just as he who can be so intimidated or coerced, has so far lost his personal liberty, even so he who seeks, directly or indirectly, to take that liberty away, shows himself to be a despot in his heart, and an enemy to the most essential rule of republican equality.

From the rights with which every intelligent citizen is thus invested, I proceed to his duties. For these should never be separated, being always, and in every case, correlatives of each other.

In the first place, then, it is his duty to *be* such a citizen as the welfare of his country requires, since otherwise, he disqualifies himself for the proper exercise of his rights as "a partner of the republic." I have shown that the public welfare and prosperity are founded upon religion, morality, and intelligence; that the maxims of the best political philosophers, even among the heathen, require prudence, justice, fortitude, temperance, disinterestedness, liberality, and benevolence, from every citizen, and that the contrary vices tend to drive the country into ultimate ruin. Hence the first duty of political life is a *moral duty*, operating on each member of the republic. Every voter is bound to be faithful, in his own person, to the virtue which he expects from the public candidate. For in a government like ours, there is no difference between the personal relations of the several parties to the welfare of the whole. The people are sovereign. The public officers are their servants. They are appointed by election. But the electors have no right to ask that their servants shall be better than themselves. They may, indeed, demand of them a higher capacity for the public functions of the State, because that is a fair and just ground of choice or preference, and in that there must needs be a great variety. In *moral principle*, however, all men are capable of attaining a certain mark of reasonable consistency, and no one has a right to find fault with another, whose virtue is equal to his own.

It is, secondly, the duty of the American citizen to support such candidates as have an established moral character, based, as all true moral character must be, on a genuine reverence for the religion and laws of the country. For I have shown that the oath of office is a religious obligation, resting, for its whole force, on a religious conscience, without which such oath can have no moral force or power on the individual. No talents, no party zeal, no popular availability, should be taken as a substitute for this. And every man understands its value, in the private relations of life. The first quality which we all demand in a servant, in a clerk, in a teacher, in an agent, or in any other office belonging to the various interests of our social state, is conscientious honesty and fidelity. What right have we to dispense with this when we select our public servants, our rulers, our magistrates, or our legislators? Is a moral conscience to be required for the faithful fulfilment of every individual trust, and shall it not be much more required for those far higher trusts, which involve the interest of thousands?

In the third place, and as a necessary consequence of the rule just stated, it is the duty of the American citizen to cast aside the false and most pernicious maxim that the *private* character of a candidate for office has nothing to do with his *public* character. This is in truth a most absurd fallacy. For it is manifest that the possession of a public office cannot change the *man*. It only gives him a new field for the display of his principles, whatever they may be, and therefore, if he be a vicious or immoral man, it is impossible that he should prove to be a virtuous or a moral officer.

We have seen that, by the theory of our government, the people are the sovereign power, and every citizen is a partner in the republic. From this, therefore, I deduce the fourth duty of every American citizen, to make himself familiar with the Constitution of his country, so as to comprehend, in some reasonable degree, its true national character; since, without some clear knowledge of this, he must be incapable of understanding the questions which may be determined by his vote, or of judging, for himself, the soundness of the views presented by contending parties. Hence it is evident that our system demands a certain measure of *intelligence*, as well as virtue, in the great body of the people, if they would not be continually led astray by the arts of designing demagogues. For, no one who is altogether ignorant of the distinctive principles of our national system, can exercise his elective franchise as he ought to do. His want of intelligence makes him, of necessity, the blind tool of other men's dictation. He fancies himself a freeman, while he is, in reality, a slave. Nor can he be worthy to act as a partner in the republic, who is incapable or unwilling to inform himself concerning the high and important interests, on which the welfare and even the very existence of the republic essentially depend.

It is undeniable, however, that we have a vast amount of this deplorable ignorance throughout the country. There are, probably, millions of men, invested with the rights of citizens, who have never given a single day to the study of the Constitution, to say nothing of those who are too ignorant to understand its meaning, or even to read its language. It is evident that, under this condition of things, it is impossible that our republican theory can be reduced to practice. The power of voting is vested in the multitude, but the power of *governing the votes* is really exercised by a comparative few. Hence, the democratic element, of which we boast, sinks into an oligarchy of the worst kind, because it is altogether irresponsible. And the destiny of our country, in the eyes of sober reason, can hardly be anticipated as prosperous or successful, unless some adequate remedy can be devised and adopted for this serious and increasing evil. For this dangerous state of prevailing ignorance of what every citizen is bound to know, two correctives may be suggested, the first of which concerns our native citizens, and the second applies to foreigners seeking for the right of naturalization.

In order, therefore, to secure a proper measure of intelligence amongst our native citizens, I would earnestly insist upon a course of instruction upon the history and principles of the Constitution, in all our public schools, academies, and colleges. Our legislatures should assign the office of teacher in this department, to men of competent ability, with a salary of sufficient amount to make it honorable. A catechism on the true theory of our government should be prepared by public authority, and no one should be admitted to the privilege of a voter, without exhibiting a certificate from the teacher, that he had acquired a fair knowledge of the meaning of our great national system, between the ages of eighteen and twenty-one, at which time the mind is usually mature enough to understand the subject. In this way a reasonable measure of intelligence may easily be secured to the rising generation, for the fulfilment of their obligations as citizens. And the result could hardly fail to produce an immense improvement in every department of the public interest.

The same principle should be applied to every foreigner, who seeks the benefit of naturalization. He should be examined in the book of instruction prepared for the native citizen, and if he cannot prove his proficiency in that, he should be rejected as deficient in the intelligence which is demanded by the theory of our republic. This simple remedy would purge the elective franchise, in the course of a few years, of many evils which now disgrace our elections. It would elevate the character and influence of our great nation in the judgment of the world. It would make the people capable of performing the serious duties which the genius of our Constitution requires; and the sophistry of party spirit, the arts of the unscrupulous demagogue, and the foul corruption of bribery, would no longer dare to tamper with the sacred trust of American freedom, without meeting at once with the indignant execration which they deserve.

CHAPTER VI.

ON THE CONSTITUTIONAL RIGHTS AND DUTIES OF THE AMERICAN CITIZEN IN REFERENCE TO SLAVERY.

HAVING proved sufficiently, as I trust, that morals must be founded on religion, and that politics, in the only true sense, must be based upon morals, I should willingly leave without remark the vexed subjects of our day and country, if I were not convinced that it is a duty to contribute my share, however humble, towards the establishment of true practical principle. As a Christian teacher, I am not at liberty to pass over those errors which strike directly at the authority of the Word of God. And as a citizen, and therefore a "partner in the republic," I may not turn aside from the application of truth to that perilous topic of discussion, which threatens the Constitution itself, and, if not set at rest, may ultimately sink our national greatness into ruin.

In bespeaking, however, the favorable attention of my readers to the ensuing argument, I beg leave to premise that I have at least one ground on which I may claim their confidence in my sincerity and candor: namely, that my conclusions stand in direct opposition to my former prejudices, habits, and feelings. I have no reason to hope that they will be acceptable to those whose good opinion I should most desire to secure. Their maintenance can bring me no accession of comfort, of advantage, or of commendation from society around me. But I have not been accustomed to measure the standard of duty by the rules of popularity or worldly interest. I am too old to be drawn away from my independent regard for truth, by the fear or the hope of personal consequences. And I declare my convictions, therefore, with no other motive or desire than to discharge honestly my own moral obligation; and to aid the judgment of impartial and reflecting men, in determining the real merits of a deeply exciting and important question.

That slavery, considered in itself, is an evil, I consider to be perfectly clear and incontrovertible. But this goes a very little way towards the settlement of the point under discussion. In the present condition of mankind, we are compelled to submit to innumerable evils, in order to avoid some greater evil; and a choice between evils is frequently the only course left to human wisdom and sagacity. In this aspect of our earthly lot, we account evil to be a good, if it relieve us from a heavier calamity. Thus war is an acknowledged evil—a positive curse. Yet war becomes a good, notwithstanding, if it protect the land from tyranny or violence. The loss of a limb is an evil. Yet if its amputation be necessary to save our life, it is good to suffer the loss, without which life would be sacrificed. An unhappy marriage is an evil. Yet it may be more tolerable than the shame or penury of a divorce, and therefore it is good to endure its trials by comparison. A thousand cases might thus be put, in which evil must be preferred, and even maintained, if the consequences of our escape be the exposure to a still more deplorable catastrophe.

But these, it may be alleged, are physical evils, whereas slavery is a moral evil—a crime against humanity—a sin against God. Let us try the validity of this proposition by an appeal to "the higher law," by which alone we can test the rules of religious and moral obligation.

And here, of course, we are referred to the Bible, because we have no other declaration of His will from the Supreme Lawgiver. I am not aware that there is any "higher law" than this, since I do not hear that there are any modern prophets amongst our ultra-abolitionists, claiming a special authority from heaven, and armed, like the apostles, with the power of miracles to prove their commission. To the Bible, therefore, let us go, and learn what Moses, and Christ Himself and His inspired messengers, said and did, in reference to slavery.

First, then, we find Moses delivering the prophecy of the patriarch Noah, immediately after the deluge, in which slavery is expressly predicted (Gen. ix. 25–27).

"Cursed be Canaan, a servant of servants shall he be unto his brethren. And he said, Blessed be the Lord God of Shem, and Canaan shall be his servant. God shall enlarge Japheth, and he shall dwell in the tents of Shem, and Canaan shall be his servant."

That this curse was a physical and not a moral curse, is too manifest to need any argument. It was like the curse pronounced on the earth, which the labor of man was permitted to convert into a blessing. It was like the sentence which condemned our race to toil and death, but yet was intended to work ultimate good through the system of redemption. And to prove that it involved no moral crime or sin against the will of the Almighty, we find the principle of slavery incorporated in the divine law laid down for the chosen people. For thus we read in the Book of Exodus, ch. xxi. 2–6:

"If thou buy an Hebrew servant, six years he shall serve, and in the seventh he shall go out free for nothing. If he came in by himself, he shall go out by himself: if he were married, then his wife shall go out with him. *If his master have given him a wife*, and she have borne him sons or daughters, *the wife and her children shall be her master's, and he shall go out by himself.* And if the servant shall plainly say, I love my master, my wife, and my children; I will not go out free; then his master shall bring him unto the judges: he shall also bring him to the door, or to the door-post, and his master shall bore his ear through with an awl, *and he shall serve him forever.*"

This passage proves that the Deity authorized the selling

of a Hebrew to his brother Israelite for six years, which was the established limit in case of debt. After the six years were fulfilled, he was entitled to a release; but if he had married a female slave during his bondage, his wife and her children remained as before, the property of the master. And if, in such case, her husband loved his family better than his liberty, he was allowed to remain, but only on condition that he should become a slave for life, since he should serve his master "forever."

And here it may be well to observe, that the term *slave* is met with only twice in our standard version of the Bible. The word *servant* is applied throughout. Yet the meaning is perfectly plain. For the bond-servant was always a slave, while the hired servant was a free man.

But an Israelite could not be held to service beyond six years, without his own consent. He was also entitled to be discharged in the year of Jubilee. Neither of these privileges, however, was extended to the slaves which belonged to the heathen race of Canaan. For thus ran the divine law expressly, in the Book of Leviticus, ch. xxv. 39–46:

"If thy brother that dwelleth by thee be waxen poor and be sold unto thee, thou shalt not compel him to serve as a bond-servant, but as a hired servant and as a sojourner he shall be with thee, and shall serve thee unto the year of Jubilee. And then shall he depart from thee, both he and his children with him, and shall return unto his own family, and unto the possession of his fathers shall he return. For they are my servants which I brought forth out of the land of Egypt; they shall not be sold as bondmen. Thou shalt not rule over thy brother with rigor, but shalt fear thy God. *Both thy bondmen and thy bondmaids which thou shalt have, shall be of the heathen that are round about you; of them shall ye buy bondmen and bondmaids. Moreover, of the children of the strangers that do sojourn among you, of them shall ye buy, and of their families that are with you, which they begat in your land;* and they shall be your possession. *And ye shall take them as an inheritance for your children after you to inherit them for a possession; they shall be your bondmen forever.*"

Here is the distinction, as plain as language can make it. The Israelite could only be sold until the sixth year, which was the year of release, or the fiftieth year, which was the year of the Jubilee; and during the period of his servitude, he must be treated as a brother, and not as a bondman or a slave. But the race of the Canaanites, and their children, even when born in the land, were to be bought and kept as bondmen in perpetuity, and to be transmitted to the heirs of the Israelite as an inheritance. Thus the prophecy of Noah was fulfilled by the slavery of the Canaanites, according to the very terms of the divine law.

Where, then, was the sin of holding them in slavery? When the Almighty commanded His people to buy and own the posterity of the heathen, was it a sin to obey Him? And how could that which He commanded be a crime against morality? Where is the "law" which is "higher" than the code laid down by the Deity? Where is the rule of morals which shall claim supremacy over the Word of God?

But the absurd, though very popular notion, which regards the relation of master and slave as essentially immoral, requires a little more examination to manifest the error. What is this relation? Simply a perpetual obligation which binds the slave to serve the master for life, and binds the master to govern the slave with justice and with reason; to provide for him in sickness as in health; to instruct him in what is necessary to his moral and spiritual welfare, according to his condition and capacity; to maintain his family in comfort, and to bury him decently when life is ended. Where is the immorality in this?

It is true that the slave-holding Israelite might abuse his power, but to this the law of God gave no sanction. So it is true that every other relation may be abused. The father may grievously sin against the child, and the husband against the wife, and the employer against the operative, and the magistrate against the accused, and the teacher against the pupil, and the overseer against the poor, and the master against the apprentice, and the jailor against the prisoner. Even the judge may take bribes, and pervert justice. The city corporation may be corrupt, and league with villains against the public good. Representatives and senators may sin against their constituents, and presidents may offend against the national peace and welfare. In a word, wherever there is *power*, it is liable to abuse from human passion or infirmity. Yet who would say that the *relations* existing in all these classes of the community were therefore immoral in themselves?

On the side of slavery, however, there were reasons which fully justified the divine law. For the Canaanites were heathen, debased, corrupt, and flagitious; while the Israelites were immeasurably superior to them, in the knowledge of the true God, and in the laws of virtue and morality. Hence, while slavery might be regarded physically as a curse to the Canaanites, it was assuredly calculated to be, morally and spiritually, a blessing. Infinitely better was it for their real advantage to serve the chosen people even in bondage, than to enjoy their own miserable freedom in the wretchedness of vice and barbarous idolatry. Nay, even their temporal comfort was far more secure under the government of their Israelitish masters, than it could have been in any other attainable condition.

Thus stood the question of slavery, according to the "higher law," throughout the whole fifteen centuries of the Mosaic dispensation. At the coming of Christ, the institution was universal. In Judea, and everywhere throughout the old Roman empire,* we find no records of any nation or people without slaves. How did our Lord treat the question? Did He utter one syllable on the subject? Did He make it the topic of a single remark? We know how His sacred rebukes fell thick and fast on every form of iniquity. We know how He inveighed against the hypocrisy of the Pharisees, the infidelity of the Sadducees, the hardship of Jewish divorce, the venality and corruption which surrounded Him. But the case of the slaveholder was never mentioned, nor could any reader of the Gospels find authority for the notion that He regarded slavery as a sin against God, and a crime against humanity.

We come next, to the course of His chosen messengers, the inspired apostles. And here we find not merely that they made no assault upon the institution of slavery, but that, on the contrary, they *sanctioned it*, by laying down rules for the conduct of both the slave and the master. A few of the passages bearing on this point will be useful, as proof positive of the character of their teaching.

1 Cor. vii.—"Let every man abide in the same calling wherein he was called. Art thou called, being a servant?

* Gibbon estimates the number of slaves at half the population, or sixty millions.—Vol. i. 58.

Care not for it, but if thou mayst be made free, use it rather. For he that is called in the Lord, being a servant, is the Lord's freeman: likewise he that is called, being free, is the Lord's servant.—Brethren, let every man, wherein he is called, therein abide with God." *

Eph. vi. 5–9.—"Servants, be obedient to them that are your masters according to the flesh, with fear and trembling, in singleness of your heart, as unto Christ, not with eye-service, as men-pleasers, but as the servants of Christ, doing the will of God from the heart, with good-will doing service, as to the Lord and not to men: knowing that whatsoever good thing any man doeth, the same shall he receive of the Lord, whether he be bond or free. And, ye masters, do the same things unto them, forbearing threatening, knowing that your Master also is in heaven, neither is there respect of persons with Him." See also Col. iii. 22, for a repetition of the same.

1 Tim. vi. 1–3.—" Let as many servants as are *under the yoke* count their own masters worthy of all honor, that the name of God and his doctrine be not blasphemed. And they that have believing masters, let them not despise them because they are brethren, but rather do them service because they are faithful and beloved, partakers of the benefit. These things teach and exhort. *If any man teach otherwise, and consent not to wholesome words, even the words of our Lord Jesus Christ, and to the doctrine which is according to godliness, he is proud, knowing nothing, but doting about questions and strifes of words, whereof cometh envy, strife, railings, evil surmisings, perverse disputings of men of corrupt minds, and destitute of the truth, suppo-*

* The word here translated servant, is the Greek δουλος, signifying a bond-servant or slave.

sing that gain is godliness: from such withdraw thyself. But godliness with contentment is great gain. For we brought nothing into this world, and it is certain we can carry nothing out. And having food and raiment, let us be therewith content."

To these abundant testimonies, I add only the epistle to Philemon, where we find that St. Paul had converted a runaway slave, Onesimus, and instead of telling him that he had a right to be free, and rebuking his master Philemon for the "sin" of slaveholding, the apostle actually sends him back again, with a letter beseeching Philemon to receive him favorably.

If we go on from the days of the apostles to examine the doctrine and the practice of the Christian Church, we find no other views entertained upon the subject. Slavery continued to exist in every quarter. Slaves were held, without any reproach, even by the bishops and clergy. When the practice died out, as it did in many of the European nations, the change was gradual, through the operation of worldly causes, and without any suspicion that the institution, in itself, involved a violation of religion or morality. Hence its lawfulness with respect to the African and the Indians taken in war, was universally maintained by the Puritan settlers of New England, who claimed the closest adherence in all things to the teachings of the Scriptures. And it was not until the latter part of the eighteenth century that a doubt was expressed, on either side of the Atlantic, in relation to the perfect consistency of such slavery with the precepts of the Gospel.

Since that time, indeed, public opinion, both in Old and New England, has undergone a great revolution. But this cannot be attributed to the Bible, nor to the Church, nor to any new knowledge of the will of God, nor to the discovery of any unknown principles of moral action. All that belongs to these was perfectly familiar to the Christian world from the days of the apostles. And therefore no intelligent and candid mind can be surprised to find that the most violent opponents of slavery in the United States are always ready to wrest the Bible and denounce the Church, because they cannot derive from either the slightest real support in their assaults against the lawfulness of the institution.

It must be remembered, however, that the *lawfulness* of slavery is one thing. Its *expediency* or desirableness is quite another. Of this I shall have occasion to speak in due season. But the law must be settled first, and the expediency must be considered afterwards; because the advocates of abolition make it a question of "the higher law"—a law above the Constitution; and assuredly there can be no such law, unless we find it enacted by the authority of heaven.

CHAPTER VII.

ON SLAVERY, CONSIDERED IN THE ASPECT OF PHILANTHROPY.

There are three characters in which we may contemplate this very serious question: first, as Christians; secondly, as philanthropists; and, thirdly, as politicians. Of the first I have already treated in the previous chapter. It is doubtless to the second, that we must assign the place of the prominent leaders of abolitionism in the United States; for although many good Christian people advocate the same cause, yet it is certain that the clergy, in general, have given it very little countenance. Let us next, therefore, examine the practical system of African slavery, as it exists at the South, under the aspect of philanthropy. And in order to do this fairly, we are bound to look at the subject, not in the narrow light of a few cases of individual hardship, but in the broad relation which it bears to the welfare of the slaves themselves, and to the future results upon the vast continent of Africa.

There are two modes in which the matter may be regarded, both being modes of comparison, because we cannot view it practically in any other manner than comparatively. And it is of the highest importance to the result that we choose the right standard of comparison, since the adoption of the wrong will infallibly lead us into error.

Here, then, we take African slavery as a *fact*. We may compare the condition of the slaves with our own condition as freemen, and mourn, to our hearts' content, over the restraints, the hardships, the ignorance, the immorality of their bondage, and imagine how much happier they would be, if they were all emancipated, and placed in our own circumstances. But is this a fair or just process of comparison? Suppose them to be emancipated, would that enable them to ascend to our level? The answer is obvious when we look at those who are already free. And it is the testimony of all candid observers that the free negro, other things being equal, is in a worse condition than the slave, physically and morally—less happy, less healthy, less contented, less secure, less religious. It is notorious that many of those who had escaped have returned to their masters of their own accord, glad to escape from the wretchedness of their freedom. It is notorious that in the Southern States the slaves look down upon the free negroes with pity, and often with disdain, as being altogether in a position inferior to their own. For they feel themselves to be connected for life with the family of their master, sure of protection, sure of a comfortable home, sure of a plentiful subsistence, sure of kind attendance in sickness and old age, and sure of affection and confidence, unless they forfeit them by unfaithfulness or rebellion. These advantages are lost to the free negro, and the slaves have no difficulty in understanding that he has nothing to replace them. True, they must work. But so must the free negro: so must the laboring class in every civilized community. And when we compare their condition with that of our own hirelings, there are many points which seem to be greatly in their favor. For their work is light and regular, as a general rule. They have abundant time allowed for recreation and for holidays. They are not, like the free laborer, liable to be dismissed at a moment's warning, and forced to beg or suffer for want of work to do. They are not tempted to strike for higher wages, when the ordinary rates are too low for the necessaries of life. They are not exposed to the melancholy refuge of the poorhouse, and turned out to die in poverty and neglect, after their strength has been exhausted in a long struggle with hardship and with toil. They are not sent adrift amongst the dens of infamy and pollution which contaminate all our free cities, bidding defiance to the hands of the police and the hearts of the benevolent. And if it be indeed a disadvantage that they cannot change their masters, it is in most cases more than a counterbalance for this that they could gain nothing by the change; since every laborer must have some master in order to live, and the slave possesses the only security of always having a master who is bound to keep him from destitution, for years after the decays of nature have taken the power of earning his livelihood away.

When philanthropy, therefore, gets rid of prejudice, and surveys the comparative advantages of the two systems with impartial candor, and casts aside the odium which attaches to the name of slave, it will not appear so easy to determine that slavery is a calamity to the race of Africa. On the contrary, it exhibits the nearest approach to the patriarchal times, when Abraham had three hundred and eighteen servants born in his own house, over whom he ruled with absolute power, but with far more substantial comfort and advantage to them than if they had been a band of ordinary hirelings. For however we may talk about the blessings of individual liberty, the true interest of the laboring class demands a large amount of mutual dependence and association. The master *feels* for his slaves, because they are his own. The slaves are attached to him in turn, because they make a part of his household, bred up under his care from childhood, and directly concerned in all that belongs to him, as their ruler and protector. The *hearts and sympathies* of both, therefore, are brought into constant play by this long and close affinity of interest. And there, after all, is the surest element of human welfare and security, if it were rightly governed by the laws of religious responsibility.

But how does this element exist in the free system of the hireling and his wages? Where is the heart or sympathy between the moneyed capitalist and his operatives? The whole essence of the business is resolved into dollars and cents. The workman is discharged, if another can be found to do the same duty with greater skill or cheapness. Or he discharges himself, if he can earn a little more by going to a new employer. There is no field of personal dependence in which the feelings of either can be exercised. Suspicion and watchfulness are the only instruments relied upon by both sides, and the parties learn to regard each other with habitual distrust, dreading to be cheated in the stern contest of unmitigated selfishness, and without the slightest hope or desire of forming a lasting union of interest and affection.

These statements may appear too highly colored or otherwise, just as my readers may have been accustomed to regard the subject. But however this may be, the *fact* remains undeniable that the slaves at the South are, on the whole, the *happiest* class of laborers in the world, and the most perfectly contented with their own condition. And this fact is of more value than all the reasonings of abolitionism. That a portion of the slaves will always be found worthy to be emancipated, as being possessed of more industry and talent than the average, is doubtless true; and such cases may safely be trusted to their master's liberality, or to the interest which they rarely fail to excite amongst others. That there is another portion likely to be dissatisfied and refractory is also true, and the number of slaves who run away afford the evidence. But these are exceptions to the general rule, about as numerous, perhaps, as the cases amongst the free laborers of other countries, where a few, possessed of extraordinary energy, are seen to rise up from a very low beginning, and another few prove worthy of the penitentiary; while the vast majority continue where they were, through the *slavery of circumstances*, which proves to be about as strong as any other kind of bondage, amongst the masses of mankind.

And for that portion who desire and are qualified for

freedom, our Southern philanthropists have provided, of their own accord, the noble colony of Liberia, now advanced so far as to be an object of great interest amongst the nations, and likely, under God, to accomplish a glorious work for the whole continent of Africa, in due time. We know the history of that enlightened and truly admirable enterprise. We know that it was originated and carried forward by slaveholders, who, as a class, are far better acquainted with the characteristics, and much more occupied with the welfare of the negro race, than we of the North can be. For with them, these matters form a constant element of practical life; while with us they are rather the subjects of uncertain speculation. And we know, further, that the disposition to emancipate their more deserving slaves is common amongst our Southern brethren, and that Liberia is constantly receiving accessions from the same generous spirit to which it owes its origin.

Grievously warped by prejudice must that judgment be, in my humble opinion, which fails to see the vast superiority of this plan for the disposal of the small minority of the negro race who desire and are qualified for freedom. For experience has abundantly proved that they can never rise to the average level of the white population, amongst the free States. Their color forms an insuperable barrier, which no art or management can remove. But in the land of their fathers, the true field of upward destiny is thrown open to them. The providence of God has fitted the climate to them, and fitted them to the climate. And I doubt not that our Southern slavery has been ordained, in His wisdom and mercy, to prepare them, under the training of their Christian masters, for the grand consummation which shall yet regenerate the vast tribes of heathen and Mahometan barbarians, throughout the whole of poor benighted Africa, and display, in the eyes of the world, a splendid proof of the mercy and goodness, which direct the mysterious dispensations of the Almighty.

But the philanthropy of our abolitionists can see nothing in the slavery of the African race except evil, and only evil. If their views had governed the counsels of Providence, the negroes imported into these United States would all have remained on their native soil. And what would have been the consequence? They must have lived and died in the darkness of the grossest paganism, accustomed to the very lowest depths of savage degradation. It is only necessary to read the statements of the geographer, Malte-brun, or any reliable traveller, concerning the kingdom of Dahomey and the Guinea coast, and reflect upon the condition of our Southern slaves as compared with that of the native African, and we shall be obliged to confess that the blessings and advantages which the negroes attained by their transfer to this country, would have been cheaply purchased by the toils and sufferings of half a lifetime. And this, perhaps, is the most enlightened and rational mode of testing the question. In the origin of the slave-trade, the slaves were captives taken in war, and, if not sold to the white dealer, they would have been liable to torture and death from their own countrymen, or been spared for a slavery infinitely worse under barbarian masters, without any of the ameliorations which civilization and Christianity had in store for them. Southern slavery, therefore, has been the very means of raising them and their posterity, amounting to many millions, from this debased and wretched state, to a far higher place on the scale of humanity: and thus we may readily perceive that the reasons which were assigned to justify the divine law, in allowing the ancient Israelites to buy slaves of the Canaanites, applied, with all their force, to the heathen savages of Africa. What sort of philanthropy is that, which would rather plunge them back into their original condition? What sort of religion is that, which brands with the name of villainy and sin the only plan which the mercy of Providence permitted, in order to rescue those millions from heathen misery and ruin? What sort of benevolence is that, which would prefer that the noble colony of Liberia had never existed, and that the negro race should have lived and died in all the cruel and bloody despotism of Dahomey, rather than become fitted, in the hands of their Southern masters, to dispense the knowledge of God, of liberty, and of civilization throughout the darkest regions of barbarism?

For myself, I can truly say that I have no sympathy with those who depreciate the negro race below the true standard of humanity. I repudiate with all my heart the infidel hypothesis which denies that God hath made of one blood all the nations of the earth. I believe that the negro is capable of all the improvement of mind and moral principle which education can bestow, and am ready to welcome every proof which individual cases have afforded of his genius and his powers. But I do not admit that slavery is the cause, in itself, of either moral or intellectual degradation, if the master be not morally and intellectually degraded. The greater part of the instructors of youth, in the palmy days of ancient Greece and Rome, were slaves. Esop was a slave. The philosopher Epictetus was a slave. A large proportion of the primitive Christians were slaves. And assuredly there is nothing in the mere bond compelling one to labor for another, which opposes the love of virtue and of truth. On the contrary, if the master be a good man, the effect of such a bond must be to elevate the character of its subject; and the hardship on the one side, in the obligation to serve, is more than equalled on the other, in being obliged to maintain the servant, through every change of circumstances.

But men may differ as they please upon the point of abstract speculation. The *fact* is, that Southern slavery has raised the African far above his original condition, and enabled him to plant the noble colony of Liberia. And in this, all *true philanthropy* rejoices, and will rejoice, notwithstanding the hostility of ultra-abolitionism.

CHAPTER VIII.

ON SLAVERY, AS A QUESTION OF POLITICS.

HAVING briefly discussed this most important topic according to the two aspects of religion and philanthropy, it only remains that I examine its political bearing: and then, as I trust, my readers will be prepared to understand, with a clearer intelligence, what are the rights and duties of the American citizen, concerning its just and legal claims.

It is quite indisputable that the political aspect of the question embraces the constitutional warrant, the existing laws of Congress, and the obligation to maintain the peace and good order of the several States, in their relations towards each other. For these are included in the oath of allegiance, which lies at the base of all civic principle, and the violation of which constitutes the essence of treason.

This oath of allegiance is expressed in the law which

admits the naturalized foreigner to the privileges of an American citizen. But I need hardly say that every native is born under the very same obligation. It is a libel on our republic to publish the political heresy, that the virtue of loyalty has no place except under a monarchical system. The only difference is, that under that system, loyalty bears relation to the rightful king, while, with us, its proper object is the Constitution.

Now slavery, such as then existed (and still exists, in nearly one half of the States), is expressly recognized in the Constitution. The *word*, indeed, is not there, but the *thing* is. No lawyer ever doubted that "persons held to service" (Art. iv. § 3), were the slaves. Such has been the invariable construction of the Supreme Court; and if any intelligent man, knowing the history of the times, could doubt the meaning, he is bound by the principles of the Constitution to submit to that tribunal which possesses the authoritative right of judicial interpretation.

The same section distinctly guards the rights of the master from any interference. "No person held to service or labor in one State, under the laws thereof, escaping into another, shall, in consequence of any law or regulation therein, be discharged from such service or labor, but shall be delivered up on claim of the party to whom such service or labor may be due."

And in the 10th article of the Amendments, the right of every State to regulate its own internal policy is fully protected by these words: "The powers not delegated to the United States by the Constitution, nor prohibited by it to the States, are reserved to the States respectively, or to the people."

To these I shall only add the last clause of the 6th article, in which it is provided that "the Senators and Representatives (of Congress) before mentioned, and the members of the several State Legislatures, and all executive and judicial officers, both of the United States and of the several States, shall be bound by oath or affirmation to support this Constitution."

The rights of the slave States being thus protected by the "supreme law of the land," we may next advert to the fact that their number has since been greatly enlarged by the new States admitted into the Union, and that several acts have been passed by Congress, directed to the securing of this special peculiarity, by facilitating the recovery of their absconding negroes.

When we look, therefore, at the political aspect of slavery, it is perfectly manifest that the Constitution and the laws allow it, and guard it against invasion; and that the oath of office demands the support of the Constitution from every officer, legislative, judicial, and executive, without exception.

From this it results, plainly, that no politician can attack the lawfulness of slavery, without attacking the Constitution and laws of his country. And equally manifest it is that no man can swear to support the Constitution in good faith, and at the same time oppose himself to its provisions, without violating his oath of office. While those prominent leaders of Abolitionism who openly avow that they trample on the Constitution, and seek to plunge the nation into the horrors of civil war, in their insane zeal for what they suppose to be the rights of the negro, are indeed more honest and frank than the rest, but certainly are engaged in nothing more nor less than the instigation to treason.

For this systematic opposition to the slave States, there is not the slightest really political pretext. Whatever the evil of slavery may be, it cannot be pretended that it is relatively greater than it was at the time when the Constitution was established. Then, the slaves amounted to 600,000, in a population of three millions, which was one-fifth of the whole. Now they have have reached about three and a quarter millions in a population of nearly twenty-four millions, which is less than one-seventh. It cannot be said that their treatment is more severe, that their personal comforts are less secure, or that their masters are enabled to exercise any larger share of power, by their means, over the other States in the Union. The spirit of encroachment is all on the other side. The South has not sought to disturb the North, or to force slavery upon them. It is the North which disturbs the South, and seeks to excite the slaves against their owners. On the one side, there is only a firm adherence to the rights guarantied by the Constitution. On the other, there is a constant effort to tear those rights away, at whatever risk of blood and anarchy. The contest is between the supreme legislature of the land, the laws, and the judges; opposed by popular societies, by loud denunciation, and bitter fanaticism. The appeal made by our inflammatory orators is to a "higher law" which exists nowhere, since it is perfectly idle to say that it can be found in the word of God, and equally idle to assert that it may be discovered in the principles of enlightened philanthropy. And the object which has thus concentrated the energy of Abolitionism is such, that it would put arms in the hands of millions of the African race against their masters, and plunge the nation into civil war, without the possibility of foreseeing an end to the horrors of the conflict.

The true politician is bound to love his country, to defend its government, and promote its unity and peace. He may not believe that slavery is expedient or advantageous, although he cannot consistently deny that it is lawful, so long as it is allowed by the laws of God and man. He may think it better for the African race, and better for their Southern masters, that the institution should be abolished, as fast as it can be, with a just regard to the rights of the owners, to the future welfare of the slaves, and to the general interests of the Union. And thinking thus, he may temperately and kindly seek to impress his arguments on the intelligence and virtue of his brethren; and do his utmost, in friendly co-operation with those who are immediately concerned, to bring about some judicious plan of gradual abolition. In a course like this, I should be able to feel a cordial sympathy; and I doubt not that efforts so directed by a just and patriotic spirit, would meet a generous welcome from many of the most influential and noble-hearted men in the Southern States. But to deny their rights, to calumniate their principles, to menace their persons when they presume to seek their own under the authority of law, to upbraid them with atrocious sin against heaven and humanity, to preach insurrection to their slaves, to goad them with bitter reproach and insult, to refuse them a place in the Church of Christ, and brand them as if they were destitute of morality, justice, and religion—all this is the work of an incendiary, rather than of a politician. Its necessary result must be, and has been, to increase the evil which it designs to cure. It exasperates and alienates, instead of convincing. And if the mistaken men who have adopted this unhappy course desired to rivet the bondage of the slaves, and thoroughly disgust their owners with every notion of emancipation, they could not possibly have taken a more likely mode of effecting the purpose.

I am aware, indeed, that the term Politician is used in our day with a large latitude of meaning. It is applied to all who are active in electioneering, though it be in the narrowest circle; as well as to those who never look beyond some party triumph, and bind themselves to a contracted sectional view, without heart or brains enough to estimate the general interests and permanent welfare of the whole country. It is not in such a sense that I have used the phrase of a *true politician*, but in the broad and lofty sense of the Constitution, which embraces the *United States*—the South and the North—the East and the West, in the comprehensive and generous scope of genuine nationality. And in that sense, I regard no man as a true politician, who seeks to gain victory for a part, at the cost of the whole. The statesman worthy of the name may desire, with all earnestness, to relieve the land from the reproach and the ultimate dangers of slavery. But he will approach the subject with a just appreciation of the arguments upon the other side. He will make all fair allowance for the difficulties which surround the question. He will do due honor to the motives and the principles of his Southern brethren. He will remember that the institution is maintained by sovereign States, who alone have the right and the power to determine how it may be safely and gradually done away. He will seek to work with and for those interests which are directly complicated with the desired change, and prove his friendliness and his sincerity by that kindly feeling which belongs to all real philanthropy. And he will be patient and willing to wait, until it pleases Providence to give a lawful impulse to the cause in the right quarter; never willing to do evil, that good may come, nor trampling upon the Constitution and the oath of office, in his intemperate haste to accomplish a change, which must come slowly, wisely, and prudently, if it come at all.

That it will come, sooner or later, in the right way, by the favor of God towards our Southern States and towards the race of Africa, is my own strong conviction: and I beg the indulgence of my readers to a brief sketch of the argument of *expediency*, in the following chapter.

CHAPTER IX.

ON THE EXPEDIENCY OF ABOLITION.

I HAVE defended, frankly and fully, the *lawfulness* of African slavery, in the Southern States, from the Scriptures, from the principles of true philanthropy, and from the Constitution. The *expediency* of its continuance to the interests of the South and of the Union, is a different question; and as this is a subject to which I have given, years ago, considerable reflection,* I shall here repeat the general process of thought by which I arrived at my conclusions.

Slavery may be easily shown to have been, thus far, a benefit to the negro, when we remember the awful depth of heathen barbarism and wretchedness, from which it has raised him to his present state, in the hands of his Southern master. But it does not follow that it has been of advantage *to the owners of the slaves*. On the contrary, I believe

* A Lecture delivered at Buffalo and Lockport in 1850, which was printed by request and largely circulated, contains an examination of this matter.

that it entails upon them a very serious amount of loss, of danger, and of peculiar responsibility, which it would certainly be desirable to avoid, as soon as may be peacefully and judiciously practicable.

The loss to the master, in my humble judgment, must be considerable. Computing the price of an able-bodied slave at $900, the interest on this may be rated annually at $70 or $80; in addition to which, he must be fed and clothed, and his children must be maintained for many years before they can earn their living, and he and his wife must be supported in old age, long after they are of any use to their owner. We must also take into account the fact that it requires two negroes, on an average, to do the work of one white man. Certainly this proves that there is no laborer so dear and costly as the slave, since the same amount of toil could be obtained from the Irish or the German for less than half the actual expenditure. It is thought by many, I am aware, that the white man could not endure the heat of the southern climate. But I presume this to be a mistake, because a much warmer climate is endured by the English soldier in the East Indies, by the miners in California, and by the travellers in South America. Moreover, the white laborers have built the railroads in those very States; and the small proprietors, who have not the means to pay an overseer, are accustomed to work along with their slaves, and do it without difficulty. Here, then, it seems manifest that the planters of the South must lose largely in the heavy tax imposed upon them by slave labor.

But the second branch of the argument, namely, the danger of the system, is still more worthy of attention. Although I believe that the great body of our southern slaves are perhaps the happiest and most contented laborers in the world, yet there are always some likely to be among them of a very different temper, prone to feelings of resentment, and disposed to regard their masters as oppressors, whom it would be no sin, but a virtue, to destroy. Instances have occurred, in all ages, of the terrible result of passion and revenge on the part of slaves. The histories of ancient Greece and Rome are full of them. In modern times, we cannot fail to think of St. Domingo; and in the Southern States themselves, there have been not a few lamentable outbreaks, which carried horror and misery in their train. Hence the insecurity, the constant sense of peril, which must attend the possession of slaves, even under the best of circumstances. Doubtless, habit may go far to reconcile their owners to the danger, and even to make them altogether insensible to their risk. But I have met with cases, in my small acquaintance, where it was a source of continual apprehensiveness; and this alone would be a serious objection to the system, if there were no other.

There is another danger, however, strongly felt by many Southern gentlemen, derived from the difficulty of maintaining the slaves, in the impoverished condition of the soil which is so generally consequent upon slave culture; and this difficulty is increasing, as the number of the negroes increases, in a fearful ratio. The Hon. Mr. Shepherd, in the legislature of North Carolina, some years ago, put this feature of the case into a powerful argument for abolition, inasmuch as he predicted that the time must come, according to present appearances, when it would be totally impossible for the masters to feed the slaves, and then they would emancipate themselves of necessity, and scatter over the land, in the very wildness of starvation. If this calculation be correct, it accounts, satisfactorily, for the anxiety of our southern friends to extend the area of slavery into new States, where the strength of a virgin soil may enable them to work to advantage. But it also shows the far wiser policy, if possible, of getting rid of the incumbrance altogether.

The third head of my suggestions, namely, the responsibility which is inseparable from the system, outweighs, in my own mind, all the rest. The whole burden of this responsibility rests on the master and the mistress, because the slaves, in general, are as thoughtless and careless as children, and need to be watched over, and provided for, with a sort of care, which is enough, of itself, to wear out the firmest nerves, and break down the strongest spirit of a conscientious guardian. They have to be taught the principles of morality and religion, by oral instruction; they have to be restrained from folly and from sin; their clothing and their dwellings must be inspected; their amusements and recreations must be regulated; their tempers towards each other must be governed; and in sickness they must be attended by eyes far more watchful than their own, in order to satisfy the feelings of a Christian. The overseer can be expected to do but little of all this, for if he looks after them in their hours of labor, it is as much as he is likely to perform, and more than he always performs as he ought for the advantage of the employer. But when these other duties are discharged towards a body of a hundred or perhaps several hundred of those simple and dependent creatures, the master and the mistress become slaves in a far more painful sense, than any of those who are under their control.

In aid of these suggestions, there is surely a large measure of consideration due to the prejudice and utter opposition to the system, which are manifested by the free States of the Union; for although I have endeavored to show how unjust and unreasonable the character of this opposition has been, yet there is no ground to hope that time or argument will lessen it. This might perhaps be expected, if the abolitionists of the United States stood alone; but they are powerfully sustained by the English press, and the same hatred of slavery is shared by France, Germany, and most of the other nations of Europe. Moreover, the spirit of the age is strongly set towards every form of human liberty, and one might as well attempt to check the rising storm by expostulation, as to put back the onward movement of our times by the force of constitutional law or religious sanction.

Would it not be wise, therefore, to remove the cause of contention, if it can be done without any serious sacrifice of interest? Have the masters of our slaves any real advantage at stake, to prevent their timely action in the only course of ultimate prudence? And does not the system present, in itself, a sufficient amount of loss, danger, and painful responsibility, to demand a friendly conference among the Southern States, not upon the best mode of resisting abolitionism, or of withdrawing from the Union, but upon the best mode of ridding themselves of a clog and a hindrance, and thus advancing their own prosperity and welfare?

Six years ago, I took the liberty of recommending a plan, by which the public lands might be hypothecated for the purpose of paying the owners who should be willing to emancipate their slaves, and transporting them to Africa, at a certain rate per annum, so that in the course of another generation, between death and emigration, the country might be free, and the masters should receive the value of their property, and be able to cultivate their lands with hired labor.

The pamphlet was largely circulated at the time, and was favored with the approbation of some amongst those eminent patriots, whom the nation once delighted to honor. But the period was not auspicious for a calm and friendly conference upon any measure of radical conciliation. Nor does the present offer to the outward eye any better prospect. So far from it, indeed, that even as I write, there is an actual commencement of a struggle in Kansas Territory, which may lead to a civil war. While the violence inflicted in the very Senate Chamber of the United States, and growing out of the contest about slavery, adds fuel to the flame; and fills with alarm and consternation the mind of every friend to peace and union.*

Yet it is possible that these conflicts may be, under the wise providence of God, the necessary means of forcing the thoughtful lovers of truth to those active measures, which can alone remove this prolific root of bitterness and dissension. And therefore I venture again to raise my feeble voice, and offer my humble counsel, in the hope of aiding somewhat in the real and practical settlement of this distracting question.

I say then, that it is expedient, good, yea necessary, not only to the lasting union of this glorious nation, but to the prosperity of the Southern States themselves, that they should get rid of the slaves, and send them to Africa, as fast as possible. But this neither can nor ought to be done at the ruin of their owners. The whole country is equally

---

* Happily, by the favor of Heaven, this storm has passed away. But the elements of strife remain. And although the result of the Presidential election may calm them for a while, yet few can doubt that they are ready to renew the perilous contest.

interested in the result, and the whole country should be equally charged with the cost of the operation. Our southern brethren were led into the system by no fault of theirs. England herself introduced it into her colonies, long before the birth of our national Constitution, and at a time when it was in accordance with the sentiments and practice of the civilized world. It took a deeper hold at the South, because it agreed with the climate, and the peculiar products of the soil, the cotton-plant and sugar-cane. And the North has no right to reproach the South, for results which I have shown to be consistent with law and Gospel, and thus far highly beneficial to the slaves themselves, in the view of all true philanthropy.

But how can three millions of souls be emancipated and sent away? The magnitude of the difficulty is appalling. I grant it freely. The difficulty, however, is only increased by delay. And great as it certainly is, I do not believe that it is insurmountable. Let me invoke the kindly attention of the reader to the various modes in which I am persuaded that it may be accomplished, if the intelligent, zealous, and sincere lovers of their country, in the North and in the South, will only come together in the spirit of cordial patriotism and fraternity.

CHAPTER X.

ON THE MODE OF ABOLITION.

THE first point that demands inquiry is the pecuniary value of the slave population. And here, out of the three and a quarter millions, I presume that there is not more

than one half million worth the full average price of $900.
This would already amount to the enormous
sum of . . . . $450 millions.
Another half million might be worth the average of $450, total, ... 225 millions.
One million may be estimated at $200, . . 200 millions.
And the remainder may be set down at . . 125 millions,
many of them consisting of weak, diseased, and superannuated persons, who are rather a loss than a gain to their owners, by reason of the large expense required for their maintenance.

But this estimate gives us the alarming aggregate of one thousand millions, worth, at six per cent., an interest of sixty millions a year! What can be done with such a frightful burden? Yet it is only about one-fourth of the standing national debt of England. And I think it can be disposed of without any serious difficulty by the United States.

In order to present the matter in its worst form, I shall commence with the most objectionable mode of direct taxation, and then proceed to show how the object might be accomplished in other ways, which would impose no burden whatever on the nation. And I hope to prove that Congress has full authority to do all that is required, without the slightest risk of acting unconstitutionally.

First, then, let us examine the possibility of providing the means by direct taxation. Congress has power, under the 8th section of the 1st article of the Constitution, to "lay and collect taxes, duties, imposts, and excises, to pay the debts and *provide for the common defence and welfare of the United States.*" And no lawyer will deny, that whenever the abolition of slavery, by just and legal means, shall appear to be expedient, *to provide for the common defence and welfare of the United States*, by warding off the danger of a civil war, and preventing the dissolution of the Union, the levying of a tax for such a purpose will be strictly Constitutional. *Salus reipublicæ suprema lex.* My own humble opinion is, that we are rapidly approaching that crisis, if we have not reached it already.

Now I assume that there are five millions, at least, of taxable persons in the land.* And therefore the annual interest upon the 1000 millions of slave property, which is about 60 millions a year, would require only an average of $12.00 for each person. Is that so frightful a price to pay for unity, safety, and peace? Especially as the operation would be gradual, since the whole would not be needed until the last slave was freed, and the increase of our population would increase the number of those who should be liable to pay it, and thus the tax on each individual would go on lessening from the maximum to the end of time.

Suppose, then, that Congress should enact a law, creating a national obligation to pay a fair price for every slave, whose master was willing to free him, in *scrip*, which should bring the interest from the Treasury every year. This scrip would always be worth its par value, or rather it would soon command a premium, because, like the English Consols, it would be the surest investment for those who are able to live on the interest of their money.

Suppose that this law contained the following provisions, in order to protect, on the one hand, the constitutional rights of the slave States, and, on the other, to secure

---

* De Bow's "Compendium" (p. 50) estimates the number of white males, in 1850, above the age of 21, at 4,684,888. Five millions in 1856 is therefore a reasonable allowance.

the gradual operation of the plan, in accordance with true policy.

1. That it should be applicable to no State, unless it were sanctioned by its own Legislature, who should at the same time pass a law making free, at the age of 21, all the offspring of the slaves born after a certain day, and providing for their school instruction in the manner of white apprentices.

2. That it should not extend to more than forty thousand slaves per annum, all of whom should be transported to Africa, with the means of support for one year, under the care of competent officers, and formed into communities, in union with Liberia, at the cost of the United States.

3. That the Commissioners of the Government should select those slaves who were most intelligent, most fit for freedom, and best adapted to be of service in Africa; including, however, the young children who were dependent on their parents' care, or from whom the parents were not willing to be separated; and in no case taking the husband or the wife from the society of each other.

The first of these provisions would guard against the charge of interfering unconstitutionally with State rights, because the proposed law would only apply to such States as should be willing to concur in the relief contemplated. Some time might elapse, perhaps, before any of the slave States would thus concur, but I presume that the example would soon be commenced; and once commenced, I cannot doubt that it would be rapidly followed.

The next provision with respect to the children born after a certain day, and free at 21, with the rudiments of a common education, would put a stop to the increase of the slaves, and would further provide a class of laborers trained under proper restraints, and yet with the anticipation of freedom, so as to become useful, and well-behaved hirelings, in any community. Such individuals would constitute, through the difference in their training, a far better kind of population than the free negroes in general. And a large proportion of them would probably go to Africa of their own accord, as soon as they were able.

The third provision would limit the number of emancipated slaves to 40,000 per annum, so as to guard the Southern States from too sudden a revulsion, by removing the slave labor, faster than it could be replaced by the free. In the mode proposed, it would not be difficult for the planter to set off a portion of his fields for free culture, and hire the laborers upon that portion only, inasmuch as it would evidently not work well to have the slaves and the hirelings together. And this portion might be enlarged, as the number of the slaves diminished, until, by degrees, the whole was brought under the free system. With respect to the government, the obligation to transport 40,000 freed slaves to Africa, and support them for one year, under proper officers, would of course add largely to the expense. Supposing it to cost $150 a head, it would amount to six millions annually. But this would only add one dollar and twenty cents apiece to the five millions of tax payers, and would be repaid a thousand-fold, in a few years, by the results in African commerce and civilization.

The effect of thus withdrawing 40,000 of the young and lusty from our slave population every year, would be to take away one million in 25 years. And after that period, how many of the rest would be remaining? Probably not one. The young children would have gone with their parents to Africa. Death would have done his work upon the old and feeble. And thus the whole danger and evil might be entirely disposed of, long before the close of the present century.

Supposing, then, such a law to be enacted by Congress, the first year of its operation would require scrip to be issued for the interest of 6 per cent. on $36,000,000, the price of 40,000 first-class slaves at $900 each. This would amount to	$2,160,000
Add expenses of transportation, officers, and support for 1 year	6,000,000
	$8,160,000

The direct tax required to meet this, from 5,000,000 tax payers, would be $1.64 for each man, during the first year. The second year would add as much more; the third would triple it, until, in ten years, it would be $16.40, supposing the tax payers to remain as at the beginning. But our country doubles its population in 25 years. And of course ten years give us ⅖ to be added to our taxable citizens, who will then have increased from five millions to seven. The tax therefore for each to pay, in 10 years, would be reduced to $9.84. And supposing the whole operation to continue for twenty-five years, which I consider to be a large calculation, the extent of the burden could not exceed $20.50 a piece, amongst ten millions of tax payers, which would be the maximum. In twenty-five years more, this would decrease to $10.50. In fifty, it would be reduced to $5.25. In seventy-five, it would be down to $2.12½, and in a hundred, it would be $1.6¼, diminishing one half, of course, as the population doubled, every quarter of a century.

I have here made no allowance for the thousands of slaves

whom our Southern brethren would doubtless emancipate, free of cost, whenever they are assured that they can be safely conveyed out of the United States, and wisely planted on the coast of Africa. Nor have I asked for any deduction on account of the noble work of the American Colonization Society. But setting these aside, and putting down the whole in the form of a dry financial calculation, it is plain that we may accomplish, if we please, a clean riddance of this most perilous difficulty, which must otherwise entail upon our posterity, if not upon ourselves, the most fatal and deplorable consequences.

But I am well aware that the imposition of a direct tax is a measure so unpopular, that few could be persuaded to contemplate it with the slightest complacency. The war with England, in 1812, obliged Congress to have recourse to it, of necessity, because that war deprived the Treasury of its commercial income. The business of the country was thrown, for a time, into confusion and perplexity,—so great, indeed, that it was a pretext for the proposition entertained by the Hartford Convention, that the Eastern States should secede from the Union, in order to escape impending ruin. Yet, although our progress towards a separation of the North from the South is gradual, and many refuse to see the danger which this slave agitation is surely creating, I am persuaded that it menaces the land with a complication of horrors far more dark and fearful, than any amount of foreign war or commercial difficulty could ever equal. And if Congress was justified in laying a direct tax, and the good sense of the nation submitted to it, sooner than allow to England *the right of search*, much more would our great legislature be justified in doing the same thing, for the far more important object of securing internal peace, and putting a final end to this bitter and distracting controversy.

Happily, however, there is another mode of providing the means, without adopting this obnoxious course of direct taxation. I have stated it at large, in order to prove that it is practicable, but I rest with greater hope upon the plan submitted in the pamphlet to which I have already referred, namely, the devoting the public domain of the United States to the object, so as to render it perfectly practicable without laying any burden upon the people.

Eighty-four million acres of the public lands were given away by Act of Congress in 1851. Other large grants have since been made. But I find it stated that there are still remaining more than *One thousand five hundred millions of acres*, worth at least *Two thousand millions* of dollars! Here, then, is a substantial basis, in land, for *twice the amount* required to redeem the whole slave population of the Union, without taxing a single individual. The capitalists of Europe would gladly pour their funds into the public treasury, for such an object, if this immense domain were pledged by Act of Congress to the lenders; and a public debt thus created would stand pre-eminently before the world, as not merely the safest of all investments, but the most glorious monument of national wisdom and philanthropy.

The public debt of England is . . .	$3,822,000,000
That of France is	943,000,000
And that of Spain is	700,000,000

Yet the greatest of these is no serious obstacle to the prosperity of the British empire, although it has not a single element about it which could enlist the thousandth part of human hope and sympathy. In this aspect of the matter, it would surely seem that divine Providence has endowed us with ample means to obviate the difficulty. And nothing appears wanting but a candid estimate of the dangers on the one side, and the benefits upon the other, to insure a general willingness to employ them.

The adoption of such a measure, in my humble judgment, would produce complete internal peace, and its future advantages would probably exceed the most sanguine calculation.

1. It would put down, at once and forever, the dangerous, inflammatory, and revolutionizing plague of political abolitionism, which scatters firebrands throughout the land, and has already brought us to the awful verge of civil war.

2. It would restore the kind and fraternal spirit between the North and the South, and give a vast impulse to the influence and power of the Union.

3. It would relieve our Southern brethren from a very costly burden, give them the advantages of free labor, improve their exhausted soil, deliver them from the inevitable risks of slave insurrection, raise the price of their lands to treble or quadruple their present value, and bring to them, in crowds, the accession of new settlers, from the free States and from Europe, which the prevailing prejudice against slavery now keeps away.

4. It would elevate the character of our noble republic to the highest point, amongst all foreign nations, by removing the only obstacle which hinders their confidence in our principles of human liberty.

5. It would furnish the most sublime example which the world has ever seen, by sending forth a million of emanci-

pated slaves, under proper officers, to regenerate the land of their fathers, to raise up poor degraded Africa from heathen darkness and barbarity, and open that golden continent to the blessings of Christianity, civilization, and commerce. *There* is the proper home of the negro race, since it is the only race adapted to the climate. And there must the happy consummation be effected, which divine Providence seems to have intended in the great work of Southern slavery. For those negroes could not have been qualified for such a mission, if they had not first learned, in the South, the lessons of sacred truth and moral principle. And they could not have had the opportunity of thus learning, unless their fathers had been placed in the condition of bondmen. And the elevation conferred on them could have produced no correspondent influence on Africa, unless they had been sent, by the beneficence of the United States, to that benighted region, and thus enabled to establish themselves in the full enjoyment of freedom, and lead its pagan tribes to the knowledge of religion, arts, and government. Surely no reflecting American can dwell upon the result without a thrill of grateful exultation, when he contemplates a chain of prosperous negro communities, framed upon our own model, and planted along the old slave coast; when he thinks of Liberia, multiplied a hundred-fold, beholding her kindred tribes coming to the light of the Gospel, and learning the benefits of education, of order, and of law; and when he can look to the noble energy of his own United States, and challenge the experience of mankind to show such a glorious product of generous zeal, for the best interests of humanity.

But who, among our men of influence and talent, will rise up, with a heart of genuine patriotism, and cast himself into the breach between opposing parties, and risk his own character for courage and consistency, in the effort to reconcile them to an enterprise like this? Alas! it is a hard thing at all times to induce even the best and most gifted to lay aside their personal interests and prejudices, and consult, in a large and comprehensive spirit, for the public good. But far harder is it when the conflict has long been raging with bitterness, and the temper of accommodation has been consumed by the fierce blaze of excited passions. Yet it does not become any true American to despair of the republic. If our sins have not provoked the Almighty to chasten us sorely in His displeasure, the men will be raised up, fitted for the difficult task of mediation; and a new day will open upon the rising waves of the political tempest, bearing the promise of sunshine and of calm.

For myself, I should anticipate a good result with much confidence, if the eminent statesmen of Virginia, "the Old Dominion," united with the patriots of Kentucky, her favorite child, were roused to take the initiative in this all-important subject. In both these States the topic of abolition has been discussed long years ago, and they have not forgotten the sentiments of Jefferson, and Randolph, and Henry Clay. But it is my own strong conviction that the floor of Congress is the proper field for laying the foundation of this noble enterprise. It is there that the South can ask the North whether they are willing to pay their just share of the cost of abolition. It is there that they can frankly offer, with the best grace, to form a committee of the ablest and purest men, to recommend some plan of radical and permanent efficiency. And if the spring of healing waters can only be made to rise in that common centre of our nation's councils, the streams will flow down from one legislature to another, and the parched roots of our old Union will sprout in all their youthful vigor, and gladden the land once more with the blessed fruits of harmony and peace.

CHAPTER XI.

THE RIGHTS AND DUTIES OF THE AMERICAN CITIZEN WITH REGARD TO SLAVERY.

If my readers have perused, with attention, the previous chapters, they will be at no loss to determine the principles which should regulate their rights and duties. But for the sake of consistency with the form in which my humble work has been constructed, I shall proceed, as before, to state them briefly.

1. The American citizen has a right to form his personal opinions on the subject of slavery, provided that he does so fairly and honestly, without prejudice or passion, after a due examination of the question, with a just reverence for the sacred Scriptures, a proper respect for his revolutionary fathers, and a faithful regard for the Constitution and the laws of his country.

But he has no right to form his opinion unfairly, by listening only to the exaggerated accounts of absconding slaves, while he refuses to hear the statement of their owners. For every man of common sense must know that a slave escaped from his master cannot possibly be received as an impartial witness in his own cause; and even if he were, it is the settled rule of justice that no one can decide the merits of any case, until he has given a full hearing to both the parties.

Much less can he have a right to appeal to a "higher law," above the Bible, or to vilify that Bible because it sanctions slavery, or to wrest its plain and fair meaning, which was understood in the same way by all Christendom until our own day; or to fancy himself better acquainted with the will of God, than all the saints and martyrs who have lived before him. Such perversions as these are not adopted by *right*, but by *presumption;* and it is not easy to say whether their impiety or their absurdity is the more revolting.

2. The American citizen has a right to believe that, without assailing the *lawfulness* of slavery, it is nevertheless highly *expedient* that it should be done away, as soon as it can be disposed of legally, peacefully, and justly, with due regard to the permanent interests of all the parties; and, consequently, he has a right to discuss that question, in a friendly and a kindly spirit, and to seek for the enactment of such laws as may best accomplish the object desired.

But he has no right to abuse the Constitution, to trample it under foot, to resist the laws of the land, to oppose the officers of justice, to rescue the fugitive slave, or to vilify and threaten the master, who only seeks to recover the possession which legally belongs to him. Such acts as these are not *rights*, but *outrages.* They prostrate the whole power, on which, under God, our lives and liberty depend. For that power is the *law*, and we can rely on no other; and if the law be openly spurned at the will of an excited mob, where is the security of the people?

3. The American citizen has also the right, of course, to form the contrary opinion, that slavery is not only lawful and expedient, with reference to the past, but that it is equally expedient for the future; and thus believing, he

may consistently labor, peaceably and fearlessly, in support of the system, and oppose by fair argument every effort to do it away.

But he has no right to threaten, on this account, the rupture of the Union, since that is only another way of trampling on the Constitution, and opening the floodgates of civil war. He has no right to employ either fraud or force to influence the election in a territory, nor to lay his hand on the property or persons of abolitionists, without the regular authority of law. Neither has he any right to inflame the public mind to the work of sedition, or to encourage the fierce spirit of discord by words or acts of angry defiance, instead of striving to allay it by the counsels of wisdom and of peace. Above all, he has no right to invade the dignity and order of our highest legislature, by a personal assault upon the antagonists of slavery, since this is an open breach of every law, both human and divine.

These remarks may suffice on the *rights*, and therefore I pass on to the *duties* of the American citizen, with regard to this most difficult and distracting question.

1. And first, I consider it his duty to be just, and fair, and generous, and patient, towards those who differ from him. After all, there is no reason to doubt that every party intends what is right, although they view the subject in such discordant aspects. That these aspects are very numerous and complicated, must be admitted by every reflecting mind; and it needs much discussion, and no small amount of time and observation, to understand the whole. But the victory of truth, though often delayed, is certain, if men will endeavor to attain it, without asperity or bitterness; and therefore every citizen should examine the question in the spirit of wise impartiality, of charity, and moderation.

2. It is next his duty to stand up, firmly and openly, in support of the law, since a due respect for this is the only basis of public or private security. He may approve the law or not. He may justify its enactment, or he may wish it were repealed. But its authority is not to be measured by the scale of his opinions, nor by those of hundreds like himself. So long as it is the law, so long it is the bounden duty of the citizen to obey it, and precisely for that very reason, *because it is the law;* and he who resists it places himself, for the time, in the position of a rebel against his government and his country, violates his oath of allegiance, and exposes the whole fabric of social order to the fearful inroads of anarchy and ruin.

3. It is his duty, in the third place, to guard himself against excitement, in order that he may exercise his judgment and use his influence beneficially, in the defence of truth. For the best and clearest minds are no longer to be trusted when the feelings are intensely roused; and men will speak and act a thousand dangerous things under the sway of passion, which they would be ready, in their cooler moments, to acknowledge and deplore.

4. And, lastly, it is the duty of the American citizen to remember that this subject of slavery is the most deeply important and complicated question of our day, and should therefore be approached under the profound sense of solemn responsibility. It involves the majesty of the Constitution, the obligation of the laws, the dignity of sovereign States, the welfare of millions, both of the African race and of our own; the peace, the prosperity, and the very existence of the Union. Never should it be approached with levity, with prejudice, or with arrogant presumption. Never should it be made the stalking-horse for party politics, or the excuse

for popular displays of oratorical declamation. On the contrary, it demands the spirit of religious reverence, of enlightened philanthropy, and of patriotic devotion to the public good. God, in His wise Providence, has sanctioned it for a beneficent purpose. When that purpose is sufficiently accomplished, the same divine Providence will doubtless do it away. Meanwhile, it is our highest privilege, as well as duty, to work *with* God, and not *against* Him. May He hasten the time when His people shall be of one accord, in favor of its peaceful, just, and gradual abolition; when the South and the North shall rejoice together in the same system of liberty and law, and the whole world shall behold the happy fruits of slavery in the regeneration of Africa from her long bondage of barbarism and idolatry.

CHAPTER XII.

ON BUSINESS.

HAVING now considered sufficiently, as I trust, the two first heads of the rights and duties of the American citizen, under the titles of Religion and Politics, in pursuance of the plan laid down, I invite my readers next to the subject of Business. In its proper sense, business stands for the regular occupation of the individual, with a view to his maintenance or his office. We say, therefore, that a man has given up business, when he retires from his former professed employment, to live in the enjoyment of his fortune. And yet, if he afterwards devote his time to a systematic pursuit of art, science, or philanthropy, we say that he *makes it his business*. The meaning, however, in this case, is not that the individual has entered into business again; but only that he follows his new object with the same daily application as if it were his business, and thus *makes it his business* by adopting it as a substitute.

There is, nevertheless, a distinction generally understood which limits the term *business* to manufactures and commerce. Hence the phrase "man of business" does not apply to the farmer, nor to the mechanic, the tailor, the shoemaker, or the blacksmith. Neither is it appropriated to the professions—the lawyer, the doctor, or the clergyman; nor is it given to literary men, to the officers of justice, to the judges, to the heads of the departments in the government, or to the clerks in the public service. And yet all these have their several business, in strictness of speech. For every employment in life, in which men profess themselves to be regularly and systematically *busied*, is their *business*. And hence I have taken the word in the widest sense as the general title of the present division, under which I purpose to consider the rights and duties, with regard to business, of the American citizen. These rights and duties may be classified as general and specific; the first, belonging equally to every kind of occupation, and the second, concerning the peculiar difficulties of certain particular avocations. The present chapter is devoted to the first general right, viz.:

The Choice of our Business, or Profession.

It was the law in ancient Egypt, that every son must follow the business of his father. And a similar rule has obtained in other despotic countries. Happily, we are quite free from any restraint in this respect, and our youth are allowed to pursue their own inclinations. Yet it may not be amiss to point out some advantages which certainly belonged to the ancient system, however common it may be to prefer a very different one in our day.

The object in view, when a youth chooses his business, is to apply himself to that occupation which shall best insure his support and comfort in life, according to his capacity and circumstances. And there are very few lawful occupations which may not suffice to his support and comfort, if he conduct himself with diligence, intelligence, and persevering industry.

As a general rule, it would seem natural to expect that the business of the father should be preferred, because the son is accustomed to hear and see more of it than of any other. This early association is sure to take place, in the cases of the farmer, and of the various trades. The child grows up surrounded by the objects of his parent's toils; he learns how to handle the implements, and usually to do a portion of the work. Insensibly, his ideas, habits, and manners acquire the tone of the home circle. Long before the age of maturity, he attains a considerable degree of skill in his father's calling; and it appears almost a necessary result that he should adopt this, rather than any unknown occupation.

This course would seem natural for another reason, namely, that he can usually follow it without leaving the society of his family. There, he is amongst relatives and friends; elsewhere, he must be surrounded by strangers. There, he can be comparatively at his ease; abroad, he must be always under restraint, and fearful of offending.

And there is yet another ground on which the choice of his father's business would seem to be most acceptable: for the way to success is usually far more open to him in this than in any other—not only because he already knows it to a great extent, but because he is sure to have all the benefit of his parent's experience. He can come into possession, by and by, of the farm or the shop, by an easy and natural transition. He has a security of a certain number of friends, helpers, and customers. There are none of the obstructions in his path, which must be expected in any other quarter. And therefore it would seem that early association, habit, feeling, affection, and interest, are all united in favor of such an election.

And yet, observation proves that this course is very rare, amongst the youth of our age and country. For the most part, the business of the father is not chosen by the son. It may be well to inquire why it is, that the theory and the practice, in this matter, accord so ill together. I believe it may be owing to a combination of causes, very commonly existing, and very easily understood; although their operation on the mind and sympathies of their subject is seldom rightly apprehended.

In the first place, parental authority, in too many instances, has gone out of fashion; and in the absence of this, home has lost much of its proper character. The father leaves to the mother the management of the children. The mother, for the most part, has no idea of governing her boy when young. And when he grows older, she no longer has the power. Hence self-will, contradiction, and ill temper are but too apt to counteract the principles of filial love and duty. In a few years, the child becomes a youth. But he takes no pains to gratify his parents. He gives his confidence to others, and uses his father's house as a tavern, for eating and sleep. For he has persuaded himself that happiness is only to be found in the society of strangers, without dreaming of the reason, namely, that he takes far more interest in making himself acceptable to them, than in giving pleasure to his own family.

As it respects the effect of early association with his father's business, it is too commonly found to be repulsive, because the boy is brought up to be wilful and disobedient, and therefore the youth makes no effort to accommodate himself to his circumstances, with cheerfulness and industry. He learns to connect the labor of home with ill humor and complaint, without reflecting that he provokes them by his total want of filial principle. And he naturally acquires a disgust for work, which, through his own fault, is never accompanied with praise, but, on the contrary, with censure.

All this is apt to be more sure of its effect, when it is united with the habit of repining over their troubles, and exaggerating the hardships of their business, which parents are too often accustomed to indulge in the presence of their children. This, of itself, would be enough to make the sons regard it with aversion; but when it is added to the other grounds of dissatisfaction, we cannot wonder that the great majority of our young men become perfectly convinced of the annoyances and disadvantages of their father's calling, and instead of adopting that, resolve to devote themselves to something else, as unlike it as possible; while the parents willingly indulge them, in the hope that they will act more wisely in the hands of strangers, than they have ever done at home.

There is another cause, however, which has doubtless a far greater influence upon the ordinary inclinations of our youth, and operates even on those who are trained on better principles. And that is, the natural impulse of ambition. The village boy discovers very early, that notwithstanding the Declaration of Independence asserts the equality of all men, there is nevertheless a vast amount of inequality in their social position. He sees the storekeeper's clerk looking more like a gentleman than the son of the farmer or mechanic, and the young collegian holding himself higher still; while the student of law or medicine is plainly on the topmost step of the ladder to promotion. He knows the men who take the lead and play the orator at public meetings, and become the candidates for public offices, and get their names into the papers, and so shine like stars in the social firmament. And learning thus much even in the quiet of a country settlement, his ideas take a still loftier flight when he visits, or hears the accounts of those who have visited, the large cities of the land, where wealth, and pleasure, and luxury astonish the youthful rustic with a splendor of magnificence beyond all previous conception. Perhaps, too, a more powerful impulse in the same direction is produced by his reading the monthly magazines, which may be seen, of late years, in the house of almost every farmer. For there he finds interesting novellettes about lords and ladies, high life and fashion, romance and sentiment; all tending to cast a strong disgust over the daily circle of his home associations, even when they are of the happiest kind; and tempting him to yearn after that great world which lies beyond, and glitters to his inexperienced eyes with such varied hues of fascination.

Alas, poor youth! how little does he dream of the obstacles, the risks, the contests, the delusions, and the sufferings which lie before him! How little can he imagine that the home which Providence has given him, if cherished as it ought to be, has more of the true elements of human happiness than all that the world is likely to bestow! How little can he suspect that even the few who succeed in the struggle for its riches, its honors, and its pleasures, are forced to acknowledge, at last, the hollowness, the emptiness, the bitter disappointment which attend the whole! But this is a lesson which is rarely taught or learned, until the sad reality is known, and the battle of life is almost ended. Seldom, indeed, even then, can we find an example of that true wisdom, enlightened from above, which estimates the value of our circumstances, not by the standard of fame, of fashion, or extravagant display, but by that of piety, peace, and contented usefulness. The same pride which first roused the boy's ambition, continues to blind the man to the end of the most successful career. And he thinks that he has achieved the noblest object of desire, if he has been enabled to rear a family in the enervating indulgences of wealth, and leave behind him money enough to ruin his posterity.

Now it is very easy to conceive how the ancient law, which obliged the son to follow the business of the parent, must have operated to counteract these dangers. For under that system of compulsion, the main point was settled from the first, and so settled as to insure the intentions of every family, to live, to labor, and to thrive together. Here was the strong motive of necessity, to make home what it ought to be. The ambition of the boy was forced to unite itself with the authority of the father, and thus assisted in making him an obedient, cheerful, and trustworthy helper in the general welfare. The business was likely to prosper under this unity of government and of interest. And the tendency of the whole must have exercised a salutary influence in favor of peace, contentment, and domestic affection.

But my readers may say that it is a mere waste of thought to speculate about a system, which is so totally opposed to the free spirit of our age and country. And I confess that at first sight it appears so. My object, however, in adverting to it, is to give weight to the leading principle which I would lay down, in the choice of a business or profession. For while I should be as much averse as any one to the restoration of the old compulsion in this matter, yet I have no doubt that, *as a general rule*, our youth would act most wisely and happily for themselves and the community, by adopting the business or profession of their fathers.

1. In the first place, they would learn it with more facility, because it would fall in with all their early associations, and they would be sure to have the best, most thorough, and most kindly instruction.

2. Next, they would learn it most happily, because it would surround them with the affection and confidence of family and home, which, notwithstanding their manifold imperfections, are the strongest and most enduring ties in this world of trial.

3. Thirdly, they would be saved from the innumerable mortifications, disappointments, and temptations which are likely to attend their inexperience among strangers.

4. And lastly, they would secure the easiest and the surest introduction to the confidence of the community, which is so essential to their ultimate success.

Of course, however, as I would recommend this only as the best *general rule*, it must be open to many exceptions. It would not apply, for example, to those numerous cases of necessity, where the son is compelled to leave the parental roof, or where the father is deceased, or where, though living, he has no business in which he can support his children.

Neither would it apply where the son is evidently disqualified for it, by ill health or mental weakness on the one hand, or by a marked talent or genius for a different profession on the other. In such cases, Providence has interposed a bar, and it is wisdom in man not to thwart the indication.

Other exceptions will likewise occur, from various motives of preference dictated by convenience, relationship, and interest. But still, as a *general rule*, there is none so safe as that which I have stated, and none which can be so well verified on the broadest scale of experience and observation.

For the most part, mankind, by nature, are equally fit for any occupation. The difference lies in their education and training, and in the diligence, integrity, and industry with which they carry it on. The cases of unfitness from mental imbecility are rare, and those of marked talent and genius are yet rarer. The youth who is thinking of the choice of a business or profession, may usually take it for granted that he can succeed in any which is placed within his reach, provided this essential agency of diligence, integrity, and industry be not wanting. And he may be quite sure that if these be wanting, no amount of talent or fortuitous concurrence of circumstances can be expected to save him from total failure.

But I would warn him to beware how he rejects, without necessity, the business or profession of his father. For the most part, this is put completely within his reach, and the providence of God has given it a sort of right to his first consideration. Let no disgust turn him aside from it, without good reason. Let no youthful companions influence him to despise his family and his home. Let no visions of romance delude him to pursue a phantom. He cannot, in general, begin the business of life in any other way, so wisely and so well, as by his father's side, and in his father's occupation. And even if it should ultimately prove that he is qualified for higher eminence in a different path, he may rest assured that the order of Providence will open it in due time, after he has attained sufficient maturity of principle and experience to enter upon it safely.

And I would warn parents to beware how they expose their sons to the common perils of early waywardness and alienation, by a neglect of those wholesome rules of domestic government, religion, and affectionate harmony, without which no home can be made safe or pleasant to the younger members of the family. The mother must instil the virtue of obedience in the nursery, and continue her discipline until it is the settled habit of the child, and then it will need no further trouble. The father must set before his sons in all respects, and strictly enforce, the example which they should follow. For if there be, in the family circle, no authority to govern, no social concord of mutual kindness to attract, and no spirit of loving religion to shed its pure light within the dwelling, the alienation of the sons will follow as a matter of course, and bring along with it the usual sad but natural consequences—danger and suffering to the self-banished youth, and bereavement and sorrow to the parents.

Nor can I leave this prolific subject without a further caution to fathers and mothers, on the temper with which they bear their appointed lot. If they wish their sons to remain and take a cheerful part in the business of the family, they must not repine, and fret over the troubles, toils, and disappointments, to which every occupation is liable. On the contrary, they must bear their burdens with patience and good-humor, make as light of them as they can, and cherish a spirit of pious thankfulness for the advantages and comforts which remain, notwithstanding these drawbacks upon their prosperity. They must talk of their business, as a general rule, with commendation, dwell upon its bright side, and teach their rising family to love it, by loving it themselves. In this way, the bent of their sons will usually be inclined rightly, and they will voluntarily prefer, at the proper time, their father's vocation, unless there should be good reasons, which all the parties can approve, for a different decision.

I conclude this chapter by a brief application to the rights and duties of the American citizen, in the choice of a business or profession.

1. The youth who comes to the proper age for choosing his business, is usually in his minority, and therefore, legally, under the control of his father. But practically, he is allowed to make his own choice, by the sanction of his father, and therefore I shall consider the position of the party himself, as being chiefly responsible.

He has a right, then, to choose his business for life, since his father concedes it to him; but he must remember, that as this right is his only by the grant of his parent, it should be exercised with a filial regard to the parental judgment. It is a bad beginning for any young man, to commence his own independent course in opposition to him who is, by religion and nature, as well as law, his guardian and protector; and he may be well assured, that a course so commenced will rarely fail to be marked with misfortune and self-reproach, if it do not end in utter ruin. The duties which attend upon the exercise of this right come next to be considered, and these are obvious and unquestionable.

1. It is his duty to pray for guidance to the Almighty, who alone can see the end from the beginning, and determine unerringly what line of life he is best fitted to pursue with comfort to himself and benefit to others; and, in connection with prayer, he should advise with his parents and his experienced friends, whose judgment is most likely to assist him in this serious and important question.

2. In reflecting on the choice, it is next his duty to attach but small importance to his present taste or fancy. For this may have arisen from his partiality to a favorite companion, or from some transient impression, which will soon pass away; while a mistake in his selection cannot fail to produce many lasting consequences, involving loss of time, loss of credit, and possibly loss of character. His safest course, as I have already shown, is to choose the business of his father, and his next safest is to take such other calling as his father and friends approve.

3. But whatever business he selects, it is his duty to pursue it with faithfulness, diligence, and thorough application. He must understand that this is the only way by which he can give satisfaction to his employers or instructors, establish his own credit, and lay the foundation for success. Nothing in the shape of recreation or amusement, however innocent in itself, must be suffered to interfere with the claims of his business. Whatever sacrifices of inclination may be required, he must make them promptly and cheerfully; and he should seek the resolution necessary for this, by depending on his heavenly Father, who has promised

His all-powerful aid to those that ask it, through faith in the Redeemer.

4. Some time, however, of course, he will have, for proper recreation; and his advancement and success in life will depend greatly on the way in which he spends it. It is his duty, in this, to remember his responsibility. He must be careful to avoid all intimate companionship with young men of dissipated habits. He should abstain conscientiously from places and amusements of disreputable character, never doing in darkness what he would be ashamed of in open day. He must be manly enough to bear, without flinching, the jests and sneers which profligates are apt to utter against all who are better than themselves. He must punctiliously avoid running into debt, and confine himself honestly within his proper income. Most firmly should he repel every form and shape of intemperance, gaming, and libertinism. And in order that he may have a reasonable prospect of withstanding the numerous temptations which will be sure to attend his youthful course, he should connect himself with some Church, consecrate his Sabbaths to their proper duties, and begin and end each day in faith and prayer.

5. Lastly, it will be his duty to guard against idle and pernicious reading. He should be aware that books are companions for the time, and the most dangerous companions, if they inculcate corruption. Here, however, he can make a free choice, with the help of his wise and enlightened friends to aid him in his selection. History, Geography, Travels, Biography, the Natural Sciences, sound poetry, and novels of pure and established character, will supply copious improvement for his leisure hours, and prepare his mind for the higher intercourse of society. But

among them all, if he would be truly wise, and secure to himself the best success for the interests of time and of eternity, let him suffer no day to pass without reading reverentially a portion of the Book of books—the Bible.

The young American citizen who commences his business or his profession on these principles, and steadfastly adheres to them, may confidently trust that prosperity will attend him. Not that he can expect to escape trials, disappointments, and afflictions, from time to time. The life of man must necessarily have more or less of these, under the best of circumstances; and they are wisely appointed to teach us the virtues of patience, resignation, fortitude, and perseverance in faith and duty. But he will be brought victoriously through the whole, if he keep in the track of diligent integrity; and his days will be lengthened in honor, and end in hope and peace.

CHAPTER XIII.

THE RIGHTS AND DUTIES OF THE MAN OF BUSINESS, WITH RESPECT TO HIS SUBORDINATES.

I HAVE considered the case of the *youth*, who has chosen his business, and is in a subordinate position under the authority of others. And I shall next ask the attention of my readers to the *man*, established as a principal, and having many others under him, on whose faithfulness he is obliged, in great measure, to depend, and with respect to whom he has not only rights to demand, but duties to perform; some of these duties being of the most important kind, though very liable to be neglected and forgotten.

Look, for instance, at the manufacturer, with fifty or a hundred operatives, or the merchant, with a large company of clerks, or the publisher, with a troop of workmen, or any other individual whose lot in life is such as to make him the employer and paymaster of many of his fellow-creatures. It is obvious that such a man fills an office of real authority and power, and may exercise a considerable amount of influence, either for good or evil, upon the character, conduct, and destiny of those who are placed under his control.

It is true, indeed, that he employs them, and they serve him, only on the ground of pecuniary interest. They undertake certain duties and labors, and he undertakes to pay them the stipulated price. They are free to leave him when they will, and he is free to discharge them at his pleasure. Thus far, the engagement is a matter of simple contract, and if that contract be fulfilled, the law of the land can exact nothing more. But there is another law which bears upon the Christian's conscience, commanding him to do unto others as he would they should do unto him. And there is, besides, the high social principle which comes directly within the scope of these essays. For I have undertaken to exhibit the rights and duties of the *American citizen.* I have shown that every such citizen is a *partner in the republic.* And therefore it results, of necessity, that as a citizen of that republic, he is more or less concerned in the character and conduct of his fellow-citizens; and is responsible for the duty of making them faithful and useful members of the community, so far as he has the power.

Like every other duty, this is easily shown to be in accordance with his individual interest. For society is so constituted that no man is able, whatever his wealth or his position may be, to stand in proud independence, aloof from those around him. The peaceful security of each is liable to be invaded, at any moment, by the evil passions of others; and a single act of injustice, or word of insult, may be avenged by the sacrifice of life. A workman, defrauded or oppressed, may become an incendiary. A hired servant, too humble to be valued as a friend, may prove to be a most effective enemy. All experience has demonstrated that the terrors of the law can avail nothing, when the spirit of disorder and lustful cupidity is let loose among the people. The only real and steadfast guardian of property and life itself, under divine Providence, must be found in the general prevalence of religious and moral principle. And therefore he who has a wide control over a body of dependents is working against himself, as well as against the community, if he fail to treat them with just and kind consideration. While, on the other hand, he surrounds his prosperity with a strong defence, if he be able to command their confidence and affection.

The maxim of the Gospel, I need hardly say, is founded upon the most consummate justice, when it declares that "of him to whom much is given, much will be required." The same rule, substantially, is admitted universally by mankind. Wherever there is power, there must also be responsibility. And the extent of this responsibility can only be rightly measured by the extent of the power.

In precise proportion, therefore, to the amount of good which the man in prosperous business has it in his power to do, by the promotion of virtue, intelligence, and comfort amongst his dependents; in the same proportion he is bound, not only as a Christian, but as an American citizen, to do it. As a merchant, a manufacturer, or an employer in any other way, he has a right to insist on the fulfilment of their duty towards himself. But as their fellow-citizen, he must aid them to perform their duty to the community.

Take, for example, the ordinary case of a merchant, in one of our large cities, surrounded by his clerks and apprentices. For a certain portion of every week-day they must be at their post, and punctually devote their allotted share of industry and attention to his business. And when this is done, he may give himself no farther concern about them, and feel no interest whatever in their safety or their welfare. He knows that they are generally young, and encompassed by temptation. He knows that many of them have come from the country, and are quite inexperienced in the ways of the world. He knows that the characters of nearly all are yet in the stage of formation, when they may be easily inclined either to good or evil. But he keeps them at a distance, makes no friendly inquiry about the mode in which they spend their leisure on the Sabbath, or into the moral standing of those with whom they have taken up their abode; and contents himself with paying the stipulated value of their services, without the slightest sense of responsibility for any further act of kindness, or human sympathy. Such is one picture of life, which is unhappily too common.

Now let us imagine a different aspect of the relation between the employer and the employed. Suppose the prosperous merchant to be a man of Christian principle and feeling, awake to a high sense of his duty as "a partner in the republic"—a genuine American citizen. He regards the youthful company around him as heirs, with himself, of immortal happiness, if they be led to submit to the divine

Saviour of the world, and this gives him an interest in their religious welfare. And he also beholds in them the sons of the commonwealth, his fellow-citizens, in whose moral character and habits the whole community, himself included, have a direct stake, of far more importance than the amount of their salary. In his eyes, therefore, they stand connected with him in other and loftier relations, than the mere contract for their services. He considers himself bound to them not only as an employer, but as a friend. He cherishes a kindly personal sympathy in all that concerns their true and lasting welfare. He invites them to come to him in confidence, as their adviser and helper in every difficulty. He inquires into their personal circumstances, obtains for them a seat in the house of God, lends to them useful and improving books, gathers them together occasionally at his own house, and gives them some pleasant evenings of social intercourse. And thus he binds them to himself, in the generous bonds of affectionate attachment. He guards them against all the snares which lie in wait for their inexperience. He trains them up, not only as faithful men of business, but as the disciples of Christ, and the supporters of the public welfare. And while, by this course, he insures the best possible performance of their duties towards himself, he becomes the benefactor of their immortal hopes, the guide of their earthly prosperity, and the protector of the community and the republic, to the extent of his ability.

The contrast here is surely marked enough to satisfy any reflecting mind, without any further argument. But there is another phase of conduct which demands a passing notice, because there are not a few examples of sordid cupidity in the land, offensive to the lowest sense of humanity and justice.

We hear of cases where the weaker sex are cruelly and shamefully imposed on, by the criminal oppression of their employers. "The Song of the Shirt" has given a painful celebrity to that class of social tyrants, who draw their blood-stained income from the very lives and hearts of their miserable victims. We hear of the slow but certain death inflicted in the work-rooms, where the brilliant dresses of the opulent and fashionable are prepared by a daily and nightly drudgery, in comparison with which the slaves of the South might be said to enjoy a paradise of comfort. We hear of men who make a business of renting wretched hovels to the poor, from whom they wring the most unrighteous and inordinate profits, for accommodations which are not fit for the very beasts to occupy. I shall not ask whether such persons are Christians, since the supposition that they could be, would be a libel on the religion of the Saviour. But I ask whether they can be, in any true sense, citizens of our glorious republic? Citizens—who live on the slow tortures of their fellows in the community! Citizens—who are making money out of the health, the morals, and the very lives of their laborers! Citizens—who gain a vile profit from sufferings which force many a feeble victim into prostitution to keep soul and body together, after the paltry wages are expended that are earned by sixteen hours each day of unremitting toil! No! such men are not citizens, in the real character which belongs to that noble appellation, but vampires, preying on the life-blood of society. Their business is not business, in the legitimate meaning of the term, for it consists in the pillage of the poor. Their money is accursed, because it is coined out of the tears and sorrows of humanity. And no heart which is not utterly petrified by sordid selfishness can dwell upon their course, without feeling a bitter pang in the thought that the mothers and daughters of our land should be exposed to such grinding oppression.

I am aware that the wretchedly inadequate reward of certain kinds of female labor is said to be the result of competition, and that the employers cannot help it. But the answer is easy. They can help it if they choose. There is nothing to prevent them from meeting together, and agreeing upon such rates as shall enable them to pay fair living wages to the poor women who depend upon them. The public would certainly not remonstrate against a just price for their garments, and the employers could have as good a profit then, as they have now. Indeed, there never can be a real necessity for oppression, cruelty, or inhumanity. And the pretence would vanish at once, before a little zealous and well-directed effort. Nay, I doubt whether any individual is a gainer at last, even in this world, by the nefarious custom of beating down the worker below a just point of compensation. The laborer is worthy of his hire, and the amount of that hire should always be enough for the necessaries of life.

But here I may be reminded of the commercial maxim, that the value of every thing is just so much as it will bring. I have no objection to the rule. For ordinary purposes of trade it is doubtless available. By no means, however, is it a rule without exception. There is a well-understood *intrinsic* value, which cannot always be obtained under *peculiar* circumstances, and yet, notwithstanding this, it remains the actual value still. If, for example, the property of an unfortunate debtor be sacrificed at sheriff's sale, every one admits that it has not brought its real worth in money, although, at the time, it would bring no more. In like manner, there may be circumstances in the crowded population of our large cities which compel females to sacrifice their labor, and yet that labor may be intrinsically worth a far higher compensation. The true standard of value, as it seems to me, rests upon the principle, that society owes a reasonable subsistence to every individual who is able and willing to work for it during a fair proportion of each day. And in every case where this cannot be done, the parties are in a false position with regard to the community, and the exactor of the labor commits not only a private but a public wrong.

This is manifest upon a slight reflection. For the labor thus performed fails to support life, and therefore the laborer must either sink, a victim to premature decay, or must have recourse to immoral and dishonest means of supplying the deficiency. In both of these results, a grievous injury is done to the individual, but not to the individual alone; because society must either lose one of its members by an act of oppression, or it must suffer from the crimes which are forced upon the individual by the stern hand of an artificial necessity. But no man has a right to deprive society of its members, and no man has a right to tempt them to sin; and, therefore, no man can have a right to take the avails of human labor, without giving the laborer the means of sustaining life in reasonable comfort.

Another phase of this injustice bears upon its inevitable tendency to increase pauperism. For the miserable laborer, if death do not intervene too soon, must become eventually a burden upon public charity, perhaps after years passed in unlawful and immoral practices. But no man has a right to conduct his business in a manner which thus degrades and debases those who toil in his service; and no man has a right to create a destitution which casts upon the public the results of his own injustice. Hence it seems to me perfectly demonstrable, that the employer who takes advantage of an artificial necessity by withholding a living price from the laborer, is both a private and a public wrong-doer, although the complicated crime, like many others, be such that no human law can correct it.

From these general principles, we may easily deduce the rights and duties of the employer, in the true aspect of the business of life.

He has a right to insist on the faithful performance of the stipulated work or labor of those whom he employs, to use all lawful means to enforce his just claims, and to protect himself against idleness and imposition.

But it is his duty to regard them as his fellows, in the sight of God, and in the relation of citizens. And therefore he is bound to do for them all that he reasonably can, by the active care and influence which his circumstances enable him to exercise, in promoting their spiritual, moral, and temporal welfare.

1. First, then, he is under obligation to give them a fair, living price for their labor or service, such as he would deem just if he were in their place.

2. Next, he is bound to pay this price punctually, in money, instead of compelling them, as too many do, to take their wages in merchandise, often charged at a false and exaggerated value.

3. Thirdly, it is his duty to be their real friend and counsellor, to whom they may have recourse with entire confidence, in all their difficulties. For in no other way can he fulfil his responsibility before heaven, or guard from the

worst dangers, the peace and safety of the community in which he is a partner.

4. Fourthly, he is bound to set before them a good example, in all thé religious, moral, and legal relations of life, which belong equally to every member of society. For how can he expect them to be just towards himself, if he will not be just to the Sovereign Master of the universe? How can he ask them to be temperate and sober, if he be dissipated? How can he hope that they will regard, as they ought, their families and homes, if he be a reckless and licentious despiser of his own domestic duty? He should never forget, therefore, that his life is an open book to those around him, which they are always reading. And let him take heed that they find nothing there, but what may lead them to truth and virtue.

CHAPTER XIV.

ON THE SPECIAL DANGERS OF VARIOUS AVOCATIONS.

The Farmer.

EVERY lawful occupation in life has some advantages to recommend its pursuit to the judgment of the individual, with reference, at least, to his peculiar circumstances; and it is but reasonable to expect that it will also have its dangers and its difficulties. I propose to consider some of these, in the following chapters. And I commence with that which lies at the basis of the whole social fabric.

The farmer supplies to the community "the staff of life," because he provides the materials of our food and clothing.

Hence, of necessity, his was the first business appointed to man after the fall. Adam was a tiller of the ground. Abel was a shepherd. The patriarchs all followed agriculture. The chosen people, Israel, were specially distinguished in this, that the Almighty gave to every family its allotment of land; and even the priesthood, though supported by the tithe, had a liberal allowance of soil around their cities. Nothing, therefore, can be more evident than the antiquity, the importance, and the substantial dignity of the farmer's occupation.

We know, moreover, from history, how fruitful it was of all the nobler virtues, on which depend the welfare and safety of society. Moses, the inspired lawgiver of Israel, was trained in all the learning of the Egyptians. Yet he was not commissioned to enter on his task, until he had spent forty years in keeping the flocks of his father-in-law, the priest of Midian. Gideon, one of the most eminent of the Judges, was threshing wheat, when he was called to be the deliverer of Israel. David, the eminent king of the chosen people, came from the work of the farm to the victory over Goliath. Elisha, the famous prophet, was driving oxen, when Elijah took him to be his successor. The old Roman hero, Cincinnatus, was ploughing in his field, when he was summoned, by the decree of the Senate, to save the republic. And every American citizen must be familiar with the names of those patriots of the Revolution, who laid down the implements of husbandry, to assert the rights and to wield the victorious sword of freedom.

Happily for our country, therefore, the main pillar of its strength is our agricultural population. The farmers are our real landed proprietors, and constitute the most permanent aristocracy of our country. And hence, there is no class whose virtue and intelligence are of more vital importance to the public welfare; and none who can be trusted, with more absolute confidence, to sustain the principles of the Constitution.

There is no difficulty in perceiving the reasons why this occupation, above all others, should be deemed favorable to the qualities of a good American citizen. The farmer who is the owner of the soil, is called to the exercise of manly independence by the very circumstances of his position; while he is accustomed to act with those who are as independent as himself, and thus learns, at once, to protect his own rights, and to pay due regard to the rights of others. His labors bring him into the closest intercourse with the works of God in nature, and he owes his success to the bounty of Providence in the most direct and simple form; because he is priveleged to depend for his harvest upon the soil, the rains, the dews, the sun, and the propitious aspect of the seasons; with no superior to dictate, no humors or fashions to interfere, no popular tastes to thwart his calculations, no competition or strife to disappoint his hopes, and no change in the financial or the political world, to threaten him with failure. His condition is therefore especially adapted to cherish the strong and robust energy of principle and habit; to invigorate the domestic affections, in conjunction with industry and forethought; and to maintain strictly, all the old established maxims of law and order. While his freedom from the dissipation and over-excitement of city life, his early hours, and his systematic labors in the open air, give tone to his physical frame, and enable him to act with unfailing vigor of nerve, according to the plan which his judgment has approved.

Notwithstanding these manifest advantages, however, the

farmer is liable to some peculiar difficulties of which he should be well aware; and to these I would next invite my reader's attention.

He is in danger of neglecting the cultivation of his mind, through the engrossing nature of his toils during the busy season of the year; and hence, his views are apt to be too narrow and contracted, and his conversation too much confined to his cattle and his crops, and the political range of the village newspaper.

He is in danger of carrying too far the carelèss simplicity of his domestic manners and habits, until they settle down into an awkward rusticity which prevents him from feeling comfortable and at ease in the society of gentlemen; although there may be very few of those gentlemen superior or even equal to himself, in real elevation of character or principle.

The result of these two difficulties is, thirdly, the danger of losing the proper influence in his own family and neighborhood, to which he might otherwise be entitled, and to keep him back from a large circle of usefulness which he might worthily occupy. And hence arises the general dislike to his business which his sons and daughters are so apt to manifest, as if it were impossible, in the nature of things, that a man should depend for his living on the cultivation of the ground, without being necessarily condemned to a life of ignorance and vulgarity.

But in reality, this is a false conclusion. That there is no such necessity in the case, every one conversant with the farmers of the Eastern States, especially, must be abundantly aware. I have known many instances of successful industry and even wealth amongst them, where the diligent toil of the business was faithfully pursued, while yet the parties were endowed with a knowledge of books, and men, and manners, sufficient to bear a candid comparison with the average of the educated and refined, and to stand well in any position which they might be called to fill. There is no good reason why such should not be the general condition of the American farmer, if the course followed by these bright examples were properly appreciated. The whole difficulty might be obviated by a steady effort to adjust the labors of the body to the improvement of the mind, so that neither of these be allowed to encroach too far upon the other, and both may go on prosperously together.

The true dignity of labor is a fact, as well as a principle. But in order to understand its practical value, we must remember that it embraces all the elements of the human constitution. God has endowed us with a compound nature. He has given us a soul, a mind, and a body; and labor is the indispensable condition of welfare to the whole. The attainment of a just balance in the faculties of each, is the perfection of humanity. And an undue devotion to one, in disregard of the others, is sure to produce disease, suffering, and sorrow. The mercy of Providence has so ordered our lot that we may, if we will, cultivate them all, in mutual harmony. And we may safely assume this as a rule, to which the occupation of the farmer, at least, presents no exception.

For, first, with reference to the soul, it cannot be pretended that the business of husbandry is unfavorable to religious feeling. On the contrary, there is no mode of life more friendly to the exercise of faith, the duty of devotion, and the practice of Christian charity. The busiest seasons of the harvest allow ample time to commence each day with family prayer, and close it with the same. And no farmer could fail to find that this act of pious reverence, united with the reading of a page from the Word of God, would be the happiest and most profitable protection of his labors, and the surest warrant for their success.

Next, with reference to the mind, I would lay it down as a sound maxim, that twelve hours out of the twenty-four, during the busy portion of the year, are enough for the work of the farmer, if employed industriously; leaving the other twelve for prayer, for food, for reading, for conversation, and for needful rest. If we take seven of these hours for sleep, and three for family devotion and for meals, there will still remain two for general reading. And that is more than sufficient, if the books be properly selected, to keep the mind constantly improving.

But the busy season does not occupy the whole year. The winter comes, with its long evenings, its reduced work, and its days of comparative leisure. Here, then, the farmer has an admirable opportunity to increase his mental treasures. Let him consult his minister, his doctor, and his lawyer, as to the most useful books for his domestic library. Let him labor on these, as he would labor on the soil, until his intellectual work becomes, as it soon will be, a real pleasure. Let him seek the acquaintance of the best minds amongst his neighbors, and give himself and his family a sufficient familiarity with the customs and habits of good society, to make them feel at ease in the intercourse of the world. Let him avoid the tavern, keep clear of gaming, racing, and all gatherings whose tendency is towards low and degrading dissipation. And he may be assured that by this course, pursued with reasonable perseverance, his intellectual powers will grow and expand in their true proportion. His social character will rise in the opinion of his family, and the community around him. And he will prove, to the satisfaction of his sons and daughters, how easily and surely the labors of the body may go on, in prosperous connection with the improvement of the mind, and the solid regard of all whose praise is worth possessing.

CHAPTER XV.

THE DANGERS OF THE MERCHANT.

THE business of commerce is not only of vast importance in itself, but it is a favorite one with a large proportion of the youth of our country. And we cannot wonder that it is so, when we look at the imposing array of ships and warehouses, in the great cities of the seaboard; the colossal fortunes realized by our successful merchants, the palaces in which they live, surrounded by luxury; and the brilliant prominence accorded to their enterprise and influence, in the public esteem.

Independently, however, of this magnificent exterior, there is something positively grand in the work which commerce performs for the interests and welfare of mankind. It maintains a constant intercourse between all the nations of the earth, with mutual profit and advantage. It diffuses arts and sciences, languages and customs, inventions and theories throughout the world, as a common property. It introduces the plants, the minerals, and the animals of every region, amongst the rest, and makes them available for use and beauty. It supplies the defects of one country by the superabundance of another, and renders the various members of the great human family, to a certain extent, the objects of thought and sympathy to all their brethren. It affords facilities, which would be otherwise unattainable, for every enterprise of religion and benevolence. It gives a vast impulse to the millions employed in agriculture and manufactures. In a word, so manifold are its uses, that it is an essential element in all civilized society; and its extinction would reduce mankind to the primitive state of tribes, in the simplest form of disorganized isolation.

It seems strange enough that all this mighty work of commerce should be generally regarded as distinct from *labor*, when, in truth, it involves labor as varied and as unremitting, as any other object of human attention. For, what labors surpass the building of ships, of wharves, and lighthouses? What labors are more severe than those of the sailors on the treacherous and stormy ocean? What labors are more exacting or more perilous than those which are lavished in the voyages of discovery, stimulated and performed by commercial enterprise? What work was ever assigned to mortal men, more hard and hazardous than that which planted the Spaniards in Mexico, the Portuguese in Brazil, the French in Louisiana, the Dutch in Ceylon, the English in the East Indies, and in the colonies of North America? Nay, even the home machinery of trade is full of labor—labor of the body as well as of the mind. If we look, for instance, at the vessel coming into port, with her foreign cargo, we find the merchant and his clerks tasked far more hardly than the farmer in his harvest-field. Day and night, the pressure of work continues, straining every nerve with effort, and wearing the frame with toil. Or if we look at the ship taking in her lading, and bound to sail by a certain day, we shall hardly discover a spot on earth which exhibits more of labor driven to fever-heat, than the counting-house and the wharf display under the lash of commercial excitement. In sober truth, there are few departments of what men commonly call labor, so exacting and severe.

But I shall not weary my reader's patience by a disquisition on the idle distinction which custom has attached to this word, *labor*. Properly considered, labor is the necessary condition of human success in every avocation. It may be more or less honorable, according to circumstances. It may occupy a higher or a lower point on the scale of social intercourse. Yet it is labor still. And if, on the one hand, it offers a brighter prize to the successful candidate, it is usually attended, on the other, by a far more serious risk of disappointment and defeat. Without dwelling any longer, therefore, on this theme, I proceed to the special topic of the present chapter, viz., the dangers of the merchant.

And here, we may place, first, the fact that the business of the commercial man, generally, is to buy and sell, without producing; and the difference between the purchase and the sale is the sole source of his profit.

In the great majority of cases, he is obliged to make both the purchase and the sale on credit. Hence, he is under a necessity of selling, within a certain time, enough to meet his engagements; and this naturally produces an anxiety to sell, which tempts him to use artifice and management. A long list might be enumerated under the general title of "the tricks of trade," none of which can be reconciled with the strict maxims of honesty, although, by the general conviction of mankind, they are only too common.

Thus we have often heard of the frauds committed against

the government by the "Custom-house oath," in which the real duties on imported goods are lessened or evaded, by an actual perjury.

So, likewise, manufactured wines and cordials are sold, under the false name of the genuine article, with a full knowledge of the base imposition practised upon the purchaser, and under the risk of the most serious injury to his health, if not to the entire ruin of his constitution.

In like manner, damaged goods are passed off as sound. Old manufactured stuffs are sold under new names. The value of the articles disposed of is systematically exaggerated, until it has become the general rule of dealers to offer less than they are willing to give, in the full belief that the seller asks considerably more than he is ready to take; and neither party considers it prudent or wise to place the slightest reliance on the candor or sincerity of the other.

The habit of thus discarding strict truth in matters of business, leads the merchant, in case of embarrassment, to extricate himself by speculations, sometimes founded on deception, in the wild hope that a lucky hit, as it is called, may relieve him from his difficulties, and restore him to credit again. And when insolvency becomes inevitable, he is tempted to manage it in such a way that his creditors are the only sufferers, while he is better in his pecuniary circumstances than he was before.

How far those evils operate in our commercial community, it is not for me to say. But it is very certain that if such be the general standard of mercantile morals, the failure of the great majority might be naturally expected, because no business which is conducted without regard to moral principle, can or ought to prosper in the end. And here, I am reminded of a remarkable statement made by the late Gen. Dearborn, who was Collector of the Port in Boston for forty years together, and had taken pains, during the whole time, to keep an exact record of the names and fortunes of the commercial community. He declared that of all the merchants in that prosperous city who were in business when he entered into office, there were only three that had not failed, while many of them had failed twice and even thrice, within the period; and his conclusion was, that, so far as security, success, and comfort were concerned, he would rather see his son possessed of ten acres of ground and cultivating them for his livelihood, than behold him among the first merchants of the land. The gain, indeed, would be slow, and might never amount to a tenth or twentieth part of a commercial fortune. There would be no prominence attached to his name in public estimation, no sumptuous residence, and no fashionable dissipation or luxury for his wife and family; but he would have enough for the real enjoyments of life, and his income would be sure and steady. His mind would be free from anxiety, and his circumstances safe from the thousand perils of commerce. His domestic happiness would be secure from the intoxication of opulence and pride on the one hand, and from the blow of sudden poverty in case of failure, on the other. His morals would be undisturbed by the temptations to which the ordinary life of the merchant is so liable. His health would be more firm, his temper more serene, his spirits more equable, and his conscience more peaceful; and therefore, on a fair and calm survey of the whole, he would find himself possessed of a much better prospect, for the reasonable comforts of the present life, and the felicity of the life to come.

But however true all this may be, the world could not

do without merchants; and therefore our desire should lead us not so much to deter men from adopting commerce, as to elevate and purify the moral atmosphere which surrounds it with so much danger. And this, at first sight, would seem to be easy of accomplishment; for surely there is no real foundation for the idea that the business of trade is necessarily dependent on deceit or misrepresentation. In itself, it is an occupation which is lawful, laudable, and even indispensable to every civilized community. Why, then, should it be thought impossible to carry it on with perfect sincerity and candor?

The answer which many may doubtless give, would be, "Because we must take men as they are, and deal with them accordingly; for otherwise their craft will impose on our simplicity, and we shall be sure to fail in the unequal contest between honesty and deceit."

This logic, however, to my mind, is totally unjustifiable. It is true that we must take men as they are, and deal with them accordingly. It is true, for that reason, that we must be on our guard against every danger which abounds throughout society, through the depravity of human nature. But it is certainly not true that we are bound to imitate and encourage that depravity. I can protect myself against a thief without becoming a thief. I can guard against deceit without becoming a deceiver. I can beware of falsehood without becoming a liar; and why can I not be safe from imposition in trade without becoming, in my turn, the practitioner of imposition?

Take, for example, the case of the wine merchant, who knows, or ought to know, the adulterations and false names so current in that branch of business, and can tell how much of his stock is genuine, and how much is a miserable and perhaps dangerous fabrication. A customer applies to him for wine of a particular quality. Is he bound to tell him a lie? On the contrary, he is morally bound to tell him the truth. He may say, "The wines in general use are mostly compounded by skilful imitators, and I cannot vouch for the genuineness of any except a small portion. I will give you, frankly, all the knowledge which I have myself, and you may rely on its correctness. The article you ask for is not to be had anywhere, at present, in its pure and unadulterated state, though you will find many dealers, I fear, who will tell you otherwise. What passes for it I have, and can afford it of as good a quality and for as low a price as any in the market. But I cannot sell it to you as genuine, because I would not deceive you." Now the worst possible consequence of this candor might be that the applicant goes elsewhere, and is imposed on by false pretences, and so the honest merchant loses the sale. But if he perseveres in telling the truth, he will sooner or later *establish his character*, and that will secure him a preference in the community, which must, even on worldly principles, insure his success.

Notwithstanding all the iniquity and folly of mankind, there is no maxim better established than this: that commerce, in its whole length and breadth, depends, for its real prosperity, on *confidence*. But confidence cannot exist, unless it be founded on *integrity*. Deceit and dishonest management may seem to prosper for a while, and yet they are sure to be exposed and detested in the end. Hence the first element of mercantile success is a *character for fidelity*. Nothing is more abhorrent to men than the knowledge that they have been the subjects of imposition. Nothing excites more surely their contempt and hatred, than the artifices of the individual who has practised on their credulity. And hence we find that even in those rare cases where persons have realized a fortune by unworthy means, and gained a transient place in society by the influence of wealth and fashion, the world revenges itself by the ready voice of impartial justice; and the purse-proud millionaire is followed by the history of his baseness, and shrinks before the steady gaze of honest integrity.

We owe it solely to the wisdom and benevolence of God, that even in the corruption of the fall, this instinctive homage to truth and virtue is yet remaining. The Creator has endowed all men with a *conscience*, and although its power is not sufficient to make them what they ought to be, yet they cannot help a compliance with its dictates, as of a law written in their hearts, by which they are compelled to decide in approving or condemning one another. (1 Cor.) And hence we may easily see the ground of that rule, so universally received, that "honesty is the best policy." Just in proportion as the merchant acts upon this rule, he may hope to prosper. No man, in the long race of life, has ever gained by its violation. And it is easily susceptible of an extent which covers the whole ground of human duty. For, honesty towards God and his own soul will provide for his religious welfare; and honesty towards man will secure the confidence of the community, which is the only permanent means of commercial success.

The chief dangers of mercantile business may all be obviated, by the application of this simple and comprehensive maxim; since *honesty* determines every word and act by the *law of conscience*. Honesty will not stoop to the baseness of perjury, before the officers of the custom-house. Honesty will not lie, for the sake of gain. Honesty will not take advantage of a purchaser's ignorance, nor sell him goods which he would not knowingly buy, nor take his money on false pretences. Honesty will not speculate at the risk of others, nor trust to luck, instead of diligence and industry, nor inveigle friends by misrepresentation, nor defraud creditors by concealment, nor make profit to itself by acts of insolvency. In fine, honesty is synonymous with integrity and truth. And the merchant who is guided by these, may safely calculate upon the approbation of society and the favor of Providence, without which no amount of temporary wealth can save him from remorse, reproach, and final ruin.

CHAPTER XVI.

THE DANGERS OF THE LAWYER.

Among the learned professions, as they are called, the most attractive to the majority of our aspiring youth is the profession of the law. The reason doubtless is found in the fact that it is not only a highly exalted avocation in itself, but one which leads the successful candidate immediately before the people, and places him in the best position for public honor and office, in the government of the country.

But intrinsically, the business of the lawyer is worthy of deep respect and consideration. For it is the object of his profession to protect the rights of every member of society, when they are invaded by knavery or violence; and no individual can tell how soon that case may be his own. Hence the lawyer is the regular medium through whom the law itself becomes available. His advocacy places all the suitors upon an equal footing before the court. Through him, the ignorant may confront the learned, the poor may withstand the rich, the weak may resist the strong, and the simple and inexperienced may countervail the arts of the most subtle and crafty foe. It is his noble office to expose the villainy of fraud, to arrest the arm of the oppressor, and to point out the guilty head on which the sword of justice should descend. In the execution of his work, he is called to exercise the most varied powers. The lore of science, the records of history, the knowledge of the arts, the weight of human testimony, the insight into character and motives, the influence of the passions, are all to be displayed by the forensic orator, in union with the grace of rhetoric, and the force of eloquence, and the energy which belongs to the love of truth and virtue. In the lofty ideal of the profession, therefore, there is no lack of abundant scope for the highest eulogy; since we can find no mere human agency more worthy of regard, or entitled to a larger share of public confidence and veneration.

When we come to the reality, however, the contrast is striking and painful. The theory is admirable, but there is a sad want of conformity in the ordinary practice. Instead of the "energy which belongs to the love of truth and virtue," we are obliged to be content with the force of professional pride, waging a pertinacious contest for victory. Instead of the "public confidence and veneration," we are compelled to acknowledge a general feeling of apprehension and distrust. The community, for the most part, do not believe that the lawyer cares a straw for justice or for right, unless the money of his client pays for it; because they see that when the case is ever so unjust, the same money secures an equal amount of professional zeal and devotion. In a word, the general opinion of mankind seems to be that the lawyer will work earnestly enough for fame and gold; but that the notion of his doing any thing for the sake of virtue or of truth is the mere romance of an Utopian dreamer.

For my own part, I have no doubt that the prevailing prejudice is carried quite too far. But its existence is a fact which is too plain for denial, and proves that this important profession is liable to its full share of danger and temptation. Let me proceed to examine some of the difficulties to which it is exposed, after I have premised a few words about its rise and progress.

The lawyer, as belonging to a distinct class, does not appear in the history of the world before the Christian era. There was, nevertheless, a substantial fulfilment of the office, in all ages, by such persons as felt themselves qualified to volunteer their aid in the attainment of justice. We see the plain traces of this amongst the Israelites, in the laws of the Mosaic System; in the case of Daniel, who interfered so nobly for the protection of Susannah; and in that order of men whom the Jews styled *doctors of the law*, and who acted a prominent part in opposition to the Saviour.

In the days of Cicero, towards the end of the old Roman Republic, there was no separate profession resembling that of the modern lawyer. But every one who belonged to the Patrician order was expected to appear in defence of his clients, when occasion required; and a present was usually made, according to the ability of the party, and the importance of the trial. Long before that period, however, the Orator had become a well-known character in the republic of Athens; and the fame of Pericles, Eschines, and especially Demosthenes, had stimulated the ambition and guided the taste of their Roman imitators. But it was not until the progress of centuries, under the emperors, had largely multiplied the precedents and authorities of imperial law, that the science demanded the whole time and attention of a distinct class. The irruption of the barbarian hordes which subverted the Western Empire, and the long reign of ignorance, commonly styled the dark ages, which followed, threw the business of the lawyer into the hands of the clergy; because the little learning that remained was confined to them, and the warlike knights and barons of feudal times held the arts of reading and writing to be beneath the attention of the soldier. This condition of the matter, however, became gradually changed by the restoration of letters in the 15th century. And by degrees, the modern arrangement was perfected, which presents the lawyer as the member of a well-defined profession; though still his chief compensation is considered as an honorary gift (*quiddam honorarium*), subject to no fixed or certain standard, but left to arbitrary arrangement, as it was in the time of Cicero, nineteen hundred years ago.

It can hardly be doubted that in many respects our established system is a great improvement on the old simplicity, although it may be argued, with much apparent reason, that this improvement is more than counterbalanced by the vast increase of expense, delay, and uncertainty which impede the course of justice, and make it the interest of most men to suffer wrong, in the large majority of cases, rather than go through the process of the law, where "the game," according to the French proverb, is so seldom "worth the candle." But we must take the matter as it stands, without discussing the merits of a question which it would be so impossible to determine. It is our wisdom to be thankful for the substantial advantages of the profession, and to examine how these advantages may be better secured, by lessening, so far as may be practicable, the obstacles to its most beneficial influence on the peace, the order, and the general welfare of society.

The surest mode of arriving at a true theory of the profession, in my humble judgment, is to regard the lawyer as a MINISTER OF JUSTICE. I grant, indeed, that he is not in the place of the judge or the jury, to decide the cause. I grant that it is his duty to represent only one of the parties. And yet, I am entirely convinced that he is only authorized to act *for the purposes of justice*, and that if he be supposed at liberty to act as the minister of *injustice*, the whole argument in favor of his office is at once destroyed.

On the theory which I would maintain, the lawyer is a most important instrument in the attainment of justice, for the following reasons: because the controversy is first placed before him, and his client is compelled to put him in possession, to a great extent, of the merits of the question—because his mind is not warped by the prejudice, the passions, or the interests which may prevent that client from understanding his real position—because it is to be presumed that the lawyer, thus consulted, will advise the applicant to such a course as will be best for his own future character and advantage, and the general welfare of the community—because the learning and the honest zeal of the advocate enable him to prepare the case so as to obtain for his client a fair and impartial decision, in despite of the wealth, the influence, or the talents of his adversary; and finally, because, for all these reasons, the agency of the lawyer is the best conceivable instrument in securing the great object of all government and law, namely, the bringing strict justice home to the rights and duties of every citizen.

To prove, yet further, that the lawyer must be regarded as a minister of justice, we may next regard the conclusive fact that he is not permitted to enter on his profession until he has undergone an examination satisfactory to the judge, and has taken a solemn oath that "he will be faithful to the court and to his client, and will delay no man's cause from lucre or malice." But it is manifest that this binds him to the service of justice, because it binds him to faithfulness under a court of justice. And although it also binds him to be faithful to his client, yet this can only be understood in accordance with the same principle. For no man has a right to ask the court for any thing but justice; and no lawyer can have a right to do that for his client, which the client has no right to do for himself.

There is still another argument, however, which leads to the same conclusion. Every lawyer is a *citizen*, and therefore *a partner in the republic*, bound by his allegiance to be faithful to the government, the laws, and the public peace and order. But all of these demand the administration of justice, on which the safety of the whole depends. No good citizen can favor or assist injustice. No good citizen can desire that crime should escape, or that villainy should prosper. And the man who becomes a lawyer, is surely none the less bound to be a good citizen. His office cannot possibly be construed so as to exempt him from the universal bonds of civic obligation. On the contrary, as an admitted member of a profession, sworn to be faithful to the courts of justice, he is doubly pledged to the public welfare as a citizen and as a lawyer. And hence, if he becomes, consciously and knowingly, a *minister of injustice*, he betrays himself into a double perjury, and deserves a double measure of righteous condemnation.

Now the main danger of the legal profession arises from a misapprehension of this fundamental principle. Lawyers, for the most part, do not seem to consider themselves ministers of justice, or even citizens, when called upon to act officially, unless they are appointed to prosecute offenders under the authority of government. In all other cases, they are apt to think of nothing but the interest of their client and their own. And when they succeed, as they often do, in protecting the vilest malefactor from the righteous sentence of the law, or in baffling the plainest claim of the opposing party, by their dexterity and eloquence, they are abundantly satisfied with the result to their reputation for ability; and the rights of justice and the public good give them as little concern, as if they held no place in their scheme of social duty.

But they are so far from acknowledging any inconsistency in this, that they defend their course on the very ground of justice. Thus they will say, that no matter how great a criminal, or how manifest a knave any man may be, his case must be decided *according to law*, and he has an unquestionable right to be protected from a judicial sentence, until the course of the law condemns him. And then they tell us that the skill of the lawyer is only employed to produce this result—that he defends his client by the use of those means which the law designs to be employed. And hence, when the culprit escapes, by the dexterous use of those means, the lawyer has done nothing more or less than his duty.

No man of reflection or candor will deny that this argument is ingenious and plausible; and I do not wonder that it passes for a full justification with those, whose habits of thought and personal interests are all in its favor. And yet I presume to think, that it is nothing better than a specimen of well-constructed sophistry. My reasons may fail to satisfy the reader's mind, but I trust they will not be found unworthy of his serious attention.

The first proposition laid down in this defence of the lawyer's practice, is undoubtedly sound and correct. No criminal should be condemned—however great his guilt may be—otherwise than by the due course of law. The rest of the statement I am compelled to reject, as totally fallacious. If the lawyer only used his skill to secure a fair trial, or to prevent oppression and abuse, there would be no ground for censure or complaint; since thus far, he would only act as the minister of justice. But if he encourage his client to lie, knowing him to be guilty—if he deliberately place that lie upon the record in the face of God, and of the court to which he has sworn fidelity—if he assume that lie to be the truth in the whole course of his pleadings—if he insist upon the same lie to the end, notwithstanding the plainest testimony—if he exert his utmost skill to brow-beat and confuse the witnesses, and prevent them from speaking the calm and simple truth, so as to make its proper impression on the jury—and if, after all, he employ the most vehement and pathetic oratory to induce that jury to bring in a verdict against what he knows to be the law and the evidence—it is simply ridiculous to pretend that he has not acted as the enemy, instead of the minister, of justice. And it is equally ridiculous to say that he has only used the means which the law itself allows, so that whatever the result may be, he has merely done his duty. On the contrary, notwithstanding all this may be tolerated—notwithstanding it may be done every day, by gentlemen of the highest character, as a matter of established professional necessity—notwithstanding it may be done with fame, profit, and praise, throughout the most civilized nations of Christendom, yet I must declare, in all honesty and frankness, that it is done in the face of *real duty*, because it is done against the object of the law, against conscience, against truth, against the oath of office, against the allegiance of the citizen, against the best interest of the community, and against the real dignity and moral character of the profession.

We will suppose the ordinary case of a felon, who stands committed on the clearest positive testimony. But he is possessed of money and friends, and can afford to employ an able lawyer. The gentleman selected is of course immediately informed of the evidence, and has no reason in the world to doubt that his client is guilty, and that justice demands his condemnation. Yet the first thing that this *minister of justice* does, is to resolve that the man shall *deny the crime;* nay, even if he has already confessed it, that the confession shall be treated as extorted, or made by surprise or misapprehension, and therefore of no validity. But does *the law* sanction this deliberate lie? Does the law expect the advocate to make himself the counsellor of falsehood? The utmost extent to which the courts can go, is to authorize the plea of *Not Guilty* to be entered on the record, when the accused refuses to give any answer. But there is not a law upon the face of the earth which justifies a member of the bar in advising a plea which he knows to be untrue—a plea designed for the very purpose of defeating what he believes to be the real ends of justice.

The professional action thus commenced in falsehood, is carried through, with consistent hardihood, to the end. But how does it quadrate with the oath of office? The lawyer comes into court with a protestation of his client's innocence, and labors to convince the judge and the jury that he ought to be acquitted, when he believes in his conscience, all the while, that he ought to be condemned. Is this sanctioned by the law? Is it *fidelity to the court* to do his utmost to mislead it? Is it *fidelity to the court* to do his utmost to mislead the jury, endeavoring to persuade them to break their own oath by bringing in a verdict *against* the law and evidence by which they are solemnly bound to decide? For nothing is more common, in criminal trials, than this very thing. When the lawyer is aware that the court cannot sustain him, he never fails to tell the jury that they are the judges of the law as well as of the evidence; and exerts all his art and eloquence to induce them to disregard the opinion of the court, and take his views as their directory. But how this can be reconciled with his official oath to be *faithful to the court*, is entirely beyond all ordinary powers of comprehension.

At least, however, it is supposed to be quite certain that the lawyer, in all this, keeps the other clause of his solemn obligation, viz., to be *faithful to his client*. And I should be willing to grant this freely, if there were no judgment in the future life, and no divine standard of Christian morality. But that cannot be justly considered *faithfulness* to the client, which only tempts him to add sin to sin. If the man be really guilty, it is better for his eternal interest that he should confess it and repent, instead of trying to obtain his liberty or prolong his miserable existence by a course of lies and hypocrisy. Certain it is, that there is no principle in the law which authorizes the pronouncing of a deliberate falsehood before a court of justice. The basis of the law is religion. The oath of God is the only security for the truth of the witnesses; the oath gives validity to the commission of the judge; the oath confers force on the verdict of the jury; but all these oaths bear reference to the divine Lawgiver, and the judgment of the great day. How, then, shall the lawyer's oath, to be *faithful to his client*, be so interpreted as to exclude all reference to the same awful responsibility? Is the danger of sinning against God to affect the conscience of judges, witnesses, and jurymen, and shall it have no application to the oath of the lawyer? Is he alone at liberty to spurn the divine law of truth, and try to extricate the criminal from the temporal penalty of one transgression, by wilfully incurring the eternal penalty denounced against another?

That the license thus taken by the lawyer is totally hostile to the best interests of the community, is quite manifest to the slightest effort of reflection. For the whole security of property, liberty, and life itself, depends, under Providence, on the just and impartial administration of the laws; and that administration cannot be trustworthy, if confidence may not be placed in the principles and characters of the lawyers. I doubt not that this is the source to which we are indebted mainly for what is ironically called "the glorious uncertainty of the law." But society at large must always suffer, when villainy escapes and knavery prospers. Nothing can be done effectually by human legislation to check the progress of crime, or protect the rights of the honest and peaceable, if justice be openly evaded and the culprit be allowed to walk abroad. And it is no light matter that any man should make himself a party to all the future wrongs which a criminal, thus allowed to defeat justice, will probably commit before his race is run. This is the reason why the law visits so heavily the rescuing of the felon, because the punishment of crime is of the highest importance to the safety of the community. And marvellous it seems to me that the same effort which would constitute a grave offence in any other man, should become right when it is undertaken by the lawyer, merely because he uses a different instrumentality. Properly regarded, it is rather an atrocious aggravation of the wrong. For if the criminal be rescued by his fellows, he may be arrested again, and they are liable to suffer for their attempt to defeat the ends of justice. But if he be rescued by the subtlety of his lawyer, he is safe from further responsibility to any human power; and society suffers the double calamity of seeing justice defrauded, and of feeling the insecurity of the only means on which the citizen can rely for his protection, when the *ministers of the law* are themselves the cause of its impotence and failure.

I have said that the prevailing ideas of lawyers on this subject are hostile to the real dignity and moral character of the profession; and I have said it with perfect sincerity. According to what I hold to be the true theory of their noble calling, they are designed to be the *ministers of justice*, authorized to act on behalf of every member of society, so as to insure the best application of the law to every case, without exception. In such an aspect, they would be esteemed by the whole community as the protectors and the benefactors of the public welfare. The honest and the well-disposed would have recourse to them with confidence, and they would only be dreaded by the unprincipled and the vile. The title of lawyer would be synonymous with truth and right, which are the real foundations of law and order; and the courts of justice, instead of being shunned with fear and apprehension, would be sought with readiness as the sure resource of virtue and integrity.

But what, it may be asked, would be the effect of this theory upon the *emoluments* of the profession? I answer, that such a system would largely increase them. For, although the fees of evil men would be lost, yet the rewards of a better class would be more than equivalent. In the multifarious business of the world, there are disputes constantly arising where both parties mean to do right, although they cannot see the subject in the same way, and need the intervention of disinterested and wiser minds to decide the controversy. But prudent men are usually unwilling to employ a lawyer, lest they might be drawn into a long and perhaps a bitter contest, involving a loss of time, temper, and money, far exceeding the value of success even to the triumphant party. And hence the majority take all possible pains to settle their difficulties among themselves, preferring even to lose, rather than incur the perils of litigation. But if it were once believed that lawyers understood their oath of fidelity to their clients in the sense which I have advocated, all men would have recourse to them immediately, as the best and easiest way of securing justice; because they would then come together as friends, to compare, in the spirit of candor, the statements of their clients. In nine cases out of ten, the whole difficulty would thus be accommodated to their mutual satisfaction; and the parties would gladly pay their lawyers as much as the same labor would have been worth, in the process of a tedious legal contention.

It may be objected, however, that in such a course they

would not be acting as lawyers, but as arbitrators. And to this I reply, Not so, in strict propriety, because arbitrators are appointed under an agreement of the parties to abide by the award; whereas, in the case supposed, the clients might continue to differ, and the lawyers themselves, with the best intentions, might not always be able to agree; so that a recourse to a legal trial might sometimes be found necessary to decide the difficulty. But in a large majority of cases, the plan proposed would have all the advantages of an arbitration; and even when it failed, as it would do occasionally, the suit would be of an amicable character, prosecuted in good faith, and entirely free from trickery or evasion.

And the certain result would be, first, an immense increase of the business of the lawyers, because twenty disputes would be brought before them, if the public confidence were fixed in their honest friendliness and candor, for one which is committed to them now.

Secondly, they would be regarded with universal esteem and reverence, as the guardians of justice, peace, and good-will, throughout society; instead of being looked upon by so many as a species of human sharks, who only lived by preying upon the misfortunes, sins, and follies of mankind.

Thirdly, the labors of our courts would be greatly diminished, because, although the business of the lawyers would be vastly increased, yet it would rarely happen that recourse need be had to a court and jury. And when such recourse became indispensable, the cause would be managed on both sides with fairness, kindliness, and justice; and therefore there would be a great saving of the time so apt to be consumed in idle and trifling controversy.

And, fourthly, the lawyers would be looked upon, in the

halls of legislation, with a far higher feeling of reliance, as the great conservative class of the nation; on whose judgment and principles all men would be willing to depend in every controverted question. Even as it is, their superior learning and ability secure for them a very extensive influence in the work of government. But it is felt and understood full well that the same proclivity to follow out the wishes of their client, whether right or wrong, for their own supposed reputation and profit at the bar, too often adheres to them as legislators, degrading them to the miserable service of a party, when they should speak and act as honest, independent patriots, for the benefit of the whole.

I have already adverted to that aspect of the question, in which the public welfare is so deeply interested, viz., the certainty with which crime would be punished, if the lawyers were always disposed to act as the ministers of justice. The proofs are unhappily abundant that they are not so considered now. We have seen how often, in California, the best and wisest citizens have taken the trial of criminals out of the hands of courts and lawyers, on the very ground that justice could not be expected from them. That in New York, a notorious woman, of whose guilt the whole city was convinced, after several exciting trials, was finally discharged, solely by the skilful management of her accomplished advocate. That in Kentucky, an open murder was committed on an estimable teacher, which rang through the whole United States, and yet the culprit was acquitted by means of his lawyer's extraordinary tact and eloquence. That, in fine, the Press is constantly complaining of the perilous facility afforded for the escape of criminals, until the public mind is in danger of becoming utterly debauched, and the whole majesty of the law is sinking down in puerile weakness and imbecility.

Doubtless not a little of this growing degeneracy may be fairly imputed to the fatal mistake of making judges elective for a term of years, by the popular voice, instead of having them appointed, as before, by the nomination of the Executive, confirmed by the Senate, during good behavior, or for life. But this innovation was the work of the lawyers. Indeed, I am not aware of any defect under which the administration of justice is laboring in our day, that may not be fairly attributed to their agency. For to them, of necessity, is committed the whole management of our legal machinery. They have the largest share, by far, in the making of the laws. They conduct the proceedings from the beginning to the end, and it rests with them whether the public trial shall be a scene of serious decorum, worthy of the occasion and the place, or a display of unseemly rudeness, disorder, and levity. Nay, they determine the character of the courts, not only because the judges are always elected from the lawyers, but because the efficiency of every judge must be greatly influenced by the conduct of the bar. Hence the result seems plain, that if the lawyers, as a class, considered themselves bound to act only as the *ministers of justice*, and refused to give their aid to any cause which their own moral sense could not approve, there would be no escape for notorious criminals, no shelter for villainy, no lack of security to the virtuous and honest, no excuse for what is termed *Lynch law*, no distrust or contempt towards the regular tribunals of the land, and no inducement for the disorganizing spirit now so mournfully on the increase, which sets itself above all law, by reason of the manifold abuses in its administration.

My professional readers will probably think that these suggestions are visionary, and that my strictures are altogether too severe. I can only say that they are prompted solely by the high reverence which I entertain for the true majesty of the law, and the real esteem in which I hold that class of my fellow-citizens, who are specially devoted to its maintenance. There are other forms of government, under which a conservative power may be wielded by the throne and the nobility, strong enough to guard the general interests of the community, even when the legal tribunals are venal and corrupt. But in a republic like our own, the law is the only power which can rightly claim supremacy. And that would be all-sufficient, under divine Providence, to secure the great ends of public peace and welfare, if it were regarded, as it should be, with trust and confidence. Such trust and confidence, however, can only be expected, when the *practical administration* of the law is felt to be in accordance with the sacred rules of truth and virtue. We all know that the people at large care nothing for abstract theories. Even religion itself, though its authority be divine and unquestionable, yet depends, for the extent of its influence, on the lives of its ministers, and the strict fidelity with which their functions are performed. Much more must the law, which is human, be affected by the course of its ministers; and hence it is absurd to expect that it will ever gain its true value and importance in public estimation, so long as the lawyers are believed to be ready to sell themselves to knavery and crime.

That there are, however, a considerable number of this honorable profession, who act upon the principles which I have advocated, and never descend from their elevated position to prostitute their learning and their talents in the service of injustice, I fully believe; for I have had the privilege of knowing some such, and of esteeming them as the ornament of their class, and the strong guardians of their country's welfare. Yet the extent of the prejudice so generally entertained against lawyers, may well justify the fear that those eminent examples are only the exceptions; showing not what the great majority are, but plainly proving what they might be, on a loftier and more Christian theory. Were it possible to elevate the whole to the true level, there could be no better human warrant for our national safety. For if the lawyers were all *ministers of justice*, righteousness, order, and peace would fill the land, and we might bid defiance to the assaults of private guilt and public corruption.

CHAPTER XVII.

THE DANGERS OF THE PHYSICIAN.

NEXT to the profession of the law, stands that of medicine, in the usual order of preference. And they differ greatly in the tastes and habits of mind which are properly adapted to them; so that the kind of talent required for eminent success in the one, is usually quite dissimilar from that which is demanded for the other. The youth who is specially marked out for the bar, is shrewd, argumentative, quick and bold of speech, and fond of social disputation. While he who is fitted to excel in medicine is thoughtful, retiring, meditative, and reserved. The devotee of law looks forward to the crowded court-room, the public convention, the halls of the legislature and of Congress; where the applause of a listening multitude may hang upon his lips, and his eloquence may be diffused, by the Press, throughout the world. The devotee of medicine anticipates the quiet wards of the hospital, or the darkened chamber of the sick; where the weak voice of the relieved sufferer may give utterance to a deeper gratitude, or the feelings of the family may yield him the pure incense of honest affection. And with these he must be content, since, at farthest, he can expect no honor beyond the chair of the professor, in which the admiration of his pupils may promise him, perhaps, a distant hope of fame. But although the prize held forth to the lawyer seems far brighter to the ambitious intellect, yet that which invites the physician lays a readier hold upon the heart. It has more to do with the sympathies of home, with individual pain and suffering. It brings within its circle the winning picture of female watchfulness, and tenderness, and devotion. And above all, it stands directly connected with the mysterious powers of the mortal frame, whose wondrous organization, and the thousand calamities to which it is liable, afford, in themselves, the most deeply interesting subjects to the student, not only for the sake of others, but for his own.

For this latter reason, the art of medicine is certainly the most attractive to the contemplative lover of nature. And hence its professors usually manifest a degree of enthusiasm, which is rarely found in the other pursuits of intellectual industry.

But the dangers of the physician are not a few, and it is by no means easy to avoid them. Perhaps it may be useful to suggest some of those, which have most frequently pressed upon my mind during many years of observation. For although I am no professor of the noble art, yet I have always been one of its fervent admirers, and devoted to its appropriate learning a considerable amount of time, in the earlier part of my humble career.

The first danger which I shall specify, is inevitable; and continues, more or less, to the end. Indeed, it is inherent in the nature of the subject, which is itself a mystery. The human body, with which medicine has to deal, is not to be fully understood by any, except the Great Physician who gave it existence. To a certain extent, we can examine the inanimate corpse, investigate its anatomical structure, and describe the bones, the muscles, the tendons, the cartilages, the nerves, the glands, the arterial and venous system. We can lay open the heart, the lungs, the stomach, the liver, the intestines, and the other organs of the trunk. We can ascend to the brain, unfold its marvellous convolutions, and trace its connection with the spinal cord. And long and close is the application, in the repulsive atmosphere of the dissecting-room, which is necessary to master these branches of knowledge. But after all that can be known, how impossible is it to discover the real *causes* of disease? How and why it is that the individual, possessing the same frame, and living in the same way, shall have at one time the croup; at another, the measles; at a third, the whooping-cough; at a fourth, the scarlet fever; at a fifth, the ague; at a sixth, the rheumatism; at a seventh, the pleurisy; at an eighth, the dysentery; at a ninth, the gout; and at last die, of small-pox, or cholera, or consumption? Take even this little list, passing by a far larger catalogue of evils which threaten our wondrous organism, and what physician in the world can tell us why the human frame exhibits the various symptoms, to which these names are applied?

Absolute knowledge, then, being altogether unattainable, *conjecture* must be admitted to supply its place. And this is not to be despised, although it be conjecture only. But it is evident that there is as much impenetrable mystery about the actual cause of the cure, as there is about the actual cause of the disease. The fact that a particular set of symptoms are apparent, indicating a disorder to which a special title has been appropriated, is ascertained upon the one hand. The fact that certain medicines, applied in a certain way, have been found to alleviate and finally remove it, is ascertained upon the other. And, strictly speaking, this is all that is really known about the matter. Thus the patient has, we will suppose, the fever and ague. And what is this? Why simply the name given to a disease which shows itself by alternate attacks of burning and of chills, occurring at certain intervals with extraordinary regularity. Does any man know the internal state of the system which has caused this strange disease, and often keeps it up for months together? Not one. It is an inscrutable mystery. But experience has proved that Jesuits' bark, or its extract, quinine, or a judicious use of arsenic, cures the disorder. Does any man know *how* they cure it? Not one. This, too, is an equally inscrutable mystery. The physician wisely and properly applies the *facts*, which are known, on the ground of reasonable probability. He may *conjecture* reasons, frame ingenious hypotheses, and gain credit for a while by his learned speculations. But it is impossible, in the nature of things, that he can do more. The facts remain facts. The conjectures remain conjectures. And this compound of facts and conjectures make up the whole of medical *science*, often falsely so called. For, rightly considered, science is only applicable to what we can certainly *know;* and the term should never be used, as it is perpetually, to signify what men can only *conjecture.* Hence this word, in strict correctness, is excluded from medicine, which is an *art* and not a *science.* Yet the distinction is exceedingly apt to be forgotten amongst physicians; and this is perhaps the main cause of the fierce and contemptuous spirit, with which the various schools of medicine are unhappily accustomed to abuse each other.

Here, then, is the first danger of this most useful and important profession, viz., the liability to confound *facts* with *conjectures*, to assume a vast deal which is not susceptible of proof, and to refuse a reasonable hearing and a fair examination to other facts, as well supported as their own by a respectable amount of evidence, because the *speculative hypothesis* of those who adduce these facts does not agree with their old or favorite theory. But this, after all, is only the judgment of prejudice. And it is a proposition too plain to need argument, that the mind which is governed by prejudice, is in a very unfit state for the attainment of truth. Yet this danger, as I have said, is inevitable, because the young physician must study in some school, and must commence his practice with full confidence in its teaching. Alas! it is the work of many years and of much sad experience, to discover how much of its supposed science is merely conjectural; and how often the very course which he has learned to despise, as ignorant quackery, produces results more beneficial than his own.

Let me not be misunderstood, however, as an advocate for ignorance in the medical profession, more than in any other. On the contrary, I maintain the desirableness and the vast utility of all the knowledge which can possibly be acquired, in the most profound and extensive study. But

Even during the present century, the system of the regular school has undergone, in many respects, a perfect revolution, and may undergo another before the century has closed. Nay, it is their boast, and I repeat it to their honor, that they are ready to accept every useful discovery, and adopt every real improvement. Why, then, should not the individual physician be prepared to do the same? Manifestly he ought to practise the enlarged and comprehensive spirit which the Faculty profess. Nevertheless it is very likely that he will shrink from such a course; for he stands exposed to the second danger, viz., the being afraid to act upon his own principles, lest he should incur, for himself, the name of *quack*, if he presume to patronize any mode of practice which has not *previously* been sanctioned from the professor's chair.

And yet he knows that the Faculty consist of men who are usually too far advanced in life, too much occupied with their extensive business, and perhaps, very naturally, too fondly wedded to their own established system, to try experiments upon a new discovery. Hence, instead of being the first to ascertain the value of any alleged improvement, they are almost of necessity the last to allow its claims. In a word, they are, by habit and by feeling, *conservatives.* And therefore the whole history of medicine proves that every beneficial change has been commenced and carried forward, not under the sanction, but rather in despite of the Faculty; and it was not until it had achieved success, by the stubborn evidence of *facts*, that the Faculty yielded their reluctant approbation.

I am far from attaching any blame to our leading physicians for this conservatism. On the contrary, I should say that it is the only course which could be fairly expected from them. It is their duty to give the important art of medicine a systematic form, and to present it, in this form, to all their students. And it is absurd to ask that they should be ready to welcome an assault upon their work, or to pull down with one hand what they are building up with the other.

But the result is, that every physician, who is capable, should do his own share of thinking for himself, on his own responsibility, without waiting for the Faculty. It is only by the efforts of independent minds that medicine, like every other art, has arrived at its present stage; and the same independent efforts will be equally needed, through all future time, if it is to make any further progress.

The nineteenth century, which has been prolific of so many astonishing inventions, has introduced a great variety of novelties in the healing art, two of which—Hydropathy and Homœopathy—have made such serious inroads upon the regular school, that they have called forth a correspondent amount of opposition. It is neither my province nor my desire to attempt a settlement of their respective claims; but I purpose to suggest a few thoughts upon these controversies, in order to show the aspects in which such questions should be regarded, according to the rules of impartial reason.

The system of Hydropathy, or the Water Cure, was discovered by a peasant, Priessnitz; and has made a wonderful progress in many parts of Europe and the United States. It professes to remove all diseases that are capable of being cured, without drugs or medicines, by the daily application of water to the patient's person, in various modes; in connection with powerful friction, with a strict abstinence from all unwholesome stimulants, with simple diet, and vigorous exercise. By these means, it is alleged not only that the disorders will be radically cured, but that the whole system will be renovated and strengthened to a degree which can hardly be conceived, except by those who have experienced it.

Now of the fact there can be no doubt whatever, because the evidence is overwhelming and undeniable, if we are authorized to put any confidence in human testimony. But how do the regular Faculty regard Hydropathy? They discountenance it as a species of quackery, brought into sudden repute by a fortunate conjuncture of ignorance and presumption. They deny its success, and attribute the good effects to friction, the cold bath, temperance, and exercise, all of which were known to the world before Priessnitz existed. They deprecate the *wet sheet* and the *douche*, as actually dangerous to many constitutions; and, on the whole, condemn the system as totally unworthy of reliance.

But are we bound to adopt this sort of denunciation? If it be true that Hydropathy has actually produced the effects claimed for it, according to the universal testimony of those who have received its benefits, is it fair or just to call it *Quackery?* For this word properly attaches to imposition and deceit; whereas, in the Hydropathic plan, every thing is simple, plain, and intelligible. And what does the world care about its being the discovery of a peasant? The virtues of the Jesuits' bark were found out by what men call accident. The use of antimony resulted from the observation of a monk upon its fattening hogs. Vaccination was suggested by the fact that milkmaids were subject to the vaccine disease, but not to the small-pox; which led to the idea so happily improved by Dr. Jenner, but opposed by the Faculty for a while, with all their might, as a preposterous notion. Many valuable medicines now in use were derived from savage Indians, and the great body of the *Materia Medica* has come down to us from sources which are entirely unknown. The question that concerns mankind in all such cases, is not whether the discovery was made by a peasant or a learned physician, but, is the discovery proved to be beneficial? The gold mines of California were not laid open by the officers of the mint, nor by scientific geologists or mineralogists. But does any one, on that account, attach less value to the precious metal?

It may be very true that the good effects of Hydropathy are dependent on the bath, the friction, the temperance, and the exercise. But what then? Granting that mankind knew the salutary effects of these things already, yet it is certain that they were never so combined before, as not only to make them a substitute for medicine, but to conquer diseases by their means, which the best physicians had failed to cure. In the power of this combination lay the value of the discovery. For the art of medicine is *the art to heal;* since without that, all other knowledge, so far as the patient is concerned, amounts to nothing. And, therefore, Priessnitz attained an art of his own,—not derived from books, nor from any previous system, yet still a real art, which went far beyond their teaching, in practical efficiency.

Far wiser, then—far better and more just, in my humble opinion, would it have been, if our regular physicians had frankly admitted the facts of Hydropathy, and used them as admirable proofs of those elements in their own system, which had always set forth the benefits of bathing, temperance, and exercise; although mankind had generally been too ready to overlook them, through the pressure of business, and the temptations to luxury and indolence; and the doctors had failed to urge them as much as they deserved. They might have freely acknowledged that the Water Cure was certainly a wonderful remedy in many cases, notwithstanding its founder erred in discarding medicine altogether; a judicious use of which, in connection with the rest, must often be necessary, and for the most part, highly useful. And they might have added, with equal truth, that the system of Priessnitz required too much time, expense, and absence from other duties, to suit more than a very small fraction of society; that, as is likely in all new discoveries, he carried his confidence in it too far; that after the cure was seemingly completed, it was hardly possible to continue such a course at home, as should be at all satisfactory, because the appliances required a peculiar arrangement and attendance which few ordinary houses possessed; and finally, that if the patients would consent to use but half the strenuous perseverance in bathing, friction, temperance, and exercise, which they would be obliged to use at a Hydropathic establishment, along with gentle medicine, under the care of an experienced physician, there was no reason to doubt that the result would be more speedy and beneficial, in most cases; notwithstanding the fact that much advantage is derived from the change of air and scene, the excitement of company, and the freedom from care, which may be enjoyed by those that can afford the cost of a regular institution.

But the Faculty are still more severe upon the Homœopathic system, which they generally denounce as an unprincipled imposition upon human credulity. Here, indeed, they cannot find fault with the ignorance of its author, Hahnemann; because he was one of the most learned physicians in Germany. Neither can they accuse him of rashness in innovating upon the previous practice, because he and a circle of his friends carried on a regular series of experiments—first on their own bodies and next in the public hospitals—during forty years together, for the express purpose of testing the truth of his fundamental theory, *Similia similibus curantur*. Nevertheless, they cast unsparing ridicule upon the maxim of this new school, that the effects of every remedy are increased by the smallness of the quantity, provided it be taken in a state of exceedingly minute division. They condemn the idea that every medicine is a specific for one set of symptoms, by its power of producing similar symptoms in the healthy constitution. And they insist that the results of the Homœopathic treatment are only favorable in those cases, where the patient would have recovered without any medicine at all.

With respect to the first of these objections, which is the principal ground of attack, it does not seem to me that Hahnemann has been dealt with fairly. There is certainly nothing absurd in the proposition that the smaller the dose of a medicine, the more powerful may be its effect, provided it be taken in a state of exceedingly minute division; when we remember that in such a case it is likely to *enter the system* by absorption, and thus operate in a very different and far more thorough way, than if it passed only through the stomach and the intestines. For this is the old, well-established theory of the regular school itself, with regard to the favorite medicine, Calomel. Given in a dose of ten to fifteen grains, it acts as a purgative and passes away; but given in repeated doses of half a grain or less, it remains, is absorbed, and *enters the system;* producing that extraordinary disease called Salivation, which has been generally relied on, in extreme cases, to conquer the disorder, although it seldom fails to impress its own specific effects upon the constitution for a long while, if not for life. Here, then, is one well known and indisputable example of the Homœopathic principle, that a minute dose will operate in quite a different way, and beyond comparison more powerfully than a large one. But this is not the whole of the truth with respect to mercury; for it is known to salivate the workmen who accidentally breathe it in the gaseous form, or handle it in the silvering of looking-glasses; and physicians have often preferred to bring on salivation by rubbing it into the groins. That sulphur, taken in small doses, also enters the system and passes through the pores, is another familiar fact, in support of the same principle.

There are many other facts, however, which lead to a similar conclusion. Take the case of hydrophobia, the most terrible of all diseases, and yet produced from the very small quantity of the slaver of a mad dog, which can be introduced into the trifling wound made by the tooth of the animal. But small as it is, it operates in due time by *entering the system.* The same is true of the venom of the cobra di capello, or of the rattlesnake. In no case, however, is the principle more manifest than in the practice of vaccination, where a quantity of matter, so minute as to be taken on the end of a needle, and only inserted beneath the skin, produces such a change, that the individual is believed to be made proof against the powerful contagion of the small-pox, for life; supposing this little homœopathic dose to be administered properly.

But the same fact meets us in other forms elsewhere. How small a quantity of morbific matter in the air must that be, which produces fall fevers and intermittents, in some seasons and countries; and in others, the yellow fever, the cholera, and the plague? This last is known to be communicated even by the garments of a person who has been dead for years. Nor is this one whit more strange than the common experience of contagion from the measles or the scarlet fever. In fine, whenever the agent can be so applied as to enter the system through the absorbent vessels, or the blood; the effect must needs be most powerful and abiding. Since, then, the familiar instance of salivation produced by the small dose of calomel, as well as by the absorption of mercury by the skin, or breathing its vapor by the lungs, clearly proves the superior force of smallness of quantity over large, *on the principle of absorption into the system*, it is surely a sufficient justification of Hahnemann to say that he has thought it reasonable to regard it as the expression of a *general law*, instead of a special exception. For it is manifestly impossible to show why such should be the fact with calomel and sulphur, and yet not be equally true with every other medicine. Hence, too, the importance which he attaches to the minute subdivision; because it is evident that the more minute the particles of medicinal matter may be, the more readily they must be taken up by the delicate absorbent vessels—a fact which probably explains the admirable effect of mineral waters, where the amount of the mineral is so very small, but in a state of perfect dilution. How far this minuteness should be carried, is a question of experiment. Hahnemann may perhaps have carried it to an extravagant extreme; but granting this, it is evident that it is an error on the safe side, and therefore it is hardly worth while to cavil at it.

The next point of attack which the regular Faculty seem to think most assailable, is the homœopathic principle that "like cures like" (*similia similibus curantur*); in other words, the medicines which will cure a disease according to their system are such, that if taken by a man in health, they would produce symptoms resembling those of the disorder. The maxim usually held by the established school is the reverse, viz., that diseases are cured by their contraries. Here again, however, there seems to be enough of acknowledged facts in the older system, to warrant the principle of Hahnemann; or at least to prove that it cannot be justly charged with absurdity. Thus, cathartics are given to cure diarrhœa and dysentery. Emetics are administered in sickness of the stomach. Blisters are applied to relieve inflammation of the pleura. Spirits of turpentine is used in burns. And snow is the best remedy for parts that are frozen. But I have already shown, that the principle on which medicines operate must always be a matter of conjecture, and can only be derived from the *facts* proved by actual experiments. The mystery of the human frame is too profound for the knowledge of any but the Creator. That theory is most likely to be right, therefore, with which the facts are in the best agreement; and hence the probability in favor of Hahnemann consists in this: that his theory is in accordance with a series of the most careful experiments, conducted by himself and his friends for forty years together. On that ground, at least, it challenges an extraordinary amount of respectful consideration; because its author has set the only example, since the world began, of a systematic and persevering pursuit of such an object, through so long and laborious a course. The records of these experiments fill several bulky volumes, and form a wonderful monument of medical industry and devotion. Nor is it possible to reflect on the marked peculiarity that all these experiments were *tried on Hahnemann and his friends*, before they were tried on their patients, without a feeling of reverence for the lofty spirit of resolution and self-denial which inspired the task; and a strong conviction that no theory was ever set forth with more anxious diligence and personal suffering, for the attainment of truth and the welfare of humanity.

I have said thus much, not because I pretend to decide between the various medical systems of our day—since such an attempt would be quite out of my province—but as a matter of candor and fair impartiality. For myself, I regard them all with deep respect; and am strongly inclined to believe that there is a large amount of useful knowledge and serviceable practice in every one of them. I see no reason to doubt, that as the body may be nourished by a great variety of food, so likewise its maladies may be cured by a great variety of treatment. My only object is to show why the regular Faculty should regard their rivals with indulgence, rather than denounce them with contemptuous asperity. Their position is so strong, that they could well afford to be generous. The bitterness of controversy is never justifiable even in theological disputes, although here we have an infallible directory in the Word of God, from which it is not lawful for any man to deviate. But how much less is this bitterness to be sanctioned in the art of medicine, where there can be no revelation claimed by any party, and the most careful and learned practitioner is so liable to error, owing to the inscrutable and mysterious organism of the human frame?

Under these circumstances, I should be disposed to advise the young physician to guard against this second danger of dreading the term *Quack*, whenever he ventures to judge for himself amongst the various systems around him. He has no right, indeed, to adopt wanton changes in the old established practice; nor to condemn or set aside, in the humor of capricious rashness, the wisdom of those who are eminent, in the regular schools, for their experience and their learning. But neither, on the other hand, has he a right to suppose that all true medical knowledge is confined to the professor's chair, so that every new discovery which is not yet endorsed by the Faculty, must be treated as a vile and worthless imposition. Rather let him resolve to be kind and liberal in his feelings towards all who are laboring, like himself, in the great work of alleviating the pains and sufferings of our common nature. Let him examine their claims with candor and courtesy, even if he should be obliged to think them utterly mistaken. And thus he will be far more likely to keep his own temper of mind in the best condition for the acknowledgment of truth, and help to infuse a benevolent and just spirit amongst the members of his admirable profession.

There is a third danger which is sure to beset the physician, at every age, although the young practitioner is most likely to feel it, viz., the temptation to stimulate the hopes of the patient, by holding out a false prospect of recovery, until the last energies of nature are prostrated, and the hour of dissolution is at hand. The reasons assigned for this common act of well-meant deception are plausible. It is said that no man can be sure of a fatal result at an earlier period, since many cases have occurred where the sick man became well, even after the doctor had given him up as incurable. Moreover, there are very few patients who can bear to be told that they are in danger, without a sinking of the spirits, which is a serious obstacle in the way of their restoration. A strong hope, or even faith, that they will recover, is itself a powerful medicine, of which the physician is not justified in depriving them, a moment sooner than he is compelled, by the most stringent necessity. The same hope is a comfort to their family, and it seems cruel to take it away until it can be entertained no longer. No one thanks the doctor for being the messenger of death; and hence, in every aspect of the matter, it seems that duty to his patients, to their families, and to himself, requires him to keep back the sorrowful information as long as possible.

I shall not deny that this view of the subject is very plausible; and yet I am quite persuaded that it is altogether fallacious, on the double ground of religious and worldly duty. This must be apparent, I think, from the following considerations.

I grant, of course, that no physician can be sure of a fatal result, until the hour of dissolution is at hand. But it is equally true that every disease may prove mortal. Why, then, does not the physician state, at the beginning of his attendance, that although there is good reason to hope for a cure, yet it is only known to God whether a cure shall be effected? Why does he omit all reference to the Supreme Disposer, when his position gives him the best possible opportunity of leading his patient to look upward to the Great Physician, in faith and prayer? For it is certain that this is the best frame of mind for the success of medical skill, because it is the most free from anxiety, impatience, and perturbation. And no man who believes in the sublime truths of the future life and judgment, can doubt that it is the only frame of mind fit for the condition of a sinful being, lying on a bed of weakness and pain, from which it is at least possible that he may never rise again, in health and vigor.

But this is not the whole of the question, in a remedial point of view. If the physician be, as every physician should be presumed in a Christian community, a believer in the Gospel, he must be conscious that the whole success of his efforts may depend on prayer. And therefore he is bound to use that best of medicines, and to remind his patient of the duty of using it also. Even infidels themselves are aware of the powerful effect of this upon the feelings of the sufferer, although they regard it as the product of delusion. They know how important it is to the recovery of their patient, that he should have confidence in the skill and faithfulness of his human physician. How vastly more important that he should believe himself to be in the hands of the Great Physician, whose power is infinite, and whose mercy is divine!

And the duty is equally plain on the score of temporal interest. Every patient should be reminded, at the beginning, of the possibility of death, that he may put his worldly affairs in order. For this is the surest way to relieve his thoughts, as far as may be, from all anxiety upon the subject of his family; and save him from the risk of leaving them in confusion and difficulty, by postponing his arrangements to the last few hours before the parting struggle.

It may be said, indeed, that such suggestions do not belong to the province of the physician, whose business is with the body of his patient, and not with his soul, nor with his temporal circumstances. But to this I would reply that they belong to the physician, for the very reason that he is bound to do his utmost for the body, and knows that so long as that body is united to the soul and the mind, the condition of both must be of high importance to the patient's recovery. No physician neglects to insist on the necessity of keeping the sick man quiet, undisturbed by visits or conversation, and free from all mental agitation or excitement. So far, he is right. But why does he not go farther, by recommending that incomparably superior repose and peace, which the sufferer can only find in the calm resignation of religious principle?

It may be said again, that this course comes rather within the office of the clergyman, and therefore it should be left to him exclusively. And I answer, that although it does indeed come within the office of the clergyman, yet it is none the less incumbent on the physician, not as a substitute for the minister, nor by using his functions, but at least so far as may give the right direction to the patient's thoughts and feelings, in reference to his cure. And that this should be done by the physician, is the more evident from the fact that, in a great majority of cases, he is the only person who can do it at all. The clergyman is rarely sent for, until hope is nearly extinguished; and full often, his only knowledge of the case comes along with a request to attend the funeral. But the physician is present from the beginning of the malady. A few words from his lips come with peculiar power, far greater, in the case of most men, than a long exhortation from the pastor. How easy for him, at his first visit, after having made the usual inquiries and prescriptions, to say, "My good friend, I trust you will do well, and I see no reason to think you in danger. But the truth is, that none can foresee the result of any illness with certainty, except the Great Physician. Without His blessing, all that man can do amounts to nothing. I hope, therefore, that you will put your chief confidence in Him. You will find faith in his goodness, and prayer for his mercy, your best medicine." A little counsel like this, given in a low voice, but in an affectionate and simple way, would be all-sufficient for the occasion; and it might be followed up to any extent which circumstances might dictate, though always in the same cordial and informal manner, from day to day. And then the physician would have no reason to fear any sinking of the sick man's spirits, when he was obliged to talk of death, or to suggest the settlement of his worldly business; because he would have laid the basis of perfect candor from the first, and his course would be understood throughout, as marked by the same consistent truth, and the same genuine and kindly interest for the patient's welfare.

The system pursued by many, I am sorry to say, is one of the gravest responsibility. For it frequently happens, not only that the physician talks to the diseased man precisely as if he had no soul, and was not in the hands of any Deity; but that *all visitors*,—not excepting the clergyman,—are denied access to the patient's chamber, by the doctor's directions; so that nothing may be said which can alarm the conscience or the fears of the sufferer, until it is too late. If the consequences of death, coming in the midst of unrepented sin and thoughtless stupidity, be perilous to the hope of the future, is *he* not responsible who was chosen to watch over the victim, and who saw the approaching consummation, yet would neither give the warning himself, nor advise his patient to send for a Christian minister? Such a course is only to be justified by the assumption of the infidel, that there is no hereafter. But I have already shown that no infidel can be an American citizen, in true consistency with the Constitution. And I am equally persuaded that no man can be rightly qualified to heal the diseases of the body, who neglects or despises its union with the soul.

CHAPTER XVIII.

THE DANGERS OF THE EDITOR.

The range of avocations which make up the complex system of civilized and social life, presents no business of such extended influence as that of the editor. For his periodical issue is read by thousands, day after day; he descants upon a larger variety of persons and subjects than any other; and his opinions are received with peculiar respect from the mass of his readers, under the idea that he is an organ of public sentiment. It is usually considered to be a special privilege that the United States possess so great a number of this important class of authors; and when we remember that the newspaper forms the favorite reading of young and old, and that very little else is perused by a considerable proportion of our citizens, it is not easy to exaggerate the result produced by this most popular sort of literature.

And yet, when we come to analyze the matter, it is exceedingly difficult to define that result; or even to conjecture what its character may be, with respect to the great objects of human thought and the true principles of choice and conduct. We open the welcome sheet, in general, under the simple impulse of curiosity. First, there is the foreign news, if there have been any late arrival. Then there is a column or more of the proceedings of some public meeting, religious, philanthropic, or political. Presently we have an-

other column filled with accidents, with calamities, and crimes. Next we may come to some remarks of interest to the agriculturist; next, to extensive notices of dramatic and musical performances; next, to a review of books and pamphlets, the last issues of the teeming press. From this we turn to the proceedings in Congress and the Legislature, if they be in session. After these, our attention is invited to letters from Paris, from London, or some other quarter. The markets, the stocks, the shipping intelligence, the new inventions, the latest fashions, a horse-race, the watering-places, the crops, the weather, with twenty or thirty other items of information, fill up the rest; saving only that a due space is always occupied by an editorial, usually about political matters, and written, for the most part, with judgment and ability; while a fair amount of room is appropriated to the strains of poetry, to jokes or anecdotes; and—especially in the smaller papers of the rural districts—to some sentimental or romantic story.

The tact and skill exhibited in this wonderful variety are certainly surprising; although we know that under the admirable system of the division of labor, adopted in the large establishments of our cities, it becomes a thing of almost mechanical routine. The object is, of course, to suit, as far as possible, the taste of every reader; and this seems to be a very proper object, since all the subscribers have equal rights, and each is entitled to receive what he would esteem as the worth of his money.

Nevertheless, it is a question not easy to answer, How much real benefit is experienced from the perusal of such a motley product? Whether, in point of fact, each reader carries away some idea which may enlarge and improve his mind; or whether the very variety does not cause a con-

fused jumbling together of incongruous topics which interfere with each other, and effectually prevent any from obtaining a sufficient lodgment in the thoughts to make a clear impression. And if this last be the fact, another very serious question arises, viz., Whether the daily custom of reading this confused mass of information has not at least a tendency to weaken the common intellect; leading it off from one subject to another, and gradually increasing the difficulty of following any train of reflection, until the mind settles down, like that of a child, into a kind of impulsive imbecility?

I state the problem, without any intention of solving it. It is much more easy to pick flaws in the course of our editors, than to suggest any serious improvement. Certainly, on the whole, I have rather been inclined to wonder that they do their work so well. And considering that they are bound to furnish a variety of intelligence which is calculated for the public taste, by the very character expressed in the word Newspaper, I think there is as little ground of complaint in the management of those with which I am best acquainted, as could possibly be expected under the inevitable law of human imperfection.

That the editorial business, however, has its peculiar dangers, no one can deny. And therefore I shall proceed, in accordance with my general plan, to offer some suggestions on the moral principle which should guide the American citizen in conducting it; since the wide diffusion of its products and the daily reiteration of its teachings place it in the first, if not the highest, rank of the influences, which are constantly operating on the character and destiny of the nation, not only in reference to our internal welfare, but in the judgment of the world.

The first of these dangers arises from the temptation of

party-spirit, from which it is very difficult to guard the mind of any man standing, as the public editor must usually stand, in the position of an active leader. In the States of ancient Greece, the orators were often called "the watch-dogs of the republic," because their voice aroused the people to every peril which, either from without or from within, might threaten the common welfare. But this appellation may be still more fitly applied to our editors, who rightly esteem themselves the guardians of the land. And hence arises the duty of guarding against the errors, which are so apt to attend the influence of party-spirit.

Of course, it would be absurd to desire that there should be no parties. Wherever there is freedom there must be party, because all men cannot think alike on any question of national policy; and they naturally divide into parties, according to the varieties of opinion which attract their attention; and these parties as naturally contend against each other for supremacy. To this there can be no objection, so long as they strive only for what is honestly believed to be the public good, and employ no other means but those of fair and open argument. The danger lies in the inevitable tendency of party to produce *party-spirit*—that is, a spirit which seeks, in the first place, the triumph of the party, and is ready to use for that single end every available instrumentality, without the slightest regard to its consistency with truth or honor—without ever pausing to inquire whether any error in public policy is likely to be so fatal in the end, as the adoption of a course which must disgust the virtuous and the pure, and poison the moral sense of the vast majority.

Unfortunately, the very system of universal suffrage, which forms the glory of our Constitution, has produced the supposed necessity and the specious apology for all the machinery of party corruption. There could be no system more admirably devised, if every voter were a man of virtue and intelligence. But the masses of our national population have long been composed of very different materials from those of the last century. The influx of foreigners has been so great, that in many of our larger cities they nearly equal, and in some they even outnumber, the native citizens. Thus, by the last census, taken in 1850, it appears that

New York	contained	277,752	native born,	and	235,733	foreigners,
Philadelphia	"	286,346	"	"	121,699	"
St. Louis	"	36,529	"	"	38,397	"
Milwaukie	"	7,181	"	"	12,782	"
Cincinnati	"	60,558	"	"	54,541	"
New Orleans	"	50,470	"	"	48,601	"

The other cities contain a smaller proportion of foreigners, but all have so many as to exert a very strong influence over the native population; and I need hardly say, that, however useful and acceptable those foreigners may be in other respects, they are generally far better adapted to the monarchical countries from which they came, than to the republican theory of our political institutions.

But independently of all speculations about the *causes*, the *fact* is undeniable that universal suffrage can only be exercised under some management, by which the intelligence of the few may direct and control the action of the many. These few must be men who make politics their business, who therefore become the leaders of parties, and whose success depends upon the number of votes which they can bring into the field. To this end they often rely on the prejudices, the passions, and the personal interests of their followers, far more than on their virtue and intelligence, because they consider themselves obliged to take human nature as it is, and not as it ought to be. And as the editors occupy a most important place amongst these leaders,—the Press being an essential instrument to the plans of each party,—it results, by a species of apparent necessity, that they address the people in all the various ways which are supposed to be most available.

Hence, party is rarely maintained without party-spirit. And party-spirit is the spirit of war, which contends for victory, and holds every stratagem to be allowable by which victory may be secured. Therefore, the editor, being usually the mouthpiece of the party,—or rather, I should say, the mouthpiece of the leaders,—is seduced by his position into the whole immorality of the occasion. Truth must be sacrificed, if falsehood is more likely to prevail. The candidates selected by each party must be systematically lauded, and those opposed to it as systematically depreciated, by all the arts of unscrupulous ingenuity. Public meetings must be gotten up in as many quarters as possible, the resolutions cut and dried, and the speakers drilled beforehand, and the whole set forth by editorial skill, as if it were the spontaneous utterance of the people. Biographical sketches must be published, in which the previous life of each candidate is industriously ransacked, to find, on the one side, something to praise, and, on the other, something to vilify. The party is proclaimed, with its platform or its principles, as if the very existence of the nation depended on its success; and every other is denounced, as if it had leagued together for the ruin of the country. And the editor, in the whole, must be the Nestor and the Achilles, wise in council, invincible in the field, and always prepared, with arguments, with sophistry, with inuendo, with sarcasm, with ridicule, with sneers, with predictions, threats, promises, or any other implement of available dexterity, to marshal the trusty band of thorough partisans to the work of electioneering, and leave no effort untried, that may aid in securing the expected victory.

This is lamentable enough, and yet it falls far short of the whole practical system of political corruption, which the editors themselves charge upon the tactics of party. Thus it is averred, on all sides, that bribery is employed to a large extent; that pugilists and ruffians of the lowest stamp are hired to intimidate honest and peaceable citizens; that votes are received from hundreds and thousands who are not legally qualified; that great numbers of foreigners are naturalized, who are unfitted, both by their gross ignorance and their lack of moral character, for the duties of an American citizen; that men are brought to the polls from the lowest haunts of vice, to give their ballots at the dictation of their leaders; and that the editors whose party is worsted in the contest, and who complain loudly of the corruption of their antagonists, are never honest enough to confess their own.

The evil of this state of things is manifest, and the consequences must be ultimately deplorable, if no remedy can be applied in time. Already it is well known, that the most pure and enlightened men throughout the nation are disgusted, and keep themselves aloof from politics, because they cannot descend to the management which is thought necessary to success. Already it is confessed, that the persons elected to office are rarely taken from the class, on whose principles and patriotism the people might fairly rely. The golden age of the Republic, if there was ever such a period, seems to have gone out with Washington;

and the age of silver has gone after it, and the age of brass is now running its rapid course, to be followed by the age of iron. But the editors of the land are the most deeply involved, by their talents and position, in the management of our democratic machinery; and it lies mainly with them to reform the existing abuses, supposing that reform be possible. Alas! it may be impossible. The only real basis of our universal suffrage is in the virtue and intelligence of the citizens, united in support of the Constitution and the laws, under the sanction of the Christian religion. If that be secure amongst the great body of our people, there is no government on earth so strong as our republic. But if it fail, its place cannot long be supplied by the schemes of political expediency. A corrupt monarchy may hold together for a long season, because it combines in one head the elements of interest and power. A corrupt aristocracy may endure, if the rulers be wise enough to see that their safety depends upon their union. But a corrupt republic has no substitute for lost virtue. There, the people are the sovereign, and there is no ruling power except it be in accordance with their will. We have no throne to reverence, besides the throne of God. We have no hereditary nobles, identified, by their vast possessions and their titles of honor, with the preservation of law and order. We have no established Church, to act as a potent bond of conservatism. We have no standing army sufficient to put down the popular discontent, because with us, every citizen is a soldier. There is nothing on which we can rely, therefore, if we lose our reverence for the Constitution and the laws. And there is nothing able to secure that reverence, if we lose the sense of religious obligation. For it is this which gives a standard to virtue. It is this which bestows validity on the oath of allegiance, the oath of office, and the oath of justice; thus bringing the conscience of each individual under direct subordination to the supreme Government of heaven.

But although I confess that there is more than enough, in the present condition of our country, to fill the thoughtful mind with gloomy apprehension, yet it is not the part of any good citizen to despair of the republic. Rather let us look the evil in the face, like men of principle and courage; and see if there be not some practical mode of action, suited to our habits, by which, under favor of Providence, a better and a purer system might be attained.

The editors of our newspapers, as I have shown, are the class whose business calls them to be, pre-eminently, the guardians of the republic. Through them, above all others, the citizens of our land receive their general ideas, especially with regard to the discharge of their political duties. If the editors were always right, therefore, it is manifest that the people could not be wrong. And hence, the great *desideratum*, in my opinion, is to adopt some plan, by which those whose chosen function it is to govern the public, may first learn how to govern themselves.

Suppose, then, that this vastly important class were to become voluntarily organized into a regular society; the editors of each State holding a convention once a year, and electing delegates to a general convention of the editorial fraternity from all the States in the Union, to be assembled once in every four years, for the following purposes:

1. That the State convention of editors should nominate those candidates for all the officers of that State, which they shall think worthy of being elected by the people; not confining the choice, however, to one name, but always select-

ing two or three from those who have the largest number of votes as the fittest candidates.

2. That the convention shall establish the laws of editorial justice and propriety; forbidding all unfair management, bribery, and corruption; enjoining courtesy, moderation, and strict regard to truth; and censuring or expelling from the convention, if need be, every editor who is shown to have abused his office, by profaneness or venality.

3. That the convention shall recognize the profession of an editor according to its real dignity, as the guardian and conservator of the public welfare; pledged to raise and purify the morals and habits of the citizens, and support the honor, peace, and permanent interests of the whole Union.

4. That the convention shall freely discuss all questions involved in the range of editorial duty; not infringing upon the liberty of speech or sentiment, but seeking, by a free interchange of views, to promote the cause of truth, and strengthen each member in his efforts to sustain it.

5. And lastly, that the general convention of editors, holden in every fourth year, shall nominate, in like manner, the candidates for the offices of President and Vice President, setting forth two or three names for each, to be presented to the people: the same rules being laid down, and the same range of subjects being open to discussion, as in the editorial convention of the State.

The effects of such a plan, as it seems to my humble judgment, would be highly beneficial. And some of these I shall proceed to specify.

It has been already granted that the exercise of universal suffrage demands, of necessity, the agency of a comparative few, as leaders for the many. The business of nominating the candidates must therefore be done by a small number of managers, and to this there can be no reasonable objection. But yet, since this is, evidently, a most important work, it ought to be done by a known and responsible body; instead of being, as now, the dictate of secret and transient cliques, whose preparatory movements are shrouded in mystery, and open to grave suspicion. There is no class of citizens so well qualified for this work, as the editors of the public press, because it is their express business to watch the course of prominent individuals, and to keep a constant eye upon every thing connected with the general welfare. And therefore the nominations made by them, in a regular convention, would be entitled to more weight than those produced in the ordinary way; and be far less liable to the reproach of intrigue and corruption.

The plan proposed would have the further advantage of relieving the community from almost all of the troublesome and costly excitement, which now produces such a periodical fever through the land; calling thousands away from their business and their homes to attend political meetings, and multiplying tenfold the expense and the annoyance which the proper exercise of the elective franchise requires. For although the convention of editors would not by any means prevent or destroy the existence of parties, and therefore the candidates recommended would represent their respective parties as truly as they now do, yet the tendency of the plan would be to soften the asperity of party spirit, and counteract that violence and extravagance which are the chief support of political excitement, and thus leave the citizens to prepare for the election day by a sober use of their own judgment, in quietness and peace.

Chiefly, however, I should anticipate, from these editorial conventions, a large advance in the wisdom, the conscientiousness, and the purifying influence of this most important profession. I believe that, as a class, they have no superiors in talent, intelligence, and genuine patriotism. But they stand too much alone, to be felt as a real power in the republic. Each man, although a person of consequence in his own particular circle, is too apt to be a tool in the hands of party leaders; compelled to take their judgment, even though far inferior to his own. And therefore I should desire that our editors might rise to their true level, by the strength of association. In mutual council, they would gather knowledge, system, and confidence, for their high office, as guardians of the country, and instructors of the people. The loftier and more generous spirits amongst them, would give tone to the character of the whole. They would learn to stand by each other, as an immovable phalanx, in support of religion and morality, the Constitution and the laws, against the inroads of fanatical hypocrisy, popular licentiousness, and venal corruption. And the resolves of their assembled wisdom, sustained by each separate press, would become not only a sure dependence of virtue and intelligence throughout our own land, but a bright example in the sight of the civilized world, worthy of admiring imitation.

I have occupied more space than I anticipated, in the discussion of this topic; but yet I may not conclude without a brief notice of some other dangers which beset the editor of the newspaper, and against which a conscientious man is bound to be carefully on his guard.

It is said to be a frequent practice to have an advertisement published as an *editorial*, by paying an extra price. And it is well worth the difference to the advertiser, because he is not only sure that his puff will be read, but that the public will have far more faith in his claims to their confidence, when they see that the editor has become a *volunteer*, as they suppose, in this spontaneous commendation.

But this practice is certainly to be condemned, on the plain ground of deception. The editor takes his money for allowing the advertiser to obtain business by *false pretences*. He tells the innocent public that he approves what he has never examined. He sells an opinion which he has not formed, and he is paid for what he knows to be a fabrication. True, he doubtless thinks it a very innocent deceit. He gains his profit. The advertiser flourishes in his business. And there is no harm done. But there is always harm done when gain is made by any sort of imposition. It is encouraging evil in the party who pays for the fraud, and it is a wound to the moral sense of the editor.

Another danger lies in wait for the proprietors of our city papers, which is of serious importance. I allude to the common custom of using a large part of the Christian Sabbath in printing the issue for Monday morning; thereby depriving the workmen of their religious privileges without any real necessity, and breaking the laws of God and man. Certainly, the proprietors might at least adopt the Puritan mode, of making the Sabbath begin on Saturday, at sunset, and ending it at sunset on the following day. And even if the Monday's paper were a few hours later, it would be no real loss to the reader; nor can I believe that the public would fail to approve the act, if all the city editors should meet together, and resolve that their printing-offices should be closed entirely during that consecrated time when man is commanded to cease from his labor.

I shall notice but one more danger which demands grave

consideration from all our journalists, namely, the danger incurred by the publication of police reports, scandalous trials, and other articles, which are unfit to be read in the family circle, and improper at all times for the eyes of youth. The defence set up for this portion of our newspaper information, is that the public have a right to expect it, and complain if it be omitted. But I deny the first part of the proposition, and doubt the second. The public have no right to a kind of intelligence which cannot possibly do good to any one, and is likely to do serious evil to the rising generation. And although there may be a portion of the public who would complain of its omission, yet I cannot doubt that the *public at large* would not merely approve the change, but approve it cordially.

The same argument applies to the publication of all idle jests upon the ministers of God, all witticisms upon the Sacred Scriptures, and all light, irreverent, and profane expressions, calculated to raise contempt, or infuse the spirit of infidelity, towards the Gospel of the Saviour. These offences against the true principles of editorial duty are not unusual, I am sorry to say, even where the best principles are generally inculcated. It is not that I am opposed to genuine wit or humor. I can see no possible objection to an innocent laugh, whether it be excited over the columns of a newspaper, or in the occasional sallies of the social circle. But the laugh cannot be innocent, which wounds the feelings of a Christian heart. And wit and humor should never be tolerated, when they invade the sense of modesty, or the sanctity of religion.

Much more might be added upon this copious theme, but that I must hasten onwards to the remaining topics of my humble volume. I would only add, in concluding my remarks upon the editorial profession, that no one can hold it in higher respect than I do, or attach to its proper exercise a larger measure of importance. Let those who belong to it only understand the true dignity and extended influence of their office, and then they will seldom fail to discharge it wisely. Let them remember that they are not merely American Citizens, partners in the republic, and thus far bound to do their share for the general good; but that they are under a special responsibility from the very nature of their chosen avocation, which makes them the guardians of the national welfare, the daily instructors of the public mind, and the regular organs of the public sentiment. In their multifarious energy, nothing escapes them. They undertake to advise, direct, and censure every other class in the community, from the President, the Houses of Congress, the governors, legislatures, judges, lawyers, and physicians, down to the scavengers who clean the streets. They do not confine themselves to things secular, but favor the nation with frequent rebukes of the ministers of God, and look sharply after the teachers of religion. They pronounce upon the merits of books and literature. The stage and the concert-room are under their established patronage. Sculptors, artists, musicians, architects, orators, share the benefits of their comprehensive stewardship. Commerce and manufactures, discoveries and inventions, all the natural sciences, all the useful or ornamental arts, come under their notice. Their praise is at least a pleasant substitute for fame, and their censure is dreaded as if it were the passport to infamy. In fine, there is not belonging to this world so manifold, so diffusive, so penetrating, so active an institution as the newspaper press. Oh! how great should be the wisdom, how pure the patriotism, how lofty the principles of those who guide its energy! How worthy of all honor are the editors who reach the mark of their vocation! And how safe would be the destiny of our favored country, if the guardians of its welfare did not themselves too often lead it astray!

CHAPTER XIX.

THE DANGERS OF THE MINISTER OF THE GOSPEL.

I NEED hardly say that among the various avocations which are open to the American citizen, the highest, in its own nature, is that of the minister of religion. All the rest are useful, estimable, and important. But this transcends them, as far as the welfare of time is surpassed by the happiness of eternity. Looking no further, however, than the interests of the present life, it is certain that the laws and principles, which guard our earthly rights and enjoin our worldly duties, rest upon religion as their basis. Deprived of this, we could derive no advantage from the spiritual element of our nature. The true nobility and glory of our being would be lost. The intellect and the body might remain, but their powers would sink into brutishness. The conscience would be utterly blotted out, and we should have no foundation left for morality and virtue.

Hence, as I have already shown, the Constitution, the laws, and the entire fabric of society are protected by religion. Take away religion, and you destroy the oath of allegiance, the oath of office, and the whole administration of justice. For the oath is the religious bond, involving a direct appeal to God, and demanding our assent by a reference to the future judgment, which awaits every soul before the tribunal of the great Redeemer. The result is manifest, that the ministers of religion are an indispensable order of men in every civilized community; because all the rights, the duties, the peace, the enjoyment, and the security of that community depend on the maintenance of religious principle.

My object in these remarks is not to exalt the ministerial profession beyond its true limit of social, legal, and political value. I shall say nothing here, therefore, of the relation of the minister to the life beyond the grave. I leave untouched the precious work of conversion and sanctification in the heart, and the ineffable peace and joy of the sincere believer. For it has been my purpose, from the first, to confine myself to the connection which religion bears, of necessity, to the citizen; and to the rules of truth, justice, and morality which concern the individual man and the public welfare, in this lower world. Under this aspect of the question, I regard the minister as an important member of the State, because he belongs to a profession which is absolutely indispensable to the framework of society; and as such, he has not only his rights to claim, and his duties to perform, but he has also many dangers in his path, worthy of special consideration.

1. The first of these, and one that is very common, is the danger of *discouragement*. For the most part, in our day, the Christian minister does not find a fair measure of appreciation, as an essential *member of the body politic*. Men in general are strangely blind to the vast importance of religion, in the preservation of their social privileges. They respect the lawyer; they reverence the judge; they honor the physician; they envy the wealthy merchant; they

worship the military hero and the successful politician; but they look down upon the Christian minister as a person of small weight in the community; totally forgetting that if it were not for the work of such as he, there would soon be no judge, no lawyer, no learned physician, no rich merchant, no popular statesman, no security for property or life, no civilized community. They do not stop to think that all they value in this mortal state is the product of Christianity. They do not reflect that throughout the whole world, wherever Christianity is not, there is neither liberty in union with law, nor pure morality, nor high intelligence, nor literary culture, nor elevated civilization. They forget that our own ancestors in ancient Britain, Ireland, Gaul, and Germany, were barbarian savages in the days of the apostles; and that it was Christianity which raised their posterity from their deep degradation. And they do not reflect that if the ministers of Christ should all abandon them, the whole fabric of society would soon go back to barbarism again.

Of course, the Christian minister is prepared to a considerable degree, by the very language of his divine Master, for this marvellous stupidity and thoughtlessness of the world around him. And yet, he is exposed to the danger of discouragement, when, as often happens, he is called to struggle with cold indifference and neglect—when even in his own peculiar circle, there is but little interest in his labors—when even his own people seem to grudge the miserable support doled out for his necessary maintenance—when every other business in the community is better paid and more regarded, than that which is the very safeguard of the whole. But still, he must endure it for the sake of Him who spent His life in doing good to His enemies, in the midst of ingratitude and persecution. He must endure it for the sake of the few, who value what the majority despise. And he *will* endure it, if he leans upon the strength which is promised to his weakness; and remembers how much more was done and suffered in the Gospel ministry by thousands of his predecessors, all worthier and holier than he.

2. The second danger of the Christian minister is *fear:* not the fear of God, which is always an incentive to duty, but "the fear of man which bringeth a snare"—the fear of giving offence to the wealthy and the worldly portion of his congregation. The virtue of courage is in high honor among mankind. But there is no kind of courage so lofty in its own nature, as the moral courage required to speak the truth, when that truth is almost sure to excite dislike and opposition. Yet here, too, the faithful minister must not falter. He may be called to suffer for his honest sincerity. Enemies may be roused, and timid friends may desert him. But he knows that there is an Almighty arm raised for his protection, and that the end will be victory and peace.

3. The third danger is of an opposite character, and springs from *presumption.* This is an ordinary companion of ministerial success and popularity, when uncommon talents, united to a bold physical temperament, gain a powerful influence in the community; and the admired orator is followed by crowds, and becomes intoxicated by the incense of extravagant praise and adulation. Happily for the interests of religion, such cases are not numerous: and happily for the individual, the season of his giddy exaltation rarely exceeds a few years, and then the delusion passes away. But while it lasts, the peril is imminent that he

may be misled into serious error, and bring reproach upon himself, and on the sacred cause committed to his care.

These remarks must suffice, however, on the general dangers of the Christian minister, simply considered as it respects his relations to society. But there are other dangers arising out of a confused and mistaken view of his position as a member of the body politic, invested with all the rights and pledged to all the duties of an American citizen. And it may be well to examine both sides of this question, which is regarded in very opposite aspects by the world at large.

On the one hand, it is said that the Christian minister has nothing to do with the affairs of this life, beyond the supply of his personal and domestic wants, and the ordinary intercourse of society. He must be so entirely occupied with the duties of his sacred calling, that he can have no judgment entitled to any weight in business, and especially in politics. His avocation lies in the care of men's souls, which is quite enough for his time and attention. The care of their bodies, the rules of trade, the principles of law, the rights of property, and the conduct of government, are all matters with which he has no concern; and if he meddles with them, he should be rebuked as an unauthorized intruder.

On the other side, we are told that the Christian minister has the same right with others, in all that belongs to the interests of humanity. That his education and position in the community qualify him for a correct judgment on the whole business of life, at least so far as regards general principles. That he may introduce at his discretion any secular topic in the pulpit, which he thinks himself capable of discussing, with advantage to his people or the public at large. That if circumstances call for his services in the line of politics, he is authorized to lay down his ministerial office altogether, and go to the legislature or to Congress. That he may even march at the head of a military troop, in the defence of his country. And, in fine, that there is no difference between his duties as a citizen and those of any other Christian, since the law of the Gospel is precisely the same for the pastor and the flock.

Between these two extremes, truth, as it seems to me, would adopt a medium. I have already shown that the ministers of religion are an essential order in every civilized State. And this, in a republic, would seem to require that each member of that order must be a citizen; because if he be not, he is free from the duty of allegiance, and does not stand on equal ground with others. Moreover, if—as is usually the case, and always ought to be—he was a citizen before he was ordained, it is certain that there is nothing in ordination which takes the rights of citizenship away. He has become an ambassador for Christ, indeed; and the kingdom of Christ is not of this world. But Christ is not a foreign Potentate, whose service is incompatible with the service of our government. On the contrary, He is the Spiritual Sovereign of all the earth, and embraces the whole under his supreme dominion. In precise accordance with this, we find St. Paul claiming to be a native of Tarsus and a citizen of Rome, notwithstanding he was an Apostle.

The ministerial office, therefore, interferes with no man's rights as a citizen, save only that it *modifies the exercise of those rights* by placing them in strict subordination to his higher duty. All his conduct must be regulated, henceforth, by this rule of consistency; because he cannot depart from it without a violation of the special vows which bound him to his spiritual vocation. He is no longer free to act, in all respects, as he might have lawfully acted, if those vows had not been taken. He has accepted a commission as an ambassador for Christ, and is obliged to sustain that character in all his public services. And therefore if he voluntarily lays aside or abandons his sacred commission, in order to become a member of Congress, a Governor, or an officer under any earthly authority, he certainly seems guilty of a contempt towards the majesty of the Redeemer, and I do not see how he can be excused.

On this ground of consistency I should be obliged to censure the ordained minister, who misused the pulpit, and profaned the Lord's Day, by declaiming on any subject not connected with the Gospel; no matter how useful to the people or the public his opinions might otherwise be. For that is the day and there is the place where he is bound to appear as the ambassador of Christ; and he has no right to employ his official powers in a cause for which they were not conferred, nor to use the Lord's house and the Lord's Day in a service for which they were not intended. Such acts of desecration show a want of proper reverence for the established order of religion, and savor not a little of the character of sacrilege.

In all other respects, however, when the rights and duties of the citizen in nowise conflict with the paramount duties of the minister, there can be no good reason assigned for depriving him of their exercise; provided always that this exercise be in perfect harmony with his sacred office, and yield no worthy cause of offence to intelligent Christian people. For this is the precept of the apostle, "Give no offence in any thing, that the ministry be not blamed." And there is a certain rule of congruity to be observed in obedience to this maxim, which no minister can disregard without danger to his proper influence.

When St. Paul labored with his hands in tent-making, for example, he was not acting inconsistently; because he did it for his necessary support, and still continued to preach the Gospel. And when he assumed the office of director during the storm and shipwreck at Malta, though it was a secular matter with which he had no official concern, he was not acting inconsistently; because it was done in the service of humanity, with faith and prayer. But we do not find him meddling with matters of war and bloodshed, nor counselling slaves to kill their masters, nor kindling the flames of rebellion, nor exhorting the citizens to the strife of battle, nor exciting a mob to resist the law. For he remembered that he was the ambassador of the Prince of Peace, and, like his divine Master, he commanded his disciples to yield rather than strive,—not to "oppose evil with evil, but to overcome evil with good."

The minister of Christ, then, is a citizen of the republic, having a right to do all things which other citizens may lawfully do, with this condition—that they be not inconsistent with the superior duties of his sacred character. He is at liberty to give his judgment on every question which concerns the welfare of the republic, like any other citizen, if he have the requisite knowledge and wisdom for the task, and his design be performed in the spirit which becomes his office to promote "peace and good-will towards men." He may advise and counsel all classes of society to such a course in secular affairs, as shall be best calculated for their temporal and eternal prosperity. He may give his vote quietly for his favorite candidates, and state his reasons when required. He may deliver an occasional lecture on history, morals, science, or the arts. He may lay down general principles to statesmen, lawyers, merchants, teachers, and physicians. He may dispense medicine to the poor, and exert himself to build schools, and hospitals, and colleges. But in all that he does, his ministerial character must suffer no violence. The spirit of the Gospel, which is peace and love, must preside over the whole. The paramount obligations of an ambassador of Christ must never be set aside or forgotten. And thus he will find it practicable to unite the rights and duties of an American citizen, with his office in the Church; and furnish a proof to the world that "godliness is profitable for all things, having promise of the life that now is, as well as of that which is to come."

But still, in all this, there is danger; because mankind are rarely willing to acknowledge the capacity of any one to be useful in a variety of services, and he can seldom be regarded with respect, out of the line of his profession. Nor can we wonder at this, when we reflect upon the fact, that the ministerial office is quite enough to occupy the time and thoughts of any ordinary individual. It is not, therefore, without some reason, that men are reluctant to admit a combination of knowledge and energy which is quite out of the common track of human experience. And hence, though such an accident may sometimes occur, it is very apt to be regarded not merely with surprise, but with incredulity. A few may possibly admire, but the major part will be far more likely to censure; taking it for granted that the effort and industry demanded as the condition of success in any one department, cannot be divided among several without a certainty of failure; and that the attempt to know many things is sure to result in knowing nothing well.

I doubt not, therefore, that the safest rule for the minister of the Gospel was laid down by the apostle Paul, when he said, "I determined to know nothing else among you but Jesus Christ, and Him crucified." It is the best and the wisest course in every calling, that the talents and energies of the individual should be so devoted to his chosen business as to attract no public notice in any thing else, at least until his ability in this is placed beyond the risk of uncertainty. But this course seems especially imperative on the clergyman, whose office consists not only in securing the highest privileges for the present life, but also in a preparation for the life to come. Hence, no measure of success can warrant the ceasing of his labors; and even old age itself should show how the infirmity of the body may exist along with the growing ardor of the soul.

Such, then, is the general rule. Like all other general rules, it may have its exceptions. Yet if the well-known maxim be true, that the exception proves the rule, it will be found pre-eminently true, to a far wider extent and for a much more important class of reasons, in the work of the ministry.

CHAPTER XX.

ON THE DOMESTIC RELATIONS.

From the large range of business, in its various aspects, it is time to pass onward to the far more interesting topic of the domestic relations, for the sake of which the American citizen usually toils with the most constant diligence. To the great majority, there is no incentive so steady and so sure as the necessity of providing for the family, which Providence has made dependent on the industry of the husband and the father. The welfare of that family forms the most precious motive which stimulates exertion. In the circle of home centers the little world of comfort and enjoyment which fills the heart. For it he is ready to labor, to struggle, to suffer, to endure disappointments, vexations, losses, contests, poverty, and pain. He lives for it, rather than for himself; and only realizes the value of life in proportion as he can secure its peace and prosperity.

But it is not the father and the husband alone, who has a deep stake in the domestic relations. For, the family is the first and most effective training school for all the duties of society; and on it depends, in the vast majority of cases, the character which stamps the future course of the individual. Nothing therefore can be more essential to the American citizen than a true appreciation of the mutual connection between the husband and the wife, the parent and the child, the teacher and the pupil, the master and the servant. The whole process of education belongs to the same comprehensive range; and the entire man, spiritual, moral, intellectual, and physical, is moulded by its powerful influence, either for good or evil.

The vast extent and importance of the principles which should regulate the domestic relations may be further shown, by the impossibility of finding, in this world, any substitute. There is no remedy for the misery of a disorderly and ill-governed family, in wealth, in honor, or in fame. And he whose home is not happy, whatever may be the measure of his success in the other objects of life, has lost the dearest prize of his earthly labor.

The consideration of the numerous questions, which arise

under this prolific branch of rights and duties, will require several distinct divisions: and the natural order of the subject presents, in the first place, the inquiry, whether youth is the proper season for entering into the matrimonial state, to which I shall devote the remainder of this chapter.

It is common, in our days, to consider early marriages as imprudent and even unjustifiable. Physicians condemn them on the ground, that the constitutions of the parties are not sufficiently mature to produce a healthy and vigorous offspring. Economists condemn them, because young men are rarely in circumstances which will bear the expense. Many others condemn them, because they see so much disappointment and trouble arising out of matrimony, when the wedded pair are deficient in sense and true principle, that they naturally conclude it to be far better to postpone this most serious of all relations until a riper age of experience and discretion. And there are not a few who are disposed to prefer the freedom of a single life, as far less liable to suffering and sorrow.

But all these reasons seem to me of little weight, when opposed to the manifest designs of Providence, the general authority of Scripture, and the instincts and affections implanted in the human heart. With respect to the first objection, the physicians know perfectly well that the delay of marriage is no safeguard against the fearful risks of youthful licentiousness; which are not only fatal to the strength of the constitution, but often lay the foundation for the most terrible diseases, and thus doom the unhappy offspring of a late marriage to an inheritance of debility and premature decay. Nature points to early marriage as the true normal condition of our race; and experience proves it to be the best practical protection of health, of reasonable continence, and of sound morality. We find, accordingly, that the people of Israel held this to be a settled rule, in pursuance of the divine law laid down in the beginning. We see the apostle Paul, also, notwithstanding his individual preference of celibacy, establishing the same practice, where he saith: "Let every man have his own wife, and let every woman have her own husband."* This is further confirmed by his emphatic declaration, "Marriage is honorable in all."† And the design of the Creator is wonderfully manifested to this day from the well-known fact ascertained by the published statistics of all civilized nations, that the males and the females born in every country are almost precisely equal in number. What general maxim of human society can be more fully proved than this, when the voice of religion, the results of experience, and the fixed order of divine Providence, concur so harmoniously in the same conclusion?

The second objection, namely, that early marriage is to be avoided "because young men are rarely in circumstances which will bear the expense," is doubtless more operative in a multitude of instances. This, however, when fairly examined, will be found to be only true, through the prevalence of those luxurious and effeminate habits, which are hostile not merely to marriage, but to all the solid comforts and sober virtues of life. If our young women were educated in the love and practice of domestic labor, with a wise contempt of the costly ornaments of fashion, and a fixed determination to disregard the notions of the vain and silly society around them, devoted to the rules of duty, and the peaceful enjoyments of home, there would be no

---

* 1 Cor. vii. 2. † Heb. xiii. 4.

ground left to fear the expense of early marriage. For on the true theory of wedlock, the wife would be a *help* and not a hindrance, earning her appropriate share of all temporal necessaries, and cheerfully resigning the poor ambition of being a fine lady, for the far higher praise of being an associate in the work as well as in the pleasures of her husband. And thus it would be found perfectly practicable to have a home and raise a family, on a smaller income, than a majority of our single men now throw away on boarding-houses, with the adjuncts of amusement and dissipation.

That this is no impracticable notion, is sufficiently demonstrated by the facts which are notorious amongst all observers. The laboring class are usually married in early life, and contrive to live and raise up large families, upon an income of two or three hundred dollars a year. How is this? Simply because the wife works in her sphere as hard as her husband, and they are content with the reasonable comforts, without the idle superfluities of life.

But this kind of argument, I am aware, would revolt my readers. They repel, at once, the idea of living on a level with the vulgar, the uneducated, the unenlightened mass, which constitutes the lower orders of society. Let me ask their attention, then, to the condition of the clergy, whose salaries, on a general average throughout the land, do not exceed six hundred dollars. Yet these men are usually married early. They are educated, often highly. Their wives are educated, and quite equal, in refinement of intellect and manners, to the best standard of society. And these, too, contrive to live and train up a numerous offspring. How? By the same management precisely. They dispense with superfluities. They do their own domestic work. They help themselves and each other. They teach their children to do their share of the common labor. And thus, by a well-regulated system of economy, by diligent industry, and by limiting their expenses to what is strictly necessary for the decent comforts of life, they accomplish what our objector holds to be simply impossible, without descending, at once, to the lowest level of the community.

This class of facts, then, is conclusive of the question. If any young man be afraid of an early marriage, on account of the expense, or the possible degradation of the educated lady whom he might choose for his companion, let him reflect upon the condition of the clergy, on the broad average of actual experience, and he will see that the difficulty lies not in the subject itself, but in the perverted notions and habits of fashionable society. And then, if the maiden of his choice be a true woman, and if he frankly state the amount of his income, and leave it to her option whether she will submit to the necessary labors of wedded life, and do as much on her part as he expects to do on his, he will find her ready and willing to make the sacrifice, in the performance of her duty. It may be, indeed, that he will be disappointed. She may refuse to give up her wretched slavery to frivolity, luxury, and ease; and resolve only to accept him when he is able to support her in idleness and vanity. But if so, let him thank Providence for his escape; and be grateful that he is not tied for life to one of those unhappy specimens of modern education, who are utterly unfit for the sacred relations of wife or mother.

The third objection to early marriages arises from the results which observation presents in too many instances, where trouble and misery attend the matrimonial state, because the wedded pair are deficient in sense and true principle. The remedy for this, however, is not to be found in the postponement of marriage; since it would usually be seen that the party or parties in fault needed a far more serious improvement of character, than the mere lapse of time could have supplied. If the husband or the wife be foolish or unprincipled, they cannot be expected to live happily together, whether they be old or young. And it would be the height of absurdity to suppose that age alone could supply the want of sense or virtue.

The remaining class of objectors, who abjure matrimony altogether, because they think that the freedom of celibacy is far more exempt from suffering and sorrow, stand so directly opposed to religion, reason, and sound morality, that there is no need of argument to manifest their error. But here we must make a distinction. I allude only to those wild and radical innovators, who declaim against wedlock on the ground of its supposed despotism and unnatural restraints; and contend for the fancied superiority of a promiscuous intercourse, to be continued no longer than it might suit the caprice of personal inclination. The case of those who only claim the right to remain unmarried in consideration of their own peculiar health, or tastes, or circumstances, is quite a different matter. These persons do honor to matrimony as the general rule, and merely ask the privilege of being exceptions. And assuredly there are many such exceptions who are in nowise blamable; but, on the contrary, by a life of purity and active benevolence, are entitled to the affection and gratitude of all around them.

Having thus replied to the objections, I conclude by a brief summary of the advantages, which, on the average survey of human life, would justify the choice of early marriage in the American citizen.

In the first place, it would concentrate his feelings and his habits in the circle of his own home; and secure him from a thousand snares, temptations, and dangers, to which the single man, especially in the season of youth, is always liable.

Secondly, it would afford the strongest earthly motive for steadfast diligence, prudence, and economy.

Thirdly, it would be far more likely to secure that mutual spirit of kindly accommodation, which is so essential to the happiness of the wedded state. For, it is in the time of youth that the heart is most warm, and the habits most flexible. The connection then formed has the strongest power to assimilate the parties to each other. And hence they become most truly ONE, in sentiment, in principle, and in affection. We all know the enduring force of early attachments in friendship. We all acknowledge how superior they are apt to be, when compared to those of later life. And there can be no reasonable doubt that the same difference exists in early love. Why should marriage be deprived of this surest principle of constancy and union?

Fourthly, the young man, *married*, has a much surer hold on the good-will of society. He is rightly regarded, by those around him, as being comparatively safe from the risks of dissipation and licentiousness, and more worthy of trust and confidence. His success gives far higher pleasure to his neighbors and his friends. His misfortunes excite a far deeper feeling of commiseration. For matrimony invests him with a double life, and therefore he reaps a double harvest of human sympathy.

Nor is this the whole of his advantages. What contrast

can be stronger than that of the young man, *before* marriage, who seeks his boarding-house at the close of his daily labor, without a solitary bosom to respond to his hopes or his anxieties; and the same young man, *after* marriage, when he can hasten to his home, in the full certainty of finding the companion of his heart, ready to share in all his trials or his joys, with perfect unity of feeling? In the days of buoyant health, what countenance, like hers, can reflect his look of animation? In the hours of sickness or of pain, what hand, like hers, can be laid upon his brow—what care, like hers, can minister to his wants, with tender watchfulness and assiduity?

And lastly, in the event of offspring, the superiority of early marriage is almost beyond comparison. For the children are generally far more vigorous, in consequence of the greater vigor of the parents' constitution. The mother is more likely to accommodate herself to the care of their education; and the father has a much better prospect of seeing them fairly launched into the business of the world, and aiding them by his experience and his counsel. And then, when old age steals on; and the whitened locks, and the dim eye, and the feeble step lead those parents gently towards the grave; the children of their youth will be in the vigor of a ripe maturity, able to cheer and sustain them through the period of decline, and stand around their bed of death in the solemn sweetness of filial love, and hallow their tomb with the tears of true and deep affection.

How infinitely is all this to be preferred before a marriage postponed to the prudent age of worldly competency! How sad the thoughts of the father who is about to die and leave his little ones, in childhood, delicate in frame and weak in constitution, to the cold care of executors and guardians, to the uncertain charity of strangers, or to the transient pity of the world! Surely, there is no comparison which can do justice to the contrast. But these reasons must suffice to prove the vast advantage of early marriage, although much might be added to the imperfect exposition. I pass on to the important topic of the choice of a wife, and to this I shall devote the following chapter.

CHAPTER XXI.

ON THE CHOICE OF A WIFE.

It is quite evident that the choosing of a partner for life properly implies some reasonable action of the judgment. And it is equally evident that as the bridegroom is bound to love and to cherish his bride, there must also be a reasonable measure of personal affection. And both should concur in the selection, if the American citizen would really desire to enjoy the true comforts and blessings of the marriage union.

Yet I have just recommended an early marriage, as in all respects the more advantageous and hopeful. Who can expect the exercise of judgment, from the youth of twenty-one? Is it not manifestly absurd to ask it at an age, when there can be so little experience in the knowledge of human character? Does it not need long years of acquaintance to form a correct opinion even of our daily associates? And how, then, can such an opinion be formed in reference to a female, with whom her admirer can have so little familiar intercourse before they are engaged, who instinctively presents herself to him in the most amiable aspect, and whose faults, even without intending it, are carefully concealed from his observation?

Now I frankly admit that these difficulties are plausible. It would seem, at first sight, that judgment can have little place in the serious business of an early marriage, and that it must therefore be left entirely to the affections or the personal inclinations of the parties. And yet such a conclusion would be altogether erroneous, as I hope to show by a very simple course of reasoning.

I commence, then, by denying that the American youth, at the age of twenty-one, is too young to form a reasonable judgment of female character. At that age, he is old enough to assume the important relations of a citizen, to commence the practice of law, of medicine, of the ministry, or of any other business, all of which require more or less judgment of human nature. At that age, moreover, he has actually been already occupied, for many years, in this very thing, of necessity; since, from his childhood up, he has been constantly observing and judging, whether right or wrong, the characters of all around him.

I deny, secondly, that men grow wise in proportion to their years, with regard to their power of appreciating human character. It is well known that the instinctive impression of women and children is often far more correct, than the knowledge which men are supposed to derive from observation and experience. Doubtless it may be true enough that the older men grow, the more likely they are to be suspicious. It is also true that in proportion as they refuse to trust each other, in the same proportion they may secure themselves from imposition. But suspicion is one thing, and the power of judging human character is another. Indeed, suspicion is so far from aiding us to form a right judgment, that it operates, in perhaps a majority of cases, to make that judgment impossible.

Be this as it may, however, it is certain that it has no relation to my present subject. The spheres of the sexes are so different, that the experience of the one can seldom be safely applied to the other. Where woman is concerned, therefore, it rarely happens that the old bachelor acquires any peculiar knowledge which is likely to aid him in the choice of a wife. We all know, on the contrary, that he is usually far more liable to error than the young; because he is more likely to be the object of mercenary art and speculation. The lady takes him, full often, not for love, but for convenience or for money. And hence we see that there are no matches more absurd than those made by old men, in all other eyes except their own.

The result, to my mind, is very clear: that the American citizen of twenty-one, who is presumed to have judgment enough to enter, for himself, on every other kind of business, has judgment enough to choose his wife, if he will only try to use it. And how ought he to use it, is therefore the next important subject of inquiry.

Here, then, on the threshold of the matter, I would not recommend him to wait until, as the ordinary phrase is, he *falls in love.* The sudden, violent, and passionate desire which this language indicates, is rarely the safest guide to a happy matrimonial connection. It is too extravagant to last. It is too blind to estimate character. It is too deaf to hear reason. It is too headlong to think of consequences. And hence, instead of this, I should altogether prefer the gradual attachment which grows with acquaintance and esteem; which is not so strong as to render the exercise of judgment impossible, but which is far more likely to increase with time, and yield the best measure of rational enjoyment throughout the whole course of the wedded union.

Supposing then, that our young American citizen designs to take a wife—as, with very few and peculiar exceptions, it is the right and duty of all to do—and supposing, further, that he finds within the circle of his female acquaintance a maiden of suitable age, whose person and whose manners impress him favorably, he should commence at once the work of judgment, before his feelings are too far engaged, and direct his attention to those points of character which he must know to be essential to happiness in the matrimonial relation.

The first and most important point to be determined, is whether she be possessed of true religious principle. And this is not to be taken for granted because she is the communicant of a Christian Church, or an extravagant admirer of some Christian preacher, or even an active teacher in the Sunday-school, and an industrious member of a benevolent society. The real strength of religious principle is rather to be found in the sweetness of her ordinary deportment, the good sense and discretion of her discourse, the moderation of her attire, the absence of envy, vanity, censoriousness, and affectation, the strict performance of her domestic duties, and the kindly regards of the members of her own family. These are the surest tests of the practical power of her Christian profession, and yield the fairest promise of her fitness for matrimonial life.

But if, on his occasional visits at her parents' house, he find her destitute of all filial respect towards her mother, pert, and sharp, and selfish, and contradictory: let him set that down in his judgment as a strong note of warning. A disobedient and unfeeling daughter can never be likely to make a faithful wife.

Or if he observe her to be exacting, imperious, and unkind to her younger brothers and sisters, indifferent to their comfort and only intent upon her own: let him set that down also, as a sure mark of the temper which he may expect, when the novelty of wedded life is over.

Or if he discover that she is accustomed to talk in the language of extravagant hyperbole, regardless of all sobriety and truth, so that her ordinary statements deserve no confidence: he may well conclude that she is quite unfit to be the head and example of a family, or a trust-worthy helpmate to a husband.

Or if she be evidently looking out for admiration, fond of excessive show and ornament in her apparel, addicted to gadding abroad, and among the last to leave routs and parties: he should lay that up in his judgment as a most unpromising sign of a happy home.

Or if she despise the knowledge of a good housekeeper, with no wish to lessen the burden of her mother's cares, but always ready to give trouble to others, without any return of thankfulness, or any anxiety to take trouble for them: this also may serve for an admonition.

Or if she be lazy and indolent, fond of reading novels and full of affected sentimentality, while she is without relish for useful information, without any active sympathy for real sorrow, and hard and uncharitable to the poor: he may take this as another most unfavorable indication.

Or if she look down, with proud disdain, upon honest labor, and deem it beneath her dignity to help herself; if she lean upon her aristocratic friends, having no sympathy with plebeian notions of utility; if she cannot cheerfully employ her hands or occupy her thoughts, on proper occasions, with sewing, sweeping, baking, preserving, gardening, nursing, teaching, or any other of the humbler, yet most important work of ordinary life; let him beware how he connects her with himself in marriage, since it is impossible, without a radical change, that she should ever succeed in the duties of the wedded relation.

Yet it may be that many of these faults have arisen from a defective education, from the foolish indulgence of her parents, or from the example of associates and acquaintances; and still she may have a principle of religion in the heart, and native sense in the head, sufficient, if rightly directed, to amend them. In such a case, let her admirer next exercise his judgment in the experiment of instruction as a *friend*, before he commits himself too far as a *lover*. Let him honestly and kindly tell her of her faults, and observe how she takes the lesson. If she receive it in good part, and display docility and energy enough to conquer her evil habits, and attain a higher and a better character, he may safely calculate on the happiest result; and marriage may be expected to complete the desired reformation. But if she treat his remonstrances with levity or resentment, let him at once retire and direct his matrimonial plans to some other quarter. Better, a thousand-fold, that he should suffer, for a little while, in the conflict between his judgment and his inclinations; than tie himself to domestic sorrow for life, and perhaps involve a family in the sad results of maternal misgovernment and ill example.

It is obvious that the exercise of this measure of observation and judgment, at the supposed age of twenty-one, demands much seriousness of thought on the part of our young American citizen; although the several points which I have specified are all easily ascertained on a very ordinary acquaintance, if attention be directed to them. But if he be supposed, at that age, capable of transacting business for himself, and worthy of trust and confidence, he must also be capable of thinking seriously on so very serious a subject as the choice of a companion, which may determine the whole complexion of his earthly destiny. He ought not to permit himself to form such an engagement in levity or reckless presumption. He ought not to be drawn into it, without careful forethought. And above all, he ought not to conclude upon it, without earnest supplication, that he may be preserved from error. If there be any connection upon earth worthy of prayer for the divine direction, marriage is so pre-eminently; because on it may depend the happiness not only of himself, but of many yet unborn. And the youth who enters upon it without prayer, without reflection, and without grave and sober judgment, has no right to complain, if wedlock prove to be a source of disappointment and sorrow.

It is to be remembered, however, that although I have endeavored, thus far, to show how our young American may form for himself a right estimate of character, yet if it be in his power to consult his own parents on the subject of his choice, it is his duty to do so. He cannot marry a wife without giving them a daughter; and he has no right to do that, until he is satisfied that they approve the selection. And this is the more imperative upon him, since he may always calculate upon their free consent, unless there be very strong reasons against it; to which, as they proceed from his best and truest friends, he ought certainly to listen with the most respectful attention.

On the same ground, he should never dream of tempting

the maiden of his choice into an elopement. Such cases, indeed, may, and sometimes do, turn out well, in the opinion of the world. But a marriage consummated by an act of filial wrong, ingratitude, and rebellion, can hardly fail of sorrow in the end. The bride commits a grievous sin in casting off her highest obligations to her parents, and may expect a righteous retribution in the conduct of her own children; besides the bitter feelings which are likely to rise against her, in her father's heart. The bridegroom commits a grievous sin by suggesting the transgression. And if the history of such examples could be fully known, I doubt not that they would usually prove to have been attended by a curse instead of a blessing.

I would only add, that the main principle which should guide the young American in the choice of a wife, if he would enjoy the true advantages and comforts of marriage, must bear reference to those qualities of the mind, the temper, the habits, and the principles which are adapted to its proper duties. In no case, therefore, should he select her merely on account of her rank or fortune. Money is no substitute for prudence, fidelity, or love. Full often it proves, on the contrary, a prolific source of discord and dissension. The wife who brings to her husband a large accession of influence or of wealth, is very apt to remind him of the fact; and to claim a right of dictation and of government which utterly subverts the established order of the wedded state, and makes him a gilded slave where he ought to be the master. It needs a rare endowment of Christian principle to overcome such a temptation, and to enable the wedded heiress to fulfil her conjugal obligations with the same faithfulness and affection, as if the fortune had been her husband's and not her own.

Believing, as I do, that the best interests of our country at large, as well as those of the individual citizen, would be greatly promoted if early marriage were the general rule; and lamenting the increasing number of those who doom themselves to an indefinite delay, and to celibacy; I have thus laid down, briefly, the argument in support of what I deem to be the safer and the wiser course. It is hardly necessary to say that all such rules must have a great variety of exceptions, which do not require to be specified, because they provide for themselves. And I am perfectly aware that there is no subject so little likely to be governed by rules; notwithstanding the dangers which are sure to result, when the parties disregard the laws of truth and nature.

CHAPTER XXII.

ON MARRIED LIFE.

It is perhaps the chief boast of our American society that the female sex is regarded with so much kindly deference and consideration; and there are few travellers in Europe who can fail to be favorably impressed in our behalf, by the difference, in this respect, between the old world and the new. To speculate upon the causes which have produced this difference, is no part of my present object. The fact is unquestionable, and I notice it in this connection, mainly on account of its strong influence upon the ordinary ideas entertained with regard to the marriage relation.

The law of wedded life, indeed, is substantially the same throughout the United States, that has been established, for so many ages, in every other quarter of the world. That law is in precise accordance with the divine decree passed on woman at the fall, "Thy desire shall be to thy husband," saith the Almighty, "and he shall rule over thee."* Hence the right of the husband is to govern, and the duty of the wife is to obey. That duty is plainly expressed by the marriage covenant, in all the nations of Christendom, our own included. But the quality of the government on the one side, and of the obedience on the other, is subject to a most potential modification, according to the prevailing notions and customs of each community.

With ourselves, this modification has gone so far, that the law of obedience is rarely acknowledged or even thought of, as a practical element of wedded life. The American citizen, for the most part, calculates upon leaving his wife in undisputed possession of the home department; reserving to himself the management of the farm, the workshop, the counting-room, or the office, as the case may be; and usually intending her to conduct her own branch precisely as she pleases. The wife takes her accustomed position as a matter of course, and by no means as if it were a matter of concession. Both parties pay a reasonable regard to the prerogatives of each other, and seldom interfere beyond their respective spheres. They are like two equal partners who are interested alike, indeed, in the profits of the business; but who agree, for convenience sake, to divide the work between them. And the result, for aught that the world can see, is a fair amount of respectable concord and success; although there is no notion of authority on the one side, or of obedience on the other.

* Gen. iii. 16.

This state of the question usually passes for a great improvement on the system of the Scriptures. And it seems to work tolerably well, unless a young family rise up to test its practical efficiency. Then comes the discovery that there is no proper family government at all. The mother regulates the children until she can control them no longer; and that period, in the case of the boys especially, arrives very soon. The force of authority is understood by neither of the parties. The father is accustomed to the law of contract, and the power of interest, and the sentiments of honor and humanity; but the rod of parental discipline, though directed by the wisdom of Solomon, is looked upon as an old and exploded institution; and the feelings of his wife would not suffer him to use it, even if he were convinced of its propriety. The mother is accustomed to the management of the home department, and thinks herself at least as competent, or rather a good deal more so, to judge of the best plan for managing the children. And the ordinary conclusion of the matter is, that the self-will of the young people gains the victory over coaxing, bribery, and moral suasion, mingled, occasionally, with an angry lecture, which only irritates the temper; until at length, if the parents be poor, they send their children out to serve strangers; and if they be rich, they commit the juvenile rebels to a boarding-school. And so the lack of government breaks up the true bond of family love and union; and home loses its proper character, as a centre of attachment and affection.

Now this is all wrong, though it is, unhappily, very common. The whole difficulty proceeds from the false delicacy which keeps the husband from asserting his lawful authority, and the pride of independence which prevents the wife from acknowledging it. But the law of God, which first instituted marriage, is the only law which can be safely taken for its government. It is perfect folly to suppose that this can be either rightly or successfully superseded by the notions of the world. The man is constituted the head of the woman, in all that relates to the married state. And neither can set that rule aside, without losing incomparably more than can be gained by the violation.

If, then, the husband, by the very terms of the wedded union, possesses the *right* to govern, it is his *duty* to claim it on the ground of the divine law; and it is his further duty to learn *how* that right may be religiously and conscientiously exercised. As the head of the wife, it is his place to instruct her in the article of obedience; and it is hers to accept the lesson, as a manifest branch of Christian obligation. And both the parties may easily understand the true quality of their mutual relations, if they will seriously study the language of the original law of marriage and the precepts of the apostles; as they are faithfully embodied in the expressive form of the Protestant Episcopal Church, and legally recognized in every Christian country.

The husband, in his wedded vow, has solemnly promised to "love and to cherish." The wife has promised, before God, to "love, honor, and obey." By the express terms of this sacred contract, both parties are bound; and therefore it results, of necessity, that the man has *no right* to give up the office of government, and the woman has *no right* to oppose its lawful fulfilment. It is very possible, indeed, that he may be inferior to her, in strength of intellect, and in general education. It is very possible that she may be better qualified to be the teacher than the taught. But that has nothing to do with the question of *authority*. The prime minister, in a monarchical government, may know a vast deal more than the king, and may often be obliged to instruct the monarch in his duty. And yet, it belongs none the less to the king to decide, because it is his place to govern; and whether he chooses to adopt the counsel of his minister or not, that minister is required to obey. So, in an ordinary court of justice, the lawyer may know more than the judge, and be abundantly qualified to give him the best instruction. But still, it belongs to the judge to decide, by virtue of his official *authority;* and whether he decide right or wrong, the lawyer must submit. So, in the general, commanding an army. The colonel may be far better versed in the art of war, and be able to give lessons to his superior officer. But the *authority* is vested in the general; and although the colonel may be ever so convinced that his commander is mistaken, yet he is bound to execute his orders notwithstanding.

It is quite easy to conceive that the husband, who is conscious of his wife's superiority of education, may give up his authority on that very ground, and fancy himself justified in doing so. And it is equally easy to conceive that the wife who has married a man intellectually inferior to herself, may think it perfectly right to claim the government of the family, for the same reason. But in truth they only involve themselves in a dangerous fallacy. They ought to have considered the relative fitness of their education and understanding, before they were married. The man would certainly have been wise in declining the office of government, which he could not expect to discharge with satisfaction. And the woman would as certainly have been justifiable in refusing to promise honor and obedience, to one whom she felt unwilling either to honor or obey. But after marriage, it is too late to consider the difficulty. The relation has now been formed. The irrevocable vows have been taken. And whatever trouble the parties may experience from the ill-matched conjunction, they must learn to discharge their duties, as honestly as they can; instead of committing the far graver error of supposing, that because they have disregarded the rules of prudence in undertaking such a union, they may try to remedy the matter by living in a constant violation of its established law.

Nor is it so difficult as it may seem, even under these circumstances, to perform their duty. The husband, like the king, may be perfectly conscious of his intellectual inferiority. The wife, like the prime minister, may be quite conscious of her ability to instruct him. Let her do so, then, as the prime minister would do, with a faithful and professed acknowledgment of his authority; and all will be well. But let her carefully avoid twitting her husband with his ignorance. Let her advise him in the constant recollection that she has promised to honor and obey. Let her present her counsel, *as counsel and not as dictation*, without temper, without sharpness, without direct and provoking contradiction. Let her tell him often, and with entire sincerity, that she considers him as the master of the family; and that she desires his authority to decide, after he has heard her reasons with attention. And she may be well assured that she will never lose a particle of her proper influence by such a course, but, on the contrary, will increase it, more and more; besides the inestimable benefit of having the approval of her own conscience, and the sure promise of the divine blessing on her union.

And the husband, on his side, may readily understand his duty of government, however willing he may be to lean on the judgment of his wife. He may and ought to consult her on all his affairs, and, like the king, resolve on nothing of importance without hearing his prime minister. And yet he should never suffer his authority to be set aside, or wantonly disregarded; because that authority is established by the decree of the Almighty, and has been solemnly acknowledged in the marriage vow. Hence, if at any time the wife forget it, he should kindly and calmly, but firmly, remind her of her obligation. And thus he may easily unite the highest regard to her superior knowledge, with a strict conservatism of his own superior power.

But now let us consider the result of this true matrimonial system, on the training of the children. The cardinal defect of our age and country lies in this very point of *authority*. The principle is dismissed, almost as if by common consent, from the family circle. They never hear of it from their parents' lips, in its connection with domestic government. They are brought up in the most perfect ignorance that God has fixed the strictest laws of subordination for the domestic relations, by which the mother is subject to the father, and the children to both. *She* cannot be expected to inculcate this duty on their part, if she be hostile to it on her own. Nor can *he* be expected to insist upon it, on the only proper ground of religious obligation, when he is quietly submitting, every day, to the independent dictation of the very wife who has solemnly promised to honor and obey him; and who, nevertheless, continually shows, in the presence of those children, that she has not the slightest idea of doing either the one or the other. They grow up, by necessary consequence, without any knowledge of this first principle of duty, *obedience to parental law*. And this inevitably leads them into all the dangers of self-will, headstrong resistance, and rebellion, which are but too apt to follow them through life, and perhaps lead them to utter ruin.

Suppose, however, on the contrary, that the authority of the husband were properly understood from the beginning, and openly acknowledged by the wife, as the fundamental rule of the marriage union; and it will be manifest, at once, that the children would understand, most fully, its application to themselves, as the established law of God, from which escape was utterly impossible. They would hear the principle of obedience honored by their mother's lips, and see it in her conjugal example. They would learn to accept it as a gift of the divine wisdom, without which there could be no government, nor order, nor peace, even in the little circle of the family. And thus the rule of submission to rightful authority would become engrafted in their hearts, and produce the best fruits in all the future relations of life, and spread its reverential influence over their memory of a father's watchful care, and a mother's devoted affection.

It is commonly believed, indeed, that this assertion of the husband's authority is inconsistent with the law of love; which is doubtless the great law of marriage, as it is of every other Christian relation. But no mistake can be more manifest, if the subject be rightly apprehended. There is no love on earth equal to the love of Christ. And yet He lays down certain precepts for His people, and expressly saith, "If ye love me, keep my commandments."* Here, therefore, *obedience to commandments* is imposed by perfect love on the one side, and made the very test of love upon the other. The apostle Paul applies this analogy to

* John xiv. 15.

the relation of marriage, where he saith, "As the Church is subject to Christ, so let the wives be to their own husbands in every thing."* And then immediately afterwards, he adds, "Husbands, love your wives, even as Christ loved the Church, and gave himself for it."†

Clearly, then, there is no contrariety between love and obedience, since it is love which issues the command, and love which is expected to fulfil it. And this is, therefore, the sentiment which, if it were as operative as it ought to be, would make the yoke of marriage a true bond of the happiest union. For love does not destroy authority, since that authority is established by the love of God, and must, consequently, be the best instrument for promoting the highest objects of the married relation. Neither does authority destroy love, because it must be regulated by love, exercised in love, and obeyed in love. But love itself cannot secure the welfare of the family, unless it works by the agency of government. Yet there can be no government without authority. And there can be no authority, unless there be some established power to enforce obedience. Hence the necessity of authority, in the family, grows out of the principle of love; and proves the perfection of the analogy which the apostle so plainly declares, between the obedience of the wife to the husband, and the obedience of the Church to Christ.

I have treated this important subject on the ground of religion, because there is no other mode of ascertaining its proper character. Marriage is a divine institution, having its whole sanction from the law of the Creator. Its great object is to provide, in the best and happiest manner, for

---

* Eph. v. 24. † Ib. v. 25.

the increase and training of the human race. No mortal ingenuity can improve its condition, by departing from the maxims of the New Testament; and the attempt is sure to be followed by danger, by suffering, and by sorrow. Alas! it is but seldom that we can find its rights and duties understood or appreciated, even among Christian people. And to this fact, perhaps, more than to any other, may be attributed the decline of piety in the Church itself; and the increasing progress of social depravity in the world around us. Doubtless there is no topic on which the arguments of the moralist are less likely to produce reformation. But I may not, for that reason, shrink from the defence of truth. It is for my readers, and not for me, to decide how far that truth shall be acceptable.

I conclude, then, with a practical summary of the whole matter. The American citizen has an unquestionable *right* to government in his own family. It is also his *duty* to claim and exercise that right, by the express law of the marriage relation; and he cannot be justified in delegating his authority, unless by some unavoidable necessity, either to his wife, or to any other.

But it is his *duty* to administer this authority in *love.* Hence, it is no license for tyranny, for harshness, for ill-temper, for caprice, for selfishness, or for any shape or form of oppression. He is bound to govern his wife, but he is also bound to *love and to cherish* her, and neither of these obligations must be allowed to nullify the other. If she be a thoughtful and consistent Christian, sincerely desirous to fulfil her wedded vow, the task of government will give him no trouble. If she be, on the contrary, self-willed, high-spirited, and contradictory, it may give him a great deal. Yet even so, he may hope to succeed, if he persevere, with kindness, calmness, and firmness, in placing her duty before her, on the true foundation of religion and conscience, sustained by reason and by law. And if he fail, after a due trial, it is better that he should have recourse to a quiet separation, than give up his rights, or use any unmanly violence, or live in constant dispute and contention. But there are few women who will continue to resist the just authority of a husband, if he know how to use it. For the most part, the fault is not so much in their wilfulness, as in the want of proper and affectionate instruction in the true meaning of the marriage vow. And if the man be ignorant of his own duty, or careless about its proper exercise, he deserves to bear the blame; as he will surely have cause to rue the consequences, in the loss of his domestic peace, and the final wreck of conjugal affection.

It is impossible, however, to succeed fully, in the establishment of this domestic government of love, unless he be willing to take his wife into his *confidence.* He should show her, therefore, that he regards her as his *other self*, his best friend, and his favorite companion. To this end, he should consult her about his business, so far as she can take interest in it. He should abandon all societies, clubs, amusements, and pleasures, in which she can take no part; and give up his leisure hours to the far higher and safer gratification of making his home happy. He must not forsake her in the evenings, and leave her solitary and sad, because he may prefer the excitement of some other company. He has promised to *love and to cherish her*, and he cannot do that, unless he consults her happiness, in union with his own. Doubtless, it may require, at first, some self-denial to resist this too common habit of seeking amusement after marriage, in the same manner as before.

But he will find himself amply rewarded in the end, for the trifling sacrifices which it may cost him. For this is the point at which we may usually date the beginning of estrangement and complaint. The young wife feels herself neglected. She naturally remonstrates. Her husband resents the expostulation as a restraint upon his liberty. And love, on both sides, sustains a wound which continues to bleed, until it exhausts the fountain of affection. And so, by degrees, the sacred bond of wedlock falls away from the heart; and marriage sinks down into a miserable state of mutual license, or cold conventionality.

Of course, there may be some difficulty in this important matter, which demands the exercise of reason and judgment. Love is often exacting and troublesome, and needs to be regulated, on both sides, by discretion and good sense. But there will be no danger of any serious error, so long as the parties keep in view the great maxims of the wedded covenant, and honestly strive to fulfil them conscientiously. They will be liable, assuredly, to make occasional mistakes. The art of a happy marriage is not to be learned immediately. Experience, observation, and care are needed by both, that they may understand and accommodate themselves to one another. And here is one of the advantages of an early marriage, which I have already noted—that the young are far more likely to acquire this important art of accommodation, than those whose habits have been fixed by long-continued celibacy. But if these mistakes of the parties, when they do occur, be frankly acknowledged and explained, as they always should be; and if both are truly anxious to perform their respective duties, time and association will accomplish the work. Love will gain in mature strength, far more than it loses in intensity. And marriage will prove to be the safest and the happiest school of human comfort, sympathy, and virtue.

I have said that this subject of marriage can only be rightly considered on the ground of religious principle; and I shall close this chapter by a repetition of the same truth. If the young American will rush into wedlock without caring whether his wife be a Christian—if the maiden of his choice will marry, under the foolish expectation that the man who has no conscience towards God will yet manifest conscience towards herself, and love his wife although he refuses to love his Saviour—there is no firm basis for peace and enjoyment to rest on. Weddings of this sort are unhappily too common. And sad experience proves that as they commence in sin, so they usually end in sorrow.

CHAPTER XXIII.

ON THE EDUCATION OF CHILDREN.

The great objects of marriage, as a divine institution, being the increase and nurture of the race, it results, plainly, that the proper management of the offspring stands in the first rank of its obligations. And as this is, confessedly, a matter of serious and increasing difficulty, in our age and country, it needs the lessons of instruction, and the hand of judicious reform, at least as much as any other interest of society.

Like the previous topic of wedded life, this topic of education must be treated religiously; because it is also a divine institution, and the laws of God cannot be disobeyed without the certain consequence of evil, even in the present world; however men may presume to promise themselves a larger amount of ease and self-enjoyment, by their violation. The formation of the sexes, and the mysterious commencement of human existence, are amongst the most wonderful works of the Creator. And it is obvious that His will must be followed in the management of the offspring, if we would secure the result which can alone make the gift of life a blessing to its possessor. Alas! it is a melancholy reflection that there are so many thousands, even in our Christian land, who have reason to look back, in bitterness of soul, upon the false indulgence of their parents; and to wish that they never had been born!

In every work of importance, it is allowed to be a point of great judgment to *begin rightly*. And in nothing is it more essential to full success, than in the task of education. For it is the universal maxim of experience, that the earliest impressions are the strongest. And this maxim is founded on the well-known fact that, in old age, when memory fails, and the long and busy scene of mature life is blotted out from recollection, the events and lessons of childhood come out in vivid relief upon the tablet of the mind, and are usually the last to fade away from the intellectual vision. In this we have the most convincing proof of the abiding power, which attaches to the *first training*. And therefore we have here the explanation of the influence which a wise and pious mother may exert upon the whole future life and character; by the right employment of the early period, committed, in the order of Providence, to her especial care.

She may be young, indeed, and quite lacking in maternal experience. But in this there is no real difficulty, if she follow the natural instincts of a mother's heart, and pray for strength and guidance, in reliance on the plain precepts of her Bible. Let her only remember that God has given her this little one, in order that she may bring it up for Him, and consecrate it to the service of the great Redeemer. To this end, she should lose no time in dedicating the infant to Christ, by the holy sacrament of Baptism. And she should resolve to secure the benefits of this sacred act, by a consistent course of watchful care and instruction.

Supposing her circumstances and her health to justify the employment of a nurse, she should be well assured that this nurse is worthy of her confidence, and she should warn her of the responsibility of the office, and sedulously examine, day by day, the mode in which it is fulfilled. Nothing is more common, I fear, than the carelessness of youthful mothers in this important matter. It is usually thought to be enough, if the nurse be of a good physical constitution, and reasonably attentive to the bodily wants of the child. But, in truth, it is quite as important that she should be pure in her moral principles, and religious in her habits; since, otherwise, there is little ground to hope that she will perform her duties conscientiously. Moreover, if the child is to draw its nourishment from the nurse's breast, there is a strong probability, at least, that it will be influenced by her temperament. For my own part, I would far rather see it dependent on the milk of an innocent cow, than have it suckled by a woman wanting in moral worth, subject to high passions, enslaved by superstition, or in any degree addicted to intemperance. The organization of the infant is so exquisitely susceptible, that too much caution cannot be employed in this very serious matter.

It is not easy to say how early in life the mother should

begin her great duty of education. But it is quite certain that it may and ought to be commenced as soon as possible, and much sooner than most persons believe that it can be really commenced at all. The first and most important habit of *obedience to authority* may be formed, to a considerable extent, before the child is weaned; and long before it can understand the duty. This, I am perfectly aware, will be regarded as a very extravagant assertion, and yet I know it to be strictly true. And any one may perceive its truth, who will call to mind the ordinary process, by which obedience is taught to the young of our domestic animals. Every observer knows how soon, and how perfectly, the horse or the dog learns to know and submit to his master. And it is certainly paying a poor compliment to the intelligence of the infant, when it is supposed that he cannot be taught the same lesson by his mother, if it be inculcated with equal care.

The error in this, and many other points, lies in the common mistake, that *habits* cannot be established without *principles*. This, however, is a perfect misapprehension. In the training of children, habits should be formed first, and principles should be inculcated afterwards. The reason is found in our double nature—the bodily, which resembles the brutes; and the spiritual, which resembles the angels. Of these two natures, the bodily nature is susceptible of training first, because it is first developed. And if it be rightly trained from the beginning, the mother will find one of her greatest difficulties removed, in the subsequent work of intellectual and moral education.

But many of my female readers will probably conceive a strong disgust at the idea of teaching submission to an infant, on the same plan that we should teach it to a brute.

To their tender sensibilities, such a course would appear cruel and unreasonable. Yet in truth, it is the ordinary course which deserves these epithets. If the child, for instance—suppose at the age of six or seven months—should get hold of his mother's watch, and refuse to let it go, why may he not be taught a lesson of obedience? Let her take the watch firmly out of his little hand, and if he screams in passion, let her look calmly into his eyes, and bid him hush; and if he refuses to obey, let her tap him gently, but sufficiently to give a little pain, at intervals, when he stops to take breath for another fit of crying. And after a few such contests, at farthest, the infant will learn to submit immediately; and thus be saved from the much greater suffering which he would otherwise endure, from his own wilfulness. But in order to succeed, the mother must be perfectly consistent and persevering in her system, and never desist from the exercise of proper authority, on account of his passion or his struggles. Her power once established, she must not suffer it to be disputed. And thus she may easily establish her maternal empire over the habits of her little one, and secure to it a happy freedom from an evil temper and a rebellious will; which are the greatest plagues through life of the majority, amongst ill-trained children.

If this course be adopted from the first, and steadily maintained, the main difficulty in the subsequent education will be conquered. The habit of obedience will prevent all the innumerable contests, which would otherwise cloud the happiness of that interesting period; and the mother may keep the household atmosphere pervaded with the sunshine of order and affection. And this, therefore, is true love to the child, because it promotes his enjoyment and his cheerfulness. The lesson of submission must be learned at some time, if the parent would have any real government; and it is cruelty to the little one to delay it needlessly. When this lesson is taught from the beginning, the painful duty of correction, in later years, becomes almost unnecessary. A word and a look will usually suffice to recall the child to duty. And when he is old enough to be taught the *principle* of obedience, there will be no obstacle to its reception; because the *habit* is already there, and has been instilled so early that it has become a sort of second nature.

In this important point, the aid of the father will rarely be needed, during the first few years; but it is quite essential that he should strengthen the authority of the mother in her good work; and carefully avoid the least appearance of encouraging the child in opposition. Yet so perfectly thoughtless are married people upon this subject—though, on every other, they appear to be persons of intelligence and sense—that I have frequently seen the father take the young child out of the mother's arms, and stimulate the passion of the little culprit against her, and even call her "naughty mother," and pretend to beat her, in order to restore him to good humor! And I have found nothing more unfortunately common than to see the parents, in later life, quite divided about the children; and effectually destroying their own peace and the future welfare of their offspring, by mutual contradiction, indulgence, and partiality.

A wise and thoughtful husband will adopt a very opposite course; and give all proper weight to the mother's authority, by the addition of his own. With his encouragement, she may rise above the prevailing error of our days; and success will usually crown their united efforts. But woe be both to parents and to children, when the concord of domestic government is wanting; for the result can hardly fail to be strife and contention, self-will, headstrong obstinacy, rebellion, and estrangement. While the law of obedience, taught in time, and maintained consistently, produces harmony and cheerfulness, industry, affection, and peace.

I pass on, however, to the period, when the mind of the child is sufficiently developed to make him capable of religious instruction. And this, too, may be at a much earlier age than is commonly supposed. In two or three years, and sometimes even sooner, he may receive his first lessons in prayer, and in the idea of that kind Father in heaven, who watches over him, and loves him, and takes care of him by day and by night, and gives him his parents, and provides every good thing with which he is supplied. The history of Christ may next be explained, in language suited to his capacity; and all his conduct may now be connected with the great truth, that the eyes of the Lord are constantly beholding him, in darkness as well as in the light; that his parents gave him up to his Saviour in Baptism; and that he should live as one of the adopted children of the Almighty King, who knows all things, and will do all things to make him happy, if he be faithful and obedient. In this way, his little heart may be led to put its trust in the Redeemer, with more earnest sincerity than even his teachers realize. And thus they may keep the precept of the apostle, which commands Christians to "bring up their children in the nurture and admonition of the Lord," in perfect accordance with the rule laid down by our divine Master where He saith, "Suffer the little children to come unto me and forbid them not, for of such is the kingdom of heaven."

And why should it be otherwise? Religious faith, in its

essence, belongs mainly to the heart; and love to Christ is its most important element. Why should not the heart be possessed with that sacred affection in the tender years of childhood? Do not the parents know, that this is the surest period to gain the love of their offspring for his father and his mother, although the little one does not yet really understand the proper meaning of the words? Would they be willing to postpone the influence of filial affection, until mature years; in order that before their child should be taught to love them, he should first be instructed in the anatomy of the human form, and in all the mysteries of the wedded relation, so as to be fully aware of the strict signification of the terms, *father and mother?* By no means. They are perfectly satisfied that love, in their own case, should be taught as soon as possible; without waiting for the knowledge of a riper age. And why can they not see that in teaching their offspring to love Christ, before the period of complete intellectual apprehension, they are only acting on the same obvious and beautiful principle?

A little later comes the time, when the child may be taught the alphabet and learn to read. And this he may do at the mother's knee, by short and easy intervals, to the best advantage. But here I would caution her against the indiscriminate use of story-books for children. She may easily find, if she will look for them, some good ones; and a large variety of cheap pictures, which will fill the young and impressible mind of her little boy with useful truth. And she should give him no others: for nothing can be more absurd than the popular notion, that folly and lies are equally fit for that early age, if they be only amusing. It would be just as wise to plant weeds on purpose in our gardens, in order that we may afterwards enjoy the pleasure of pulling them up. On the contrary, the parents should never present to the mind of the young child *any ideas on any subject*, which they do not intend to remain there; because they must be aware that at this period, all ideas are received *as true;* and there is neither knowledge nor judgment sufficient to enable the understanding to discriminate. I have already shown that the earliest impressions are the strongest and the most abiding, of necessity; because the condition of the brain and of the mind in childhood is the most tender and susceptible. And hence, when we call to our recollection the preposterous jumble of notions which are commonly infused into children, by the nonsense of Mother Goose, Jack the Giant Killer, and fairy tales; assisted by the superstitious stuff of St. Nicholas, and the black man, and goblin stories, detailed by the servants and the nurses; it is little wonder that the great majority of mankind prove so careless of truth, especially of religious truth, to the end of life; and that so few amongst them are fond of sober thought, or sound reflection.

Let the child, then, have books and pictures in abundance. But let them all present something worth learning, useful and true. Pictures have a wonderful power to seize hold upon the tender mind, when the mother takes proper pains to explain them. First should come the large collection which belongs to the narratives of the Bible. Next, pictures of birds, beasts, reptiles, fishes, flowers, fruits, and trees. Thirdly, as he advances, books illustrating geography, beginning with that of the holy land, and passing on to the manners and customs of nations. Then, little works on travels and history, and in due time, biographies of good and useful men, voyages of discovery, descriptions of the various arts and trades, &c. The object of the whole being the same, viz., to store the mind with *truth*, and gradually develop the powers of reason, in connection with sound judgment and right feeling; while we keep away, as carefully as possible, the notions of falsehood and error, and so build up the enduring basis of principle and habit, for the future life.

In all this, I propose not only the course which is plainly dictated by the precepts of religion, but that which is equally required by a strict analogy with the laws of bodily health and vigor. Every physician insists upon the food of children being simple, pure, and wholesome; absolutely forbidding the hurtful indulgences of old persons, in spices, stimulants, elaborate cookery, sweetmeats, sauces, highly seasoned dishes, and confectionery; which may, indeed, be allowed in moderation and with safety, after the constitution becomes mature, but should never be permitted while the frame is growing. No intelligent physiologist doubts that the common violation of this essential rule is one main cause of the multiplied diseases of society; producing, inevitably, the dyspepsia, fevers, liver complaints, and various forms of organic debility, which interrupt so sadly the duties and true enjoyments of life, and consign such multitudes to suffering and premature decay. But shall unwholesome food thus injure the body, and will it not, still more surely, injure the mind and the soul? Is not knowledge the meat and drink of our spiritual nature? And if this knowledge be unwholesome in its quality—not good, but evil—not true, but false—not calculated to strengthen but to weaken the intellect—not adapted to elevate and purify, but to degrade and even poison the thoughts and the affections during the same all-important period of early development—who can doubt that it must introduce a correspondent amount of mental disease, disorder, and debility? Who can question the likelihood of the wretched result, which ends in the total lack of virtuous energy, and high-toned principle?

I am well aware, however, that the system which I advocate is opposed by a variety of objections. Some wise arguers will say that it is all nonsense to lay down such strict rules for this early period—that children are children, and it is folly to desire that they should be men and women before their time, or to attempt to put old heads on young shoulders.

To this very popular and convenient style of argument, I answer, that it is the duty of the father and the mother to lay down strict rules for their children, because they alone are able to enforce them; and the responsibility of their early training rests upon the parents, whether they will or not. That *children are children* is indeed most true; and if they were any thing else, the task of educating them would be impossible. But that the effort to bring them up in the knowledge of truth and virtue is likely to make them men and women before their time, is mere absurdity. *That* cannot be done, simply because it is contrary to nature. The objector must mean, therefore, that the plan proposed would have a tendency to make them *fancy themselves* men and women, prematurely. This tendency, however, I utterly deny. There is not the slightest danger of their forgetting that they are children, so long as they are held in the true subordination to their parents' authority which religion and reason enjoin; and are taught to look up to those parents with reverent obedience and affection.

On the contrary, it is the ordinary system of the world that makes them fancy themselves men and women. It is the preposterous indulgence which frees them from domestic restraint, and fills their thoughts with the dress, the company, the dissipation, the vanities, the fiction, and the artificial manners of mature society. It is the allowance of children's parties, and children's fashions, and children's balls, and children's flirtations, and children's novels, which stuffs their young heads and hearts before the time with ideas and feelings totally unsuited to their age and condition. And hence the result deplored by every reflecting observer, that *young America* has almost lost the period of childhood altogether. Our boys and girls assume the airs of independence before they enter their teens. Obedience to parents is stricken out of the list of youthful virtues. There is no notion of government connected with the name of home. And "old heads are effectually put upon young shoulders," when the children are encouraged to think for themselves, and act for themselves, and choose their companions and amusements for themselves; without reference to the authority of either father or mother, and with a full persuasion that the main duty of both the parents is to let them do precisely as they please.

Another objection to the system would doubtless be, that it is impracticable. It runs counter too much to the prevailing custom of the world. It lays too great a burden on the wife and mother. It requires too constant and watchful a degree of attention. Neighbors, friends, and servants would all help, in their several ways, to counteract it. And it must of necessity be relinquished, when the children are old enough to be sent to school. This is a plausible statement, I admit; and demands a fair and full consideration.

In the first place, then, let it be granted that the task of education, rightly performed, *does* run counter to the custom of the world—that it lays a great burden on the mother—that it requires a constant and watchful attention, and that neighbors, friends, and servants would help, in their several ways, to counteract it. What then? That all this renders it a work of great difficulty is admitted; but does that make it absolutely impracticable? Duty is always difficult, when it differs from the practice of the world; but does that make it less a duty? And with respect to that pre-eminent duty which involves the virtue, the health, and the ultimate happiness of children, will the world give either to them or to their parents any equivalent, for the woeful and ruinous results of failure in their education?

It should further be considered that if there be difficulties on the one side, there are far greater difficulties on the other. The true system would usually result in the formation of the children's character, so that their parents would derive from their future course the highest earthly comfort and satisfaction; while, during the whole process of their training, their temper, their habits, and their reverential affection would make a comparative paradise of home. The ordinary plan, on the contrary, is a constant source of trouble, disorder, and anxiety. The parents, instead of being the governors of their children, often become their slaves. And their heads are frequently bowed down in grief, and their hearts are well-nigh broken, by youthful immorality, ingratitude, and rebellion. Are there no difficulties here? And when they recur, will the world be able to afford the father and the mother any consolation in their wretchedness, since not only are they conscious that it is the natural result of their own careless indulgence, but the children themselves, when they begin to feel the consequences of the mistake, are apt to upbraid them as the causes of their ruin!

Whatever, then, may be the amount of care, attention, and labor which the true system costs, the object to be accomplished is well worth it all. True, indeed, it is, that the best-directed endeavors of the father and the mother may fail, on account of the counteracting influence of others; and perhaps still more, by reason of their own defect of wisdom and consistency. Yet it is a great matter to have a high and just *ideal* of the rule; since the nearer a conscientious parent can approach to this, the greater the likelihood of success in the important undertaking. Perfection is not to be expected in any thing belonging to humanity. But it is none the less our duty to aim at it, in all things; and to advance, by diligent care and attention, in the path which leads to virtue and to truth.

With regard to the last branch of the objection, namely, that the strict system must of necessity be relinquished when children are old enough to be sent to school, I should say that it is wholly gratuitous and imaginary. As a general rule, the boy should be kept at home, until he has learned to read, and his habits have all been rightly formed, under strict parental authority. The age of eight years is quite early enough to enter the day-school; and this should be one where the pupils are about the same age, not too numerous, and kept by an experienced, or at least a conscientious and religious teacher. The mother should send him, and require him to return, with punctual regularity; on no account allowing him to play and loiter in the street. She should give an hour, in the evening, to examine his lessons and his progress; and have a daily report, marked on a card, of his conduct in the school. She should attend, as before, to his performance of his religious duties, and listen to his remarks on the events of each day, so as to form his judgment and his principles, in their new application to strangers. And in this, she will have an excellent opportunity to teach him the virtue of charity and allowance for the faults of others, and of strictness towards his own, by telling him that the children who went wrong had not the same advantages as himself, and were therefore ignorant of their duty; so that he should look on them not with anger but with pity, and remember that if he had been brought up as they were, he might not only have been no better, but perhaps far worse. Hence, instead of feeling proud or vain of his superiority, he ought rather to thank God who had given him the instruction of His holy Word, and the careful teaching of his affectionate parents; and pray to Him for the help of His Holy Spirit, that his own conduct might be always answerable to his privileges; since otherwise he would be condemned to a much severer punishment, in the judgment of the great day.

In this manner, the wise and careful mother may easily preserve her authority over her son, during the years of adolescence, and effectually guard him from the snares of evil company. But she will need the co-operation of the father, and should always have it when required. And if, at any time, there be manifest the temper of rebellion, notwithstanding all their care; or if, without any open resistance, there be laziness, inattention, or wilful neglect, the father should tell him of his fault, read to him the instructions of Solomon, and calmly but firmly administer the rod of correction, in the fulfilment of his own parental duty. This painful but indispensable part of a true system of education, should indeed be well understood, from the earliest years of childhood. The boy should regard it as it really is—the express command of the Almighty, from which no conscientious parent has a right to deviate. It should never be administered in passion, but in marked displeasure, mingled with sorrow, and followed by prayer. And it should be repeated—like medicine in the hand of a careful physician—until the disease of self-will and disobedience is conquered, and the boy seems fully sensible of his transgression, and resolved to commit it no more.

Nothing can be more dangerous and unjustifiable, in any Christian parent especially, than the notion that this wholesome discipline can be superseded by "moral suasion," as it is called, or by any other scheme of human discovery. The idea that it was only suited to the severity of the Mosaic ritual, and was virtually done away by the more merciful spirit of the Gospel, is a pure absurdity. Our divine Saviour Himself made a scourge of small cords, to chastise the buyers and sellers who profaned the temple.* And St. Paul, illustrating the paternal love of God in punishing His children, asks the emphatic question: "What son is he whom his father chasteneth not?"† Human nature is precisely the same since the advent of Christ, that it was before; and there is not a shadow of apology for the popular folly of supposing that it does not require the same kind of correction, whenever the self-will or disobedience of the child or the boy resists the law of rightful authority.

The education begun and steadily continued on these true principles, would insure to the American citizen, who is married and has a family, the best and happiest results, in that which forms the dearest object to every father's

---

* John ii. 15. † Heb. xii. 7.

heart—the character and welfare of his children. It is his duty, therefore, to understand the subject well; because, although the agency of the mother must be chiefly employed, particularly in the earlier years of childish training, yet she will usually need his counsel and advice, and always his entire and harmonious co-operation.

I shall not, indeed, undertake to say that the fruits of such a system will always be satisfactory. Obstacles may intervene between the parents and the child. Strange and untoward influences may arise to alienate and corrupt him. And often, when he leaves the refuge of his father's roof, the pleasures and allurements of the world may appear, for a while, to carry him away. But it will be only for a while. The inspired proverb of Solomon contains a precept and a promise: "Train up a child in the way he should go, and when he is old, he will not depart from it."* WHEN HE IS OLD! He may depart when he is young, through lack of experience. But the hand of God will lead him back, after he has found that the world has nothing but disappointment and grief to offer. Like the prodigal son, he will return to his Father, for he learned to know that heavenly Father in early life. And therefore he will retrace his steps in humility and penitence; and he will be welcomed with joy; and the remainder of his days will prove the power of that divine truth which he was taught in the beginning.

To realize all this in the consistent plan of education, is no light nor easy undertaking. I have admitted it already, and I admit it now again. It requires piety, reflection, and prayer, that the parents may have wisdom for the task, and

---

* Prov. xxii. 6.

carry on their work in the spirit of love, with patience, perseverance, and confidence, to the end. To those who will not employ these only lawful methods, I have nothing to say in favor of any other. The same Creator who made man, and who alone comprehends fully the infirmity of his understanding and the corruption of his heart by nature, has laid down the law for his education; and from that law no human power has a right to deviate, nor can it deviate with the hope to prosper.

But to those parents who will devote themselves to the work in a true religious temper, the reward is sure, even in the happiness of the present life. What possession is so precious as the grateful love of our children? What spectacle so delightful as to see them walking in the ways of virtue, usefulness, and truth? What wealth so great as the treasure of their integrity and honor? What suffering so deep, as the knowledge of their misery and shame? Shall the mother shrink from the trouble demanded in their nurture? Shall the idle intercourse of society, or the empty pleasures of the world, or the habits of easy indolence, be allowed to come between her and this most sacred of all her duties? Shall the father cut himself off from his share in the work, for the sake of his evening amusements, his gay companions, his games and dissipation? Alas! for the parents who thus decide. Alas! for the children whose rightful protectors have so deserted them.

Nevertheless, I mean not to condemn those, whose circumstances are such that they are really unable to perform aright this all-important duty. Doubtless, there are very many who cannot discharge it in their own persons, either by reason of ill health, or lack of knowledge, or want of the faculty of domestic government, or other difficulty which may be, in their case, insurmountable. The only resource, in these instances, is the substitute of the Boarding-school. And to this I shall devote the following chapter.

CHAPTER XXIV.

ON FAMILY SCHOOLS OF EDUCATION.

I HAVE endeavored, in the last chapter, to show that the most important and abiding part of education should be performed at home, through the affectionate authority of the father and the mother; and it is quite obvious that when circumstances render this impracticable, the Boarding-school, which is presented as the substitute for home, should preserve as many of its proper characteristics as possible. I say its *proper* characteristics, because I use the term, *home*, in the sense which it ought to bear; and not in that which is too commonly affixed to it, in the loose and dangerous license of our day. Rightly understood, home is not merely the place of the parents' residence; but it is also the place which should possess the largest amount on earth of Christian government, united with love, order, and growth in knowledge and virtue.

Under this aspect of the matter, the master and mistress of the boarding-school become the temporary substitutes for the parents of the boy committed to their care. They are invested, for a time, with the same power, and assume the same responsibility. Hence they are bound to treat him as they ought to treat their own child; and if they fail in this, they are lacking in the fundamental point of a most serious obligation.

Of course, I do not mean that they should love him as they would do, if he were really their own; nor that he should transfer to them the filial affection which he should have for his own father and mother. This would be equally impossible and undesirable, and does not come within the range of contemplation by either party at the time. I have therefore said precisely what I mean, that they should *treat* him as they *ought to treat their own;* with the affection which will tenderly provide for his comfort and welfare, and with the constant care of his improvement in religious principle, in sound morality, in knowledge, in habits and deportment; so as to qualify him, to the extent of their power, for the subsequent duties of life. More than this, no reasonable parent could desire. Less than this, ought not to satisfy the conscience of any Christian teacher who conducts a boarding-school.

Such being the basis of the true system, the first result would seem to be that it cannot be extended to a very large number. How large, indeed, it would be difficult to prescribe; because there is so great a difference in the capacities of men for the government, the inspection, and the quick insight of individual character which the task requires. Much would also depend on the fidelity and watchful attention of the other instructors. The famous Pestalozzi contrived to manage, with eminent success, a hundred boys. But he was a single man, and entered into the work with a rare enthusiasm. He lived in their constant society, slept in the same apartment, was the companion of all their sports and plays, and gave himself wholly up to them in every thing. The plan, in his hands, seemed to prosper admirably: so admirably, indeed, that it became, for a little while, known and praised as the Pestalozzian system. It was soon found, however, that it depended solely on a kind of energy which nothing but his own enthusiasm could supply; and, therefore, after his death, it sunk into oblivion. Nor is this to be regretted, because it was his aim to make education a matter of pleasurable excitement rather than of patient industry, to render discipline unnecessary, and to form the habit of exertion by the stimulus of social ambition, without the only enduring support of religious principle.

This example, under these circumstances, proves nothing on the point of numbers. We must take men as they are, and estimate their powers by the fair average of capacity, rather than by the transient success and popularity of a rare exception. And if we assume this average as the safest standard, we shall probably come near the mark by saying that twenty-five boys are quite enough for one man to govern, with real parental care; unless he can command a degree of zealous and conscientious fidelity in his subordinates which is seldom to be expected.

I am aware that many of my readers will think this a very low and absurd estimate. In our age, we are accustomed to do these things on a magnificent scale, and to calculate their worth according to their cheapness and their magnitude. But it must be remembered that I am speaking of a boarding-school which is to be a substitute for home, and conducted on parental and religious principles. I am also considering the question with reference to boys rather than to girls, who are much more easily governed and restrained. And I am not at all concerned with the question of numbers in those establishments which offer a cheap opportunity of education to young men and women, at that riper age, when, as in our colleges, they are presumed, whether justly or otherwise, to be capable of governing themselves.

In this restricted view of the subject, I think that the care of twenty-five boys will be found sufficient for the average capacity. Of men whose minds and energies far exceed this average, I have nothing to say beyond the homage of admiration. The first Napoleon was endowed with such astonishing faculties for government, that he was able to exercise an influence over every individual soldier in a vast army; and knew more of their character and circumstances, than an ordinary captain knows of the members in a single company. And, doubtless, we may have, now and then, a Napoleon in the government of schools, whose intellectual vigor places him far above the sphere of probable calculation.

But even on this moderate scale, the master of a true family seminary will be found to be engaged in a most important work for the community. For supposing him to receive his boys at the age of ten, and to dismiss them, rightly educated, at sixteen, ready for the college, the office, the counting-room, the farm, or the manufactory, and let him be thus occupied for thirty-six years, and the aggregate would be one hundred and fifty youths trained to be examples of religious principle, sound knowledge, and industrious habits, a blessing to their parents and to society. This is enough for the labor of any ordinary lifetime; and would produce more real good than if a thousand or ten thousand had passed through his hands, with the common amount of irreligion, ungoverned license, and worldly indulgence, which prevail so largely amongst the rising generation of our country.

I proceed, in the next place, to consider some specific

points belonging to this system of family education in the boarding-school.

And here, all agree that there must be a due amount of religious instruction. But this, as usually understood, would fall short of the true idea. The morals and motives of the Gospel are rarely appealed to in the practical work of education; and hence the religious teaching is very apt to sink down into a dull, formal routine, which goes in at one ear, and out at the other, making little impression on the intellect, and still less upon the heart. Instead of this, it should be regarded as the rule of the daily life, and thus become the actual standard of feeling and of principle; holding up the Saviour as the great model of imitation, and trying every question by the light of His precepts and example.

This, however, should be done without gloom, austerity, or unreasonable strictness; which only tend, with young persons especially, to make religion odious and repulsive. The Gospel is the religion of light and love, and can always be best inculcated in the spirit of kindly and cheerful affection. It was the declaration of the Saviour Himself, that His yoke is easy and His burden is light. And therefore the pupils should understand the value of His precepts as the only way to real happiness, by which they may conquer sin and selfishness, which are the worst enemies to peace and true enjoyment even in this world; and attain that pure and benevolent habit of the heart and mind which repels the desire of doing evil to others, and rejoices in goodness and in truth.

With this view, there should be no appeal made to the motive of emulation. For this motive is thoroughly antagonistic to all Christian principle, and only operates by the stimulus of contest and pride; while the reasons held out for diligence and industry by the Gospel are infinitely superior, and, when once implanted, remain through life. The boy should be taught, therefore, that he is not required to *excel* his young companions, because he is told to "love them as himself,"* and Christians are commanded "in honor to prefer one another."† Besides, it is impossible that all should excel; because it pleases God to endow them with very different measures of talent and capacity. Hence all that the pupil has to do, is to use the ability which the Lord has seen fit to bestow, *as well as he can*, on the true ground of duty. He is the servant of Christ, who will demand a strict account of his time and occupations. He is bound, moreover, to fulfil the reasonable hopes of his parents, who sent him to school in order that he might learn as much as possible. He is further bound to set a good example to his companions, by his diligence and application. And lastly, he is bound to exert himself, that he may be fit for usefulness to the world when he becomes a man. Meanwhile he must not be discouraged, if he cannot do as much or as well as others. Neither must he envy their superior powers, nor be discontented with his own. For God has given him enough, if he do but use them wisely. And those who have the brightest abilities are often found, in the end, to be far less happy and prosperous than their fellows; because the pride of their talents is so apt to carry them away, and lead them to place all their confidence in their own capacity; instead of trusting in the blessing promised to persevering industry and virtue.

These are the motives and the feelings with which the

* Mark xii. 31. † Rom. xii. 10.

teacher should labor to inspire his pupils. They are in strict harmony with the precepts of religion, and furnish the conscience of the boy with principles of action, under every circumstance of his future career, as well as during the course of youthful instruction. I regard the ordinary system of emulation, on the contrary, as altogether hostile to the injunctions of Scripture, injurious to the improvement of the young, unjust in its results at the time, and eminently instrumental in producing all the selfish contests and strifes which, in after life, deform society. But this system is so strongly rooted, and the truth, as I regard it, is so likely to be unacceptable, that it may be necessary to discuss the subject fully, before it is dismissed.

Let it be carefully remembered, then, that the object of education is to prepare the boy for the duties of the man, and to make him what he ought to be, in all the relations of his being. This, to be effected rightly, plainly demands not only the cultivation of the intellect, but the implanting of moral principles in the heart. Of these two, there can be no controversy about the comparative importance. We all know that it is not intellectual ability, but moral principle which forms the good citizen, the faithful husband, the affectionate father, the true friend, the kind neighbor, the honest man of business. Intellectual ability, *without moral principle*, does nothing of all this; but on the contrary makes men rogues and sharpers, fraudulent schemers, false in every social relation, pests to their family, and plagues to the community around them. It results undeniably, therefore, that the implanting of moral principle is the first and highest object of true education; while the cultivation of the intellect, though of great value, is yet a subordinate and inferior concern.

But there is no system of moral principle in the world which can be placed in competition with the Gospel. Infidels themselves always acknowledge this, for even when they cavil at the divinity and miracles of Christ, they never fail to confess the superior purity and sublimity of His moral teaching. Hence arises the necessity of taking the precepts of the New Testament as the rule of moral principle; and thus far the system which I advocate is placed beyond the reach of doubt or disputation.

Let us next see, therefore, whether the popular plan of emulation is in accordance with this order. What is its practical method of proceeding? First, in the class, boys are ranged together for the convenience of the teacher, according to the measure of their intellectual attainment. Out of the members of that class, some two or three are nearly equal in ability; and they contend as rivals for the place of honor at the head. The rest, being inferior in talent, in memory, and perhaps in age, have no chance in the struggle; and therefore the stimulus of emulation does not reach to them, but exhausts its power upon the two or three antagonists. And the successful pupil is sure to be elated with pride, *because he has excelled his competitors;* and they are apt to be filled with envy and mortification.

Thus matters go on, day after day, until the time of public examination; when the intellectual attainments of the most proficient scholars are ostentatiously displayed, and the triumphant candidates are graced with prizes and rewards, not because they have done the best in their power, but simply *because they have excelled the others.* How do those others feel, in being totally passed by? Some are depressed by shame, some discouraged by failure, while the majority, who had no hope of success, and yet had no other motive addressed to them except that of emulation, are more indifferent than ever towards the task of learning, and dismiss the effort from their thoughts, as not worth the trouble.

Now I ask, who in that school—who amongst the crowd that attended the examination—nay, who amongst the teachers themselves, have remembered for a moment that the first great object of education is not intellectual ability, but MORAL PRINCIPLE? What share had moral principle in the daily teaching of the class? What share had moral principle in the prizes and the honors of the successful candidates? What share had moral principle in the applause of the assembled company? None whatever. From first to last, the intellect filled the whole sphere of effort and of praise. And moral principle was as completely out of sight and out of mind, as if it had nothing to do with the business of youthful training.

But this is not the whole, for I have shown that moral principle, by universal consent, is based on the precepts of the Gospel; and hence I contend that this system of emulation is not only destitute of moral principle, but actually opposed to it. For the apostle Paul expressly ranks emulation among the works of the flesh, and puts it along with strife, hatred, and other deadly sins.* And in this he is fully justified, when we reflect, that the youthful competitors for the prize of scholarship are not expected to exert themselves on the score of duty, but simply in order that they may *excel* the rest. The motive is therefore plainly that of *pride*, and the selfish *love of distinction;* which is totally at war with the love of our neighbor, and derives its pleasure

---

* Gal. v. 20.

from another's pain. Moreover, the successful candidate is usually indebted to his superior talents; and may be far inferior in real worth of character, to many of those whom he has excelled in intellectual display. And since the prize of honor is awarded to the result of those talents, notwithstanding, is there not an open slight offered to moral principle, when that is not thought worth inquiring after, while the other is hailed with admiration and applause? What can more manifestly tempt the inexperienced mind of boyhood to form the dangerous conclusion, that goodness and virtue are of no account, if they can only attain a certain measure of intellectual ability? And how, in the name of common sense, can such a system be expected to educate our youth in the love of sound morality; or send them forth with those habits and principles which deserve the confidence of mankind?

There can be no doubt, therefore, as it seems to me, that this whole matter demands a total reformation. Moral virtue, based as it must be, on the Gospel, should be set forth as the first element of youthful training; and no prize should ever be given to any pupil, without a satisfactory examination in the principles and practice of goodness and of truth. Talents are laudable. Learning is laudable. But the morals of Christianity should be held in higher esteem than either; because on them, at last, we must depend for the ultimate success of every individual man, and for the peace and welfare of the community.

That this true theory of education is the only one which can rightly carry out the idea of a family school, must be obvious to the slightest reflection. We have already seen that the father gives his authority to the master of the school; and along with this, he transfers, for the time, his parental responsibility, in the expectation that his substitute will treat the boy as he would treat his own. But what judicious father would consent to leave his child to the ordinary stimulus of literary emulation, without any special enforcement of moral principle? What mother would be willing to rate the learning of her son higher than his virtue? And how shall such teachers fulfil their parental duty, if, instead of raising the standard of Christian morality to its proper height, in the judgment and feelings of the children intrusted to their care, they are content with appealing to pride and selfishness, on the old plan of emulation; and give their public honors to the few boys of superior talent, without regard to the infinitely more important *moral character* which must determine their safety and happiness through life, besides involving the peace and comfort of all connected with them?

The danger of encouraging emulation, however, is further manifest, when we consider that it is the very principle of strife and competition, and makes the great bulk of mankind the enemies, rather than the friends, of those who are engaged in the same profession with themselves. The moral precepts of Christianity teach us to rejoice in the prosperity of all around us, forbid us to covet their possessions, and command us to exert our powers on the ground of our individual responsibility to God and to society; without seeking to rise above the rest, or wishing to depress them, in order to gratify our personal ambition; but rather taking pleasure in their success, and accepting our own share from Providence, in the spirit of thankful contentment. Emulation, on the contrary, is always intent upon drawing comparisons with others; and is never satisfied unless it can overtop them, and cast them into the shade. Hence, its very genius is contention, opposition, and struggle for mastery. The successful youth, therefore, who has borne off the prize from his school competitors, too often sustains a moral injury; because he is apt to be a slave for life to the same consuming and unhappy anxiety for distinction. He is puffed up with the pride of his superiority, and as it has once been so publicly acknowledged, he expects it to be always conceded as a settled fact. He commences the real business of the world, accordingly, with the worst possible preparation of feeling; and instead of understanding that his success must depend, under God, upon the diligent labor of persevering duty; he calculates upon his presumed merit, looks unkindly upon all who are unwilling or unable to see it, grows impatient at their envy or stupidity, feels vexed at the slowness and difficulty of his progress, and disgusted at the difference between his past honors and his present insignificance. And the frequent result is that he falls into low companionship and dissipation, as a relief from his morbid and disappointed temper. He is dissatisfied unless he can be "king of the company," and cannot be happy without some field in which the spirit of emulation can enjoy applause. And thus it is, that in a large number of instances which are known, and doubtless in thousands which have escaped observation, the flattered youths who have gained at school the prize of public honor, have been betrayed by that very means into ruin and disgrace; while the undistinguished mass, who aspired to no superiority, have gone on with humble diligence, and far outstripped them in the ultimate attainment of credit and success.

The vast importance of the subject may be lastly regarded with respect to its extensive influence on the interests of society; for the evils of emulation may be seen amongst them all. It is emulation which stimulates the ambitious politician, and makes such small account of lies, and slanders, and bribery, if they can only help his progress to distinction. It is emulation which excites the man of business to outstrip his competitors, and tempts him to employ the tricks of trade, and the arts of dishonesty. It is emulation which sets physicians by the ears, and produces the bitter animosity of those who are enlisted in the support of contending systems. It is emulation which reigns over the oratory of the bar, and makes the attainment of justice seem of little value in comparison with personal triumph. It is emulation which prompts the extravagance of fashion, and dooms the fairer sex to a wearisome rivalry of dress and ornament, in the desire of superior notoriety. It is emulation which squanders such millions in the building and furnishing of our merchant palaces, where prudence and benevolence are so often sacrificed to contentious ostentation. It is emulation which governs the halls of pleasure, and plants the thorn of envy in the heart of seeming gayety, and darkens the brow of youthful beauty with resentful discontent, when it cannot obtain the expected prize of admired distinction. Nay, it is emulation which even enters the sanctuary of God, and converts it into a theatre of proud display, and tempts the preacher himself to labor after striking novelties for effect, instead of solemn truths for edification. In a word, it is emulation which fills the world with the fruits of pride, vanity, contest, strife, envy, hatred, malice, and revenge, in the selfish indulgence of some petty and miserable ambition. Who can wonder, then, that St. Paul included it amongst the works of the flesh, and condemned it as altogether hostile to true Christian principle!

This false and dangerous stimulus, therefore, should be altogether banished from every school which claims to be conducted in accordance with pure morality; instead of being actually adopted into the very system of education, and praised as a motive for exertion, and rewarded with public honors, as if it were a virtue. There is more than enough of it—God knows—in every human heart; without this studied effort to nourish and enlarge its baleful influence. The whole strain of a sound and faithful training should be to root it up, as far as possible, and plant in its place the true principle of DUTY. This is the embodiment of all practical morals, which should be incessantly inculcated on the rising youth of our country—duty to God, duty to parents, duty to teachers, duty to their associates, duty to themselves, so as to prepare them for their duty to society. They should be taught to understand that there is no other road to real happiness, for all selfishness, pride, and worldly ambition are sure to lead to disappointment and misery, while the path of duty is the path of peace and lasting pleasure. It may seem rough and rugged in the beginning, because nature is depraved, and the conquest over its opposition cannot be achieved without constant self-denial. But the victory is sure to every youth who takes the Saviour for his guide, and faithfully seeks, in daily prayer, the strength which He has promised to bestow on those that ask it. And as he proceeds, the path of duty will grow more and more easy, until, at length, it will be covered with the flowers of truth and the fruits of virtue; and he will be safely led through all his troubles to the best portion of solid enjoyment in the present world, and to the heritage of certain felicity in that which is to come.

If it were possible, then, it would be my most earnest

desire, as a friend to the best interests of the rising generation, to see the true order of education arranged upon this principle. Christian morality first, and useful learning second—both governed by the same rule of DUTY. The application of the maxim to common-schools, where the work of training is performed for the benefit of the many; as well as to colleges, where it is completed for the advantage of the few; must be reserved for the following chapter.

CHAPTER XXV.

ON COMMON-SCHOOLS AND COLLEGES.

THE boarding-school which aims at securing, to a moderate number of young persons, the advantages of a family, is always the private enterprise of the individual undertaker. The common-school and the college, on the contrary, are subjects of legislative care and regulation. I have therefore classed them together, for this reason; because it belongs to every legislature to provide for their modes of instruction, at least so far as the public interest may require, until they are brought to the highest attainable point of practical efficiency. But yet there is so wide a difference between their respective systems, that it will be well to consider them separately.

It is an admitted principle, throughout the United States, that it is the special office of government to furnish the means of gratuitous education to every child, in the more useful and ordinary branches of reading, writing, arithmetic, &c., so that the poorest may have sufficient cultivation to discharge their social duties in the republic; and acquire a respectable measure of intelligence, as citizens and parties in the general welfare. To this end, convenient districts are marked out; school-houses are erected and furnished; books, materials, and teachers are provided; all out of the public funds. And many of our most useful and distinguished men have had no other aid than this, in their preparation for a course of success and honor.

So far as it goes, all this is well. The defect is that it does not go far enough to attain the object. If reading, writing, and arithmetic, with a slight sprinkling of grammar, geography, and history, were sufficient to qualify the boy for the duties of a good and honest citizen, nothing more would be required for the great body of the people. But the fact is quite certain that neither these, nor any other branches of mere secular art and science, can produce such a result. It needs something more, and that something is a regular system of *moral training*, on the principle treated in the previous chapter. Nor can the Legislature fulfil its proper obligations in this all-important matter, until some plan be devised and carried into effect, by which this lamentable deficiency may be supplied.

Before I enter upon this, however, it will be proper to notice a practical defect, which prevents the children of the poor and the dissolute from deriving any benefit even from the existing system.

As the matter now stands, there is no sufficient mode for securing their attendance, when, as often happens, their parents are quite indifferent to their learning, or when they are too impoverished to supply them with decent clothing for the purpose, or desire to employ their time in begging or even pilfering. The children themselves cannot be expected to care for the privilege, and would rather stay away. And hence there is a large, and I fear an increasing proportion of the rising generation, to whom the common-schools are practically inaccessible.

This is, unquestionably, a great public evil, which it lies upon the Legislature to remedy. For many of these children grow up to maturity, in ignorance of every thing but vice and wickedness. They become liars, thieves, shop-lifters, counterfeiters, gamblers, ruffians, familiar with the grossest forms of licentiousness, and ready for every act of violence and blood. It is from this class that our elections, in the larger cities especially, derive their disgraceful character of fraud and disorder. They supply the chief share of work for our police, our magistrates, and our criminal courts of justice. They are the ready tools of villainy, in all its lower forms. And they constitute a perilous nuisance, more or less known and dreaded, in every community. Is it really necessary that our country should bear this frightful burden? Can the government do nothing to purify this pestilent abomination, and effectually stop the alarming increase of juvenile depravity? In my humble judgment they can; and assuredly, if so, it cannot be denied that it is a matter of high legislative duty.

It was one of the laws of Lycurgus, the famous legislator of ancient Sparta, that all the children born in the republic should be trained by the State, as the children of the commonwealth, on the system laid down by public authority. And no parent, however high his rank, was allowed to interfere. So effectual did this regulation prove, that the government of Sparta remained firm and unchanged for 500 years together; and the people preserved a greater unity of character and principle than any other nation of antiquity.

From this well-known example, our Legislators may certainly derive a hint worthy of serious consideration. Why cannot they adopt the principle, with reference to that class of unfortunate children, who have no parents or guardians to provide them with instruction; or whose parents are unable or unwilling to fulfil their duty to their offspring, and therefore either train them to vice, or abandon them to ruin? Why should the laws not require strictly that an annual inspection be made in every school district throughout the State, with especial reference to this matter, that every father who keeps his children from school, during six months of the year, unless from sickness or other actual necessity, should be held guilty of a misdemeanor, punishable by fine or imprisonment; and that all children who are vagabonds, or orphans, or beggars, should be taken and enrolled as the children of the commonwealth, maintained and instructed at the public expense, until they are old enough to be bound as apprentices?

That such a law would be of vast benefit to the individuals and to the public, can hardly be disputed by any reflecting person; because it would clear the community of numbers who would otherwise be sure to inflict upon it the worst evils of vice and disorder, by converting them into worthy men and honest citizens. The cost would doubtless be considerable; but it would be as nothing in comparison with the increased peace and security; the saving of the property now destroyed by theft, fraud, licentiousness, and every other form of depredation; and the immense sums required to keep villainy in check by the hand of justice.

I come next to consider the defect already intimated,

which deprives our common-schools of their proper efficiency, namely, the want of any regular system of *moral training*, without which it is mere folly to expect that they can prepare the pupils for the duties of good and trusty citizens, or fit them for the various relations of their future life.

But here, on the threshold of the argument, it may be said that the public schools are only opened during certain hours of the day; and that the children have their parents, and their families, and their Churches, for the purpose of learning morality. In truth, however, this is nothing to the purpose, when we know that they are not likely to learn morality without other help than these; since neither family nor parents are usually able to teach them, and the Churches have not the opportunity, through the loose practice of allowing them to waste and profane in amusement, if not in mischief, the Christian Sabbath-day. The object of the government, therefore, is not attained, and cannot be attained upon the present system. Provision is indeed made for a certain amount of intellectual culture, and even that is far from being as good as it might be. But there is no provision whatever for what is infinitely more important, not only to the children themselves, but to the public welfare, namely, *moral training and supervision*, on the basis of the Gospel.

Here again, however, I may be met with another objection. For the Constitution secures equal rights to every form of Christianity, and forbids the Legislature to favor one before another. How, then, it may be asked, can the Gospel be introduced into the public schools, when all the various Churches and sects throughout the land understand it differently?

The answer to this specious but shallow argument is very plain, and in my humble judgment, incontrovertible. The point to be attained is Christian *morality*, founded on the precepts and example of the Saviour. In this, ALL CHRISTIANS AGREE. The questions on which they dispute are dogmas of faith, forms of government, and modes of public worship. But they all acknowledge the same Redeemer. They all admit the same Bible to contain the Revelation of God. And therefore the public schools, in training up the children of the commonwealth according to the *morals* of the Gospel, would not interfere in the least with the equal rights of Churches, and sects; because they would only inculcate those principles in which all are of the same mind, and would leave untouched the points in which they differ.

The Roman Catholic, however, objects again, that the translation of the Bible used by all the rest is erroneous; and that he cannot conscientiously consent to have it read by his child, nor used, in his instruction, as a book of authority. This cavil is also specious, and yet it is perfectly absurd to rely on it, as a valid obstacle to the exercise of Legislative duty.

For, in the first place, our English Bible is only a translation; and there never was a translation of any book, since the world began, which might not be made a subject of dispute, on the point of strict verbal accuracy. But we cannot use the Scriptures, for the public benefit, in any other language than that which the people understand; and therefore we are forced to employ an English version. Morality must be taught by some means. It can only be taught, amongst a Christian nation, by the divine authority which all profess to reverence; and hence the Legislature are bound to use a translation, and can only be reasonably asked to use the best which exists, in the general judgment of the vast majority.

In the second place, the Legislature act as the representatives of the people. Under our republican government, the people are the sovereign power; and they have, long ago, settled the whole question as to the English Bible which they and their forefathers accepted, as a true and faithful version of the Word of God, and to which alone they appealed, for religious and moral instruction. It was that Bible which was everywhere established in the schools, and no man dreamed of introducing any other. It was on the basis of the same Bible that all the laws concerning religious duties have been passed. And, therefore, there seems to be a surprising amount of recklessness in undertaking, at this day, to raise any controversy about the matter.

But, thirdly, the Roman bishops have not a shadow of real ground for the pretence that they cannot conscientiously allow their people to use our established version, on the score of fidelity. For it is not only much superior to their own, in general style, but agrees with it substantially, in meaning. The exceptions to this agreement are very few, and in these, our established translation is fully justified, on a fair appeal to the Hebrew and Greek originals. In fact, the controversy between them and other Christians does not turn on the contents of the Bible, but on the authority of *Church tradition*, *outside of and beyond the Bible.* There is not a single point involved in that controversy, which depends on the difference between their version and ours. And hence, their real object in raising the difficulty is not to adopt a better translation than that which is already established, but to get rid of the Bible altogether; lest the children might insensibly learn to look to the Bible for their system of *religious faith*, as well as for their principles of *moral practice*. Whether their apprehensions of such a result are well founded or otherwise, I shall not now inquire. For myself, I can only declare that I regard them as wholly imaginary. So long as the child of a Romanist believes that his *faith must be founded on the teaching of his Church*, which he is to receive as the *unwritten* Word of God, *because that Church is infallible*, the reading of all the Bibles in the world can never move him. But it is sufficient for my argument to say, that the fears of a small body of ecclesiastics about a possible future result, can never be taken as a valid reason for depriving the public schools of the Word of God, in the form which has always been approved by the great body of the nation. Indeed, the very idea seems monstrous in absurdity; since it is evident that if the fears of a minority are to neutralize the judgment of the majority, we never could establish any law or system whatever.

In the last place, however, it is answer enough to reply that the sole object for which the Bible is to be used in our common-schools, is the establishment of *moral principle;* and therefore, unless the Romanist can point out some passages in which our established version *perverts the morality of the Gospel*, he has no pretext for objecting to its use, for purely moral purposes, by the public teacher.

I recur, therefore, to my proposition—that the great defect of our common-schools, founded for the education of the mass of our population, lies in the want of moral training and supervision on the basis of the Christian Scriptures. The question arises, How may that defect be supplied?

The Bible must be retained, of course. But the mere

reading of a chapter in the Bible is a small part of the work required for the moral training of children. It is the foundation, indeed, but it requires the superstructure to be raised, before it can be available; and that can only be done by making it the *practical rule of life*, which is the most difficult, as it is the most important matter to be accomplished, in the task of education.

The first thing demanded for this great object, in my humble judgment, is to make the morals of the Gospel a distinct branch of instruction; to be held forth, in all our public schools, as the primary and essential subject of attention, to which every other must be subordinate.

To this end, books should be prepared, rising in extent and thoroughness, presenting a detailed and complete course of Christian morals, beginning with a catechism for the younger scholars, to be followed by a grammar of morals for American youth, adapted to the more advanced pupils. And every class should be put daily through some portion of this course, as the most important part of their training.

This would insure the attention and the knowledge required, and go far towards inclining the thoughts and improving the habits of the pupils, by the regular reiteration of instruction. But in addition to it, the teacher should be obliged to keep a daily record of moral conduct for each scholar; and at the end of every term, the moral character should be made the first and most serious part of their examination, and should occupy the leading place in the certificate given by the master of the school.

The next thing required would be to provide for some effectual supervision of their conduct, during the remainder of their time. And for this purpose, there should be an inspector appointed in each school-district, whose duty it should be to make himself familiar with all the children, and to exercise a salutary government over their general behavior, both in their families and abroad. It should further be his care to have them entered as scholars in the Sunday-schools of their parents' choice, and to require a weekly report of their attendance and conduct on the card which each should receive from the superintendent. The first business at the opening of the public school, on Monday morning, should be the handing in of this card by every pupil, as the roll is called; and the memorandum should be set down upon the conduct-book, and a list made for the inspector, of those whose attendance at the Sunday-school could not be proved. And on every Saturday the inspector should visit the school of his district; examine the conduct of the past week, according to the record; call the delinquents to account, give commendation to the good, and rebuke the disorderly and disobedient. He should also, once in a month, or more frequently, if need be, visit the home of every pupil; and lend his influence to the authority of the father or the mother, as the case might require, for the benefit both of themselves and of their children.

For examples of special obstinacy, disobedience, habitual idleness, or direct rebellion, a further provision would be necessary. The Legislature should establish a place of discipline for obstinate delinquents, where a moderate degree of confinement, with a diet of bread and water, might suffice to correct their waywardness in time; instead of their being suffered to go on in an evil course, until they commit some act of villainy. As a general rule, this place might be the domicil of the inspector; and he should be authorized to take charge of every pupil whose wilful opposition to the regular course of training rendered it, in his judgment, necessary. And the fear of this punishment, if seasonably applied, would be quite enough to insure success, in those occasional cases of youthful obduracy, which might otherwise bid defiance to all that his instructions or the authority of their parents could do to reclaim them.

And on the 4th of July, in every year, it would be well to have a public procession of all the schools within a convenient distance; each school being attended by the inspector and the teacher, and a banner with some suitable device being carried at the head, by the best pupils. The choice of the bearer might be by ballot, given by the scholars themselves, but confirmed by the inspector, in order to prevent improper influence. And a short address might be made to them, and some simple refreshments provided; and then, when they had returned to their respective school-houses, and deposited their banners, they might be dismissed for the remainder of the day. Cases of serious delinquency should be excluded from this annual festival, which would render it a useful adjunct to the influence of salutary discipline. And the effect would be to raise the system of our common-schools in the public estimation, and especially in that of the parents and the scholars; so as to make it more and more appreciated as one of the most important elements of the national welfare.

Such is the outline of a plan which would seem to me adapted to correct the defects of our common-schools, and make them what they ought to be; namely, an adequate course of instruction in the intelligence and virtue demanded by our republican Constitution from every American citizen. There is no subject so grave and important on which the wisdom of our Legislatures can operate. On the training of the children in this generation depends the future prosperity, and perhaps the very existence, of our Union. And the acknowledged progress of youthful license, immorality, and irreligion, taken in connection with the general inefficiency of our common-schools, certainly warns our rulers, with fearful emphasis, to remedy the growing evil before it is too late. It rests on them to devise and apply the proper corrective, because it can be done by no other authority. They have undertaken the work by establishing the common-schools, and in this they have done well and wisely. But they are pledged, for this very reason, to go on and perfect the system, until the object is really effected; and I do not understand how, if it be in any way within the scope of their lawful powers, they can evade this most weighty responsibility.

It is very possible, doubtless, that the scheme which I have presented may be quite unsatisfactory; and I am perfectly aware that many of my readers may be disposed to dismiss it at once, as too stringent on the one side, or Utopian and visionary on the other. But I hold it to be a very idle exercise of time to expose a public evil, without devising some appropriate remedy. As an humble citizen, but yet as "a partner in the republic," where all the people are sovereign, I have suggested an available plan, according to my poor ability. And no one will rejoice more sincerely than myself, if the Legislatures of our land will only take up the subject in its true length and breadth, and establish some system which shall far exceed my own in wisdom and efficiency.

Nevertheless, as every man who proposes a plan of public improvement is naturally desirous to be fairly understood; I must request the attention of my readers to a brief explanation of those points which are most likely to be supposed objectionable.

The first of these would probably be the strict requisition on every parent to send his child to the public school, (unless he be able and willing to pay for his education in some other) during the six years between the ages of eight and fourteen, *on pain of being fined or imprisoned for a misdemeanor.* This, of course, would seem to many minds extravagantly despotic and severe. Yet I have no doubt whatever that such a law would be not only just and beneficial to a large number of children, who are now growing up, through their parents' fault, in ignorance and vice, but that it would be in fair analogy with other parts of our established system.

The law of the land now takes cognizance of the parents' conduct towards his child, in several particulars. The father has an undoubted right to chastise his son; but if he does so with cruelty and unreasonable excess, he commits a misdemeanor, and may be punished by fine and imprisonment.

The law of the land also permits the father to regulate the food and clothing of his son, according to his circumstances. But if he *purposely* keeps him in starvation and nakedness, he commits a misdemeanor again, and may be punished by fine and imprisonment.

But does the father owe nothing more to his child than the absence of brutality to his body? Is he not equally bound to treat him as an intelligent being, endowed with the rights of a citizen? Does he not know that the law designs his son to be trained up, by the use of the means which the State has provided, in the knowledge and the principles which may enable him to fulfil his duty? And is he at liberty to expose that son to the inevitable alternative of ruin to himself, and injury to the public? Shall the father be liable to punishment because he is cruel to the person of his child, and shall he not be at least equally liable to punishment if he be yet more cruel to his whole lifetime?

There are two great principles in the old civil code, familiar to every lawyer: "*Sic utere tuo ut alicui non lædas,*" and, "*Salus reipublicæ suprema lex;*" both of which apply directly to the subject. The first lays down the principle that the citizen must "so use what is his own, that he does no injury to another." And the second prescribes the great rule of all legislation, that "the safety of the commonwealth is the highest law." The father may count as his own the time and labor of his child; but he may not use his rights to the public injury, by bringing him up in ignorance and vice. And "the safety of the commonwealth" is so absolutely dependent on the right education of its members, that the system which provides for this must be respected as a portion of its "highest law;" and therefore the father who stands in the way to prevent its execution, and thus treats it as if it were a nullity with respect to his own son, is justly to be regarded as an enemy to the commonwealth, and guilty of an aggravated misdemeanor.

It is on these principles that we are able to justify the laws made to suppress intemperance. A man has a right to buy what he pleases. Therefore he may buy intoxicating liquor; and when thus purchased, it is his own. But he is forbidden so to use it as to commit drunkenness, because he injures others. He is even forbidden, in some of the States, to sell it by retail, lest the buyer may be tempted to commit the same sin; and if he violates this law, it is a misdemeanor, punishable by fine or imprisonment. Yet how trifling is this offence against public morality and order, in comparison with the course of the father who keeps his own son from access to a useful education; and trains him up, not to commit the sin of drunkenness only, but to be a nuisance to the community in every form of gross abomination!

For these reasons, then, I should contend that a law compelling every parent to send his children to the public school, for six years together, under the penalty affixed to every other misdemeanor, would be neither despotic nor severe; but, on the contrary, it would be a law of justice to the children, justice to the parent, and justice to the community. It was the law of ancient Sparta. It is said to be the law, substantially, of several European nations. And yet there never was a government on earth which demanded a stronger guard upon the education of children than our own; because the virtue of our citizens is our only protection against disorder, in the absence of kings, nobles, or any other established class of fixed authority.

The next objection might be to the office of district inspector over the conduct of all children between the ages of eight and fourteen, who were, or ought to be, pupils in the public school. It may be said that such an office would be too inquisitorial in its character. It would interfere too much with the rights of parents. It would invade the privilege of every man to consider his home as his castle, and never could be made to agree with the free institutions of our country.

This is all very reasonable, doubtless; but yet I do not see that it has much practical force, when we consider that the object to be attained is vitally important to the safety of society. In my humble judgment, no good and well-disposed parent would object to an office, which could only operate to aid him in securing the morality and obedience of his children. And those parents who are neither good nor well-disposed ought to have their children subject to *some* government which might save them from the ruin consequent upon idleness and vice, and protect the community from the disastrous consequences. The inspector would therefore be welcomed as a friend by all who had a desire to see their children in the right way; and his visits would only be disliked by that class to whom they would be most necessary.

A third objection would perhaps be made against the power of the inspector to confine and punish the obstinate and refractory. But here, again, he would only be doing that which is the express duty of the parents. And hence, whenever they either fail or refuse to use the correction, which they are bound to employ, for the safety of their children and for the public good, his office would afford a legal substitute of domestic discipline.

And the fourth and last objection might be against the arbitrary act of taking under the protection of the State all children who are vagabonds and beggars, and providing for their maintenance and welfare. Yet here, also, it is manifest that some such provision is absolutely required, for the rescue of the children and the good of society. Strictly considered, the commonwealth has a direct interest in all the children, who are, by and by, to be admitted to the privileges of citizens, and thus to become "partners in the republic." And if the parents will not, or cannot, train them in the path of duty, the government is not only justified in depriving those parents of the natural right which they would otherwise possess, but is obliged to apply some humane and adequate remedy. It is precisely on the same principle that the law now authorizes the appointment of guardians over the property of the drunkard, and confines the insane. And no one can question that the abandonment of young children to a life of vagabond beggary is usually followed by far more dangerous and fatal results, than even drunkenness and insanity. Why, then, should the Legislature guard society against these, and yet make no adequate provision for the other?

To my mind these answers seem satisfactory and conclusive. But, as I have already said, I am not so much devoted to my own plan, that I cannot rejoice in the adoption of any other which may be deemed preferable. The great object which I propose to myself is to contribute my humble share, in calling the attention of the American citizen to the subject. The evils are manifest. They are rapidly increasing. Every man is interested, directly or indirectly, in removing them. For the public schools concern us all, because they educate the mass of the community. Those who are now in their mothers' arms will be, in a few years, the body of the nation. And just according to the character implanted by their youthful training, will the nation be.

Hence, every one is ready to allow the wisdom of establishing the common-school system for the children of the masses. But the same wisdom which began the good work, is bound to improve and perfect it, until the object is attained. And therefore it may be hoped that our Legislatures will not "grow weary in well-doing." There is no labor in which they can be employed, of so much value;

none of such deep and abiding interest, and none in which success will be followed by so large an increase of public peace and prosperity.

CHAPTER XXVI.

ON COLLEGES.

UNDER the general term of Colleges, I would include all those public schools which are incorporated, by a legal charter, for the highest finish of education; and over which the Legislature retains a just measure of general supervision and control. In these most useful and important establishments our youth are prepared for the several professions, and for the immediate introduction into the practical business of life. And there are few topics of greater interest to all thoughtful and instructed men, than a fair inquiry into their efficiency for the great objects of their institution.

No one can have a more profound respect for the presidents, the professors, and the teachers, so well and so actively employed in our colleges, than I have ever entertained; nor can any man cherish a deeper regard for their incessant and invaluable labors. Yet I must be permitted, in pursuance of my general design, to point out the defects which they have inherited from bygone ages; of which there are doubtless some that might be removed in part by their official powers, but all would be far more easily and surely corrected with the friendly aid of legislative action

The cardinal fault is the same which I have had occasion

to notice at so much length, in the three previous chapters. Education in college, as everywhere else, is confined to literary culture; and Christian morals have no distinct importance assigned to them. The inevitable consequence is what all virtuous and intelligent men lament;—that with respect to religion and morals, college life is a period of temptation. And it is hardly to be doubted that the majority of the youth who pass through it, while they carry away with them a large increase of intellectual knowledge and power, suffer also a serious decrease of moral sensibility and principle.

The causes of this are not to be traced to the indifference or neglect of their instructors, who are usually Christians, and, for the most part, Christian ministers, anxious to promote, in every way, the religious welfare of the youths committed to their care. The difficulty lies partly in the lack of previous training in the young men themselves, and partly in that want of distinct attention to the subject of Christian morals, which is chargeable upon the college system. And I shall proceed, therefore, to consider both of these causes according to this order.

I am persuaded that, as a general rule, the strong and abiding character of every youth is fixed for life, before he is old enough to enter college. But I have examined the power and permanence of early habits and impressions in the 23d chapter, and I shall not weary my readers by repeating the arguments here. Suffice it to say, that if the young Freshman does not come into the hands of the Faculty with the motives of Christian duty, the habit of subordination to authority, and the love of knowledge, industry, and order, already grafted in his heart; it is usually quite impossible for his instructors to supply the deficiency. Indeed the effort can seldom be made. He sees them only at certain hours of every day, in company with his classmates. He has no opportunity of that familiar personal intercourse, which might give them an influence over his individual thoughts and feelings. The intervals between his hours of study and recitation are passed in the society of his boarding-house, or with his fellow-students, or in such reading and thoughts as please his own fancy. These associations are generally such as lead to pleasure and indulgence. And hence, it is rarely found that he can derive any advantage from his college life, in the principles of moral virtue. On the contrary, those principles are far more likely to lose than to gain, throughout the four years of his literary course; unless there be some peculiar circumstances, not necessarily connected with that course, which may give them a better direction. And this is so well understood, that the Faculty neither are, nor ought to be, subject to any blame, if the character which the student brings with him, instead of improving, grows worse to the end.

Here, then, in the defect of his previous training, and in the tendency of his new associations, lies the first cause of the moral degeneracy which the student is so apt to experience, during college life. The second cause may be found, as I have said, in the want of that distinct attention to the subject of Christian morals, which is fairly chargeable upon the established system. And this want may be readily understood from the fact, that Morality, as founded upon the Gospel, *is not a branch of instruction*, nor is it held up *as a rule of life*, in any college or university of Christendom. In this point, the same defect meets us everywhere. The Bible is used, indeed, to a small extent, and prayers are regularly offered for the divine blessing on the Institution. But nothing is systematically done to "train up the youth in the way he should go," nor to make the precepts of the Gospel a law of daily observation.

I do not forget, however, that an approved work on Moral Philosophy is made a part of the studies of the senior year. Nor do I wish to pass over the fact that Butler's Analogy, and some author on the evidences of Christianity, are added in several colleges. But this comes too late to rectify the defect in the previous three years. And besides, it is merely gone over as an intellectual study, along with Metaphysics; and is in no way brought to bear upon the heart and life, as a rule of real and practical efficacy.

And in precise accordance with all this, is the final course of examination. There is not a word said about the Christian morals of any student. There is no attention given to his moral character at all. There is no inquiry made into even his intellectual acquaintance with the moral precepts of the Bible. But he receives his diploma with credit, as a proof that he has gone through a certain amount of literary culture; and he is considered fully entitled to his college honors, without the slightest reference to his standing in truth, fidelity, or virtue.

I have already said that the Faculty are not to be blamed for the defective condition of this matter. The fault is not in them, but in the system which they have inherited from previous ages. The college only caps the climax of the error which I have shown to prevail throughout our whole scheme of education; since, from first to last, the morals of the Gospel have been cut loose from the schools, and the work of the teacher has been limited to the mere task of literary and ornamental instruction. But the true design of education remains the same, notwithstanding. Its proper object is to prepare and qualify the youth for the duties of the man. His conscience and his heart, therefore, need to be educated, even more than his intellect. For if these be not cultivated aright, the increase of his intellectual powers will do nothing for his character. And they cannot be cultivated aright, except by a diligent and constant training in the moral precepts of the Gospel.

The question, then, arises at once, Can any thing be done to rectify this defect, and make our colleges, not only schools of intellect, but schools of virtue? It seems to be a difficult, and yet by no means a hopeless undertaking, if the good and wise men, connected with those important institutions, will make the needed improvement a subject of united *effort*, as well as a subject for united *prayer*. And they will pardon me, I trust, if I, who am neither the president nor the professor of a college, should make some practical suggestions, which may at least be worthy of consideration.

My first resort would be to the Legislature, because I am persuaded that no authority less than this would be likely to effect any serious reform. In the present state of lax independence, when our youth are allowed to select what college they please, and change it when they please, no institution could be expected to set up a new and stricter standard; because it would probably diminish very seriously the number of its students, unless the law of the land made it equally obligatory on all others. And therefore, if the government cannot be induced to interfere, I should despair of any available result from individual action. I presume, however, that they would willingly adopt any recommendation which should be presented by a memorial from a respectable number of College Faculties; and in this way, much might be done, with due and persevering exertion.

Suppose, then, that the Legislature, in every State, should be requested to pass a law to increase the usefulness of the colleges and universities, containing the following provisions:

1st. That in order to open the way for all deserving youth, to the advantages of a complete and finished education, the common-schools should be extended into a higher department, where boys who had honorably passed through the present course, and were recommended for their moral character and industry in study by the inspector and the teacher, might go on with those branches which should prepare them for college, at the public expense.

2d. That in the high-schools thus constituted, the science of Christian morals should be maintained, as a leading branch of instruction; and a record kept of the moral character and conduct of every pupil.

3d. That on the final examination of the high-school, when the course of instruction was completed, one-tenth of the pupils, having passed a satisfactory examination in moral character as well as in literary qualification, should be privileged to enter college and be sustained to the end, at the public expense, as the students of the commonwealth; subject, nevertheless, to the forfeiture of their privilege, at any time, in case they should incur the censure of the Faculty.

4th. That no student whatever should be admitted into any college, unless he exhibit satisfactory testimonials of moral character, in addition to the usual literary qualifications.

5th. That every college should appoint a professor of Christian morals, whose duty it should be to instruct each of the four classes, at least once in every week of term time, in the knowledge and practice of morality, as the same is laid down in the precepts of the New Testament. And that it should further be his duty to keep a just record of the personal conduct of the students, and oversee their course, with kind and watchful attention.

6th. That in every college examination, a chief place should be given to the branch of Christian morals; and no diploma should be granted without an express testimony from the Faculty to the moral character of the party.

7th. That inasmuch as there are great differences in the diligence, the talents, and the attainments of students, and it is not just that the same testimonial be given to all alike, the diplomas should be divided into the first, second, and third ranks in the baccalaureate degree, and be distributed fairly according to the merits of each candidate respectively. And that if the candidate deserve to stand first in moral character, and only second or third in learning, or the contrary, as the case may be, his diploma should express the truth, with fairness and strict impartiality.

These regulations, recommended by the College Faculties and established by law, would produce, in my humble judgment, a great and most salutary change in the entire circle of American education, and be felt, in due time, throughout the whole range of social, political, and individual duty. For the most part, they explain themselves sufficiently. The object is the same throughout, namely, to elevate the importance of *moral character* to its true rank, in the estimation of the youth of our country; and to require such direct and positive action on the subject from the official instructors in every chartered institution, as should secure the best attainable result, for the interest and welfare of our educated men, and for the safety and honor of the nation.

The principle set forth, however, in the first three sections of the proposed law, may require some further consideration, before my readers can understand its practical value. For here I have suggested the propriety of carrying forward the provision already made in our common-school system, by establishing high-schools for the most deserving; and by giving the further privilege of college education to one-tenth of those who should pass honorably through these high-schools, at the public expense, as the students of the commonwealth. My reasons are, briefly, these:

It is a fact acknowledged by all, that the best talents, the most vigorous energy, and the purest moral dispositions, are often found amongst the masses of our population; where the opportunities of a thorough education are rarely attainable, and the individuals are consequently kept back from that degree of culture which would render them fit for the highest sphere of public utility. This ought not to be so, in a republic, which professes to secure equal privileges to all the citizens. And since it is already a settled principle that the government shall provide for a certain amount of knowledge, by our common-schools; it would only be an extension of the same wise policy which should select the best subjects of these schools, and lead them on to the full measure of instruction, to which their capacity, their diligence, and their moral character entitle them, and so train them up to be the surest instruments for preserving and advancing the true interests of the whole community.

That the youths thus trained as "the students of the commonwealth" would be superior men, seems to be a natural result of circumstances. For they would come from the masses, and would therefore be, emphatically, *the men of the people.* They would owe their education to the government, and would therefore be, on the score of gratitude, the special lovers of their country. They would be staunch supporters of pure moral principles, because their moral character, through their whole course, would be one prominent ground of the distinction bestowed on them, and habit and consistency would in their case give tenfold force to the power of duty. They would work their way without the dangerous obstacles of wealth and family position, guarded by the wholesome checks of necessity, and constantly reminded that their good conduct and industry were the only instruments of their success. And they would form a class, recognized in every State, as the pledged examples of what the best citizens should be, in virtue, intelligence, and patriotism.

The privilege thus granted by the State, would prove, moreover, to be the strongest possible incentive to morals and learning, in the public schools. It would be a prize of the brightest and the purest kind, to stimulate the most deserving. And it would so operate in bringing the college within reach of all who proved themselves worthy of the patronage of the government, that every youth of talents and of virtue would look upward to that, as his allotted reward.

To the colleges themselves it would be an inestimable benefit. For we know that as matters now stand, there are few, comparatively, who can have access to them, besides the sons of the wealthy; and these, for the reasons already assigned, rarely derive much substantial benefit, at least in the all-important point of moral principle. Hence, there is a growing indifference, or even dislike, towards colleges, in the minds of the community; because observation and experience seem to show that there is no permanent advantage for success in life, secured by collegiate training. What we need, therefore, pre-eminently, is a *steady supply of good materials*, on which the college Faculties can work with full success. The "students of the commonwealth" would furnish that supply, and their previous preparation would insure their faithful improvement, throughout the whole course. Their numbers would give new life to the college system, new strength to the college discipline, new stimulus to the zeal of the professors, and new importance to the true value of a thorough education, in the eyes of the community at large. And their subsequent course would convince the public, in due time, that when the highest training fails to produce the best result, the fault lies not in the acquisition of learning, but solely in the personal folly of those who desire to purchase the honor of a diploma, without the proper agency of talent, diligence, and virtue.

These remarks may suffice, however, with respect to the aid which the Legislature should afford in this important matter. The rest would depend on the voluntary action which our College Faculties may give, even now, to the essential point of moral principle. For, assuredly, there are no reasons why they might not, of their own accord, have a professorship of Christian morals. Nor is there any argument which I can discover to justify the general laxity of practice, in the granting of diplomas and other college honors, without any real merit on the part of those who receive them.

Take, for example, the average attainments of our Bachelors of Arts, and what proportion of them do the Professors believe to have honestly deserved the college testimonial? It is beyond all question that the general course has become so complaisant and amiable, as to make that testimonial of the smallest possible value. Many years ago Professor Stuart, of Andover, complained that few of his theological students had learned Greek enough to read even the New Testament with ease and accuracy, although they had diplomas from the best Colleges in their hands. Professor Turner, of New York, has frequently been obliged to notice the same deficiency. In Latin, there is not a youth in the Westminster school of London, or in the German Gymnasia, who is not very far superior, before he enters the University, to the great majority of our college graduates. And in mathematics, it may well be doubted whether one young man in every hundred who have gone through the course, professedly, *understands* the science at all. As to logic, metaphysics, moral philosophy, natural philosophy, history, &c., nothing can well be more superficial than the actual knowledge required; so that, on the whole, the progress of our Colleges has not been upward, towards the mark which a diploma once signified; but downward, towards the dead level of indolent facility, where the lazy carelessness of the student may be accommodated with the certificate and the name of learning, without the irksome toil and labor of its real acquisition. The degree of Master of Arts is bestowed, after an interval of three years, as a matter of course, upon every one who has received the previous degree of Bachelor, without any evidence whatever of advancement during the interval. While the honorary degrees of Doctor of Divinity and Doctor of Laws are dispensed purely as a personal compliment; and often on such subjects as provoke a smile at the strange distinction.

These incongruities, however, are by no means original with our American Colleges. Some of the Scotch universities were in the regular habit, formerly, of giving the title of Doctor of Divinity to any one who would pay the regular fee, without the slightest regard to his learning. And even the great English University of Oxford converts her degree of Doctor of Laws into a mere token of personal respect, as when she bestowed it on His Royal Highness, Prince Albert, the Duke of Wellington, and Field Marshal Blucher! The legal knowledge of the whole three, united, was probably much less than that of the meanest petifogging attorney. But that was of no consequence whatever. The University thought fit to pay them some public compliment, and this was the cheapest in her power. And so she resolved to confer upon these eminent personages a title originally designed as the highest mark of judicial learning, to which none of them had the slightest claim; although the act was entirely beyond her proper province, and the whole proceeding was nothing more or less than a solemn display of unquestionable moonshine.

It is an ungracious task, I know, to point out these abuses in the practical administration of our highest seats of learning. And if I did not feel the deepest interest in their honor and their usefulness, I should much prefer to leave it to less friendly hands. But the truth is, that unless some method can be discovered to remedy those evils, it is a pure impossibility that our colleges should secure a lasting hold on public confidence, in an age like our own; which reduces every thing to the scale of positive utility, except it be within the privileged circles of popular amusement, and fashionable extravagance. Education must be raised to its true level, by restoring its long lost element of moral principle, and then these inconsistencies will all disappear. The worthless and the lazy student will no longer claim the honor of a College diploma, nor will the Faculty be expected to sign a testimonial without any confidence in its truth. Our worthy and laborious Presidents and Professors will be relieved from the fetters of a vicious custom, which seems to compel an indulgence so foreign to their own sense of consistency. And their official approbation will be incomparably more coveted and prized, when it is only conferred on successful diligence and virtue.

One suggestion, however, yet remains, before I close this chapter; and this arises naturally out of the character of our political system, which regards the people as sovereign, and makes every citizen a partner in the republic. The course of College training, therefore, which is designed to prepare the young man for the business of life, should always include a thorough system of instruction in the Constitution of the United States, and in the rights and duties of the American citizen. He should be taught to understand his relation to the commonwealth, to love his country, to be a firm friend of law and order, to guard against the evils of party spirit, and to realize the importance of his personal course to the general welfare. For the responsibility of government rests, in part, on every member; and the measure of this responsibility increases with the amount of his intellectual culture. And hence, no scheme of education should be thought complete, unless it provides, in some reasonable degree, for the just discharge of this serious and inevitable obligation.

CHAPTER XXVII.

ON FEMALE EDUCATION.

It has given me pleasure to advert, in a former chapter, to the superior deference and respect, with which the gentler sex is regarded by every true American. And perhaps it may be, in a great measure, the consequence of this, that female education has assumed a form of such imposing proportions as to rival the male department; even in those kinds of learning once deemed to be the exclusive property of the masculine intellect. Our maidens, as well as our young men, must now be taught Latin, Greek, and Mathematics. Their public examinations must be conducted on the same plan, and in the same branches. They, too, must have diplomas, or certificates to supply their place. They, too, must read or recite their own poetry and prose before a public audience, and their names must be spread abroad in the newspapers. It is probably one natural result of this rivalry, that a few are even bold enough to claim an equality with men in every other privilege; in the exercise of the elective franchise, in the professions of law, physic, and divinity, in the government of the State and of the family. The authority of the Bible and the laws of the land are indeed directly in the way of this assumption; and therefore they are loudly assailed, with all due feminine eloquence and pertinacity, as tyrannical invasions of the true rights of woman. And societies are formed, and conventions are assembled, in the vain hope of revolutionizing the world, by the final triumph of this strange and silly infatuation.

But it is no part of my design to argue against the wild and impious extravagance of this Quixotic enterprise. The interests of education are all that I propose to consider, and these are assuredly involved, to no small extent, in the new experiment, which seeks to give our females the same kind of intellectual training as the males, along with the accomplishments of music, painting, and the modern languages; and thus, in truth, to make the attainments of the woman not only equal, but far superior to those of the man, in the same rank of society. Believing, as I do, that the laws of God, which are entirely consonant with the capacities of nature, stand in opposition to the system, I hold it to be my duty to say so frankly, and to state my reasons at large for what some of my respected readers may regard as a very unjust and illiberal opinion.

At the threshold, however, of my argument, I desire distinctly to disclaim the doctrine that there is any superiority of the male over the female, in the original design of the Creator. On this point, we have no express information in the brief record of Scripture; although I think it is not very difficult, on reasonable grounds of inference, to establish a quite contrary conclusion. Certain it is that the woman was placed under the authority of the man immediately after the fall; for thus runs the sentence of the Almighty, "Thy desire shall be to thy husband, and he shall rule over thee."* Certain it is that the inspired apostles confirm this authority, by commanding the wives to be "in subjection to their husbands,"† and by declaring that "the head of every man is Christ, and the head of the woman is the man."‡ But the right of authority is one thing, and the

* Gen. iii. 16. † 1 Pet. iii. 1. ‡ 1 Cor. xi. 3.

superiority of nature is another. The woman was the first in the transgression, being deceived by the tempter, and this may have been the reason why she was placed under subjection. And although it is very obvious that the organization of the man is such as approves, most fully, his superiority in all that belongs to government, yet this alone would not establish his superiority of nature.

For nature, as it respects the human race, includes the heart or the affections; as well as the head, or the intellectual faculties. That men, as a general rule, are superior to women in the power of the intellect, is a truth so manifest, that I should regard its denial as a perfect absurdity. But I hold it equally indisputable that women are superior to men in the warmth, the purity, and the constancy of the affections. Which is the more important of these two? Which exercises the larger influence on happiness—WISDOM OR LOVE? The latter, in my humble opinion, for several reasons. First, because love is the primary rule which the great Creator has laid down for His spiritual creatures. "Thou shalt love the Lord thy God with all thy heart, and soul, and strength. This is the first and great commandment. And the second is like unto it: Thou shalt love thy neighbor as thyself. On these two commandments hang all the law and the prophets." With these words of the Redeemer, St. Paul agrees where he saith, that "love worketh no ill to his neighbor; therefore love is a fulfilling of the law." And St. John carries the principle to its highest point, by declaring that "God is love, and he that dwelleth in love dwelleth in God, and God in him." These passages might be greatly multiplied, but they are amply sufficient for my purpose; and, on Scriptural ground, are quite conclusive to the Christian.

But the same result is easily proved by the next consideration, namely, that it is confirmed by universal experience. Love makes us happy without wisdom, while all the wisdom in the world cannot make us happy without love. Hence arises the familiar fact that the period of childhood is usually regarded as the happiest part of life, because then, the affections of the heart are in the liveliest exercise; and the wisdom of the head, which comes long after, only serves, in most cases, to chill their ardor; and establish in their place the calculations of selfishness, and the fears of suspicion.

And there is yet a third reason which may serve to prove the superiority of this principle, derived from the unquestionable fact that it is not wisdom, but love, which determines the character and governs the life, in every individual. We may imagine a man of accomplished intellect, a master in the knowledge and wisdom of this lower world: yet if he loves the indulgence of his appetites and passions, and uses his superior knowledge in the service of his own selfish ambition and base desires, his character presents an odious and fearful compound of atrocity. On the other hand, the ignorant peasant, who cannot make the slightest pretence to worldly wisdom, may have the noblest character, if he hates falsehood and vice, loves only what is good and true, and thus pursues, with honest zeal, the path of benevolence and virtue.

In fine, love is superior to wisdom in energy. For love rules over wisdom. Love conquers pride, indolence, avarice, and ambition. Love has no fear of danger, opposition, or difficulty. Love is ready to labor, to suffer, to make any sacrifice, even of life itself, for the objects of affection. It does not wait for the counsels of selfish prudence, the rules of duty, or the calculations of interest; because its own warm and generous impulse supersedes them all. Hence, love is a law unto itself; and if the world were full of love, such as the Saviour and His apostles have commended, it would need no other law. Surely, then, the question may be easily decided, between the claims of the sexes to intrinsic superiority. Man excels woman in wisdom, which belongs to the intellect. Woman excels man in love, which belongs to the heart. Of these two, I have shown that love is the higher principle of happiness, of holiness, and of virtue. And hence it results that the sex which possesses the best capacity for this, must needs be superior to the other.

Such would be my own view of this disputed point, as it respects the constitutional characters of the sexes. But this, however it may be regarded, cannot change the rule established since the fall. Both are depraved by sin. Both need the same restoration to righteousness through the mediation of Christ, in whom "there is neither male nor female, bond or free." Both are dependent on Him, who unites boundless wisdom with infinite love; and He has placed the woman under subjection. Hence, the work of education must take note of their relations, not as they might have been in the beginning, but as we see them now, under the express law of the Gospel; sustained as it is, in this at least, by the laws and customs of all mankind, without exception. The task of government is assigned to the man. The duty of obedience is enjoined upon the woman. And the system of education which tends, directly or indirectly, to run counter to this rule, is manifestly opposed not only to the revealed will of God, but to the voice of nature.

For it is obvious to the slightest reflection, that there is no discord whatever between this law and the original constitution of the sexes, but, on the contrary, the most entire harmony. The duty of government devolves on the man, because it demands the superior wisdom of the intellect. In addition to this, however, the corruption of our world is such, that physical force is indispensable as well as mental discernment. A large proportion of every community requires the strong arm of the law to keep it in order. The clubs of the police, and sometimes the weapons of the soldier, are essential to the public safety. Even the subordination of the children in the family needs the vigorous correction of the father's hand, to put down the spirit of rebellion. What could the female do with government, in circumstances like these? She must be herself dependent on the other sex for her safeguard and protection. And hence she must be under government; because, in the very nature of things, government and protection go together, and demand the exercise not only of superior wisdom, but of superior power.

Nor is this the whole. The entire machinery of life calls for the labor of the intellect and the hands which the man alone can supply. Who cuts down the forest, and builds the house, and clears the ground, and tills the soil, and gathers in the harvest? Who opens the mine, and converts the ore into metal, and makes the tools, and weaves the linen and the cloth, and slaughters the cattle, and prepares the hide, and forms the household utensils and furniture? Who frames the ship, and navigates it through the pathless ocean, and brings from distant lands the comforts and the ornaments of the family? Who ransacks the laboratory of nature in chemistry, reads the heavens with his telescope, binds to his service the electric and magnetic forces, and provides from the storehouse of his invention the countless contrivances of mechanism, which minister to the wants and pleasures of society? All these, and much more, are the work of man, and not of woman. Hence we see, again, the necessity which makes her dependent on his superior intellect; since the entire range of the arts and sciences are the fruits of his genius and his toils, without the slightest share of female participation.

But the whole of this mighty product would avail nothing to the real happiness of life, if we lacked the treasure of the affections which it is the province of woman to supply. The wisdom and the ingenuity of the intellect could do little for us, without the love and tenderness of the heart. And therefore it is, in the merciful distribution of Providence, that the inspiring motive for the mental and physical energies of man concentrates itself in the society of woman; and finds its proper enjoyment in the charmed circle of home, of which she forms the centre of attraction. It is her privilege to reward the anxieties of government, the drudgery of business, the toils of labor, and the strifes and contests of the world, with the voice of admiring praise, the feeling of cordial sympathy, and the welcome of true affection. Her gentle hand can smooth the brow of care. Her smile can scatter the clouds of disappointment. Her words of hopeful confidence can cheer the weary spirit, and strengthen the fainting resolution. Her patient sweetness can calm the chafed temper. Her trusting faith can lighten the gloom of despondency. And thus it is that the sovereign power of the masculine intellect comes gladly to the refuge of domestic love; and lays its head upon the woman's heart, as its best source of earthly joy and consolation.

Each sex, therefore, has its own peculiar sphere, and its proper characteristics are written as clearly in the intellectual and spiritual, as in the physical organization. In all the great elements which constitute humanity, indeed, they are alike; but these elements are so admirably and beautifully compounded, that the difference appropriated to the sex appears throughout the whole. Hence the instinctive disgust which we feel at the spectacle of an effeminate man, or a masculine woman. It is usually quite impossible to regard the one with respect, or the other with affection. And this alone might teach us to understand that the relative position of the sexes is determined not only by the revealed word of God, but by the voice of nature.

This fundamental principle should be the ruling maxim in the work of education, the object of which is to prepare the individual for the duties of life, or, in the expressive language of Scripture, to "train up the child in the way he should go." And it is precisely because the modern system of female education violates this principle, and aims at a result which counteracts the law of grace and the true ends of nature, that I am compelled, however reluctantly, to accuse it of serious error.

In the first place, I hold it to be a mistake, and a very grave one, to tax the female mind, as a general rule, with the study of the dead languages and mathematics; in the vain and idle expectation that their knowledge of these things may place them on a fair equality with educated men. I do not deny, indeed, that there are instances, now and then, of females whose mental structure is of a masculine stamp; and ought, therefore, to be gratified with a masculine training. So, likewise, there are examples of women with beards,—women who disguise themselves in male attire, and prefer the labors and habits of the other sex to those which are appropriate to their own—women who have played the part of sailors and soldiers, as well as that of professors and ecclesiastics, and with some measure of success. But these are rare exceptions; and the system of education is not to be adapted to them, for the very plain reason that all *systems* must be consistent with the *general rule*, and conformed to the usual course of experience and utility.

It is on this ground, therefore, that I object to the modern plan of forcing these masculine studies into female seminaries. They are not in harmony with the character of the feminine mind; and cannot be acquired, to any available extent, without a degree of painful effort, which is perilous to the pupil's health, and often fatal to the vigor of her mental and physical constitution. They demand, moreover, an amount of time and study which cannot possibly be devoted to them, without neglecting other branches of knowledge, incomparably more important to the future duties of wives and mothers. And the actual amount of proficiency is so trifling and superficial for the most part, that the pretence of having learned them at all is little better than a transparent imposition.

For the same reasons, I should banish a large list of other masculine studies, physiology, chemistry, geology, metaphysics, logic, &c., of which it is impossible for one girl in a thousand to learn enough to be of the slightest benefit to herself or to society. The attempt to cram the mind of a young female with such a variety of subjects, only results in a jumble of confusion; and the result too commonly is that she leaves the school without any real knowledge which deserves the name.

The truth is, that the whole of this ambitious effort to place the minds of women on the same level as those of men must end in disappointment, because it is contrary to nature. It would be just as reasonable an enterprise to cast their bodies into a masculine mould; and insist on making them as tall, as muscular, and as strong as the other sex, without regard to the difference in their physical conformation. Both attempts would be equally absurd, and equally abortive, save in those rare instances already mentioned, where the exception only serves to prove the rule. For in the male as in the female, there is a perfect harmony between the body and the mind, which may be seriously disturbed, although it can never be entirely destroyed, by a false education. Energy and strength are the characteristics of the one; grace and beauty of the other. Both contribute equally to the welfare and happiness of the social state, but in different departments. And it is the safest maxim which their teachers can keep in view, that the practical duties of the future life should be the main guide, in the system of youthful training.

I am well aware, however, that there is a very plausible defence of the modern system, derived from the admitted fact that the woman is intended to be the companion and helpmate of the man; and therefore it is necessary to furnish her with the same variety of education, without which, their mutual intercourse must soon become devoid of all true sympathy and interest. But this argument is formed on a radical misapprehension. For how does a miserable smattering of Latin, algebra, geometry, conic sections, physiology, chemistry, or metaphysics, qualify the woman to be the companion and helpmate of the man? What scholar desires to talk on such subjects to his mistress or his wife? Nay, what individual, in any department, would choose to bring the details of his daily business into the society of his friends? And how much less would he select those details for his domestic circle? On the contrary, he seeks his home as a refuge from the toils of his regular employment; and loves it in proportion to the relief which he feels, in its cheerfulness, its order, and its peace. Small comfort would he find there, if the work which has already wearied him, must be renewed by the ambition of his wife to show the *equality* of her understanding in the line of her husband's avocation. The experience of mankind is therefore quite opposed to the modern theory. The learned professor, who is fatigued with teaching Latin, Greek, or mathematics day by day, does not wish to be pestered by the display of his helpmate's erudition. The lawyer, who is already exhausted in the labors of his office or the exciting contests of the court, has no appetite for his wife's *sympathy* in the art of litigation. The physician who has gone the rounds of his patients or his hospital, is in no humor to listen at night to a family talk about comparative anatomy. The merchant has had enough of commerce in the hours of business, and would not thank his chosen companion for a lecture on profit and loss. The mechanist rejoices to lay aside his apron and his tools, when evening comes; but has no notion that his domestic partner should entertain him about the machinery of the steam-engine. In a word, the very charm of home consists in the grateful change which it supplies, to relieve the mind of man from the pressure of business; and strengthen him, by its affection and its pure enjoyments, for the renewal of his toils. And that charm would be wholly destroyed, if the conversation of his wife only served to weary him still more, by harping on those subjects which she can rarely understand, and of which, even if she could, he is tired enough already.

The testimony of experience, however, goes yet further, to prove the utter mistake of this modern theory. Its advocates suppose that a certain amount of masculine learning is necessary to qualify the female for the society of the other sex; when in truth, it is universally known that nothing renders her more repulsive and disagreeable. A learned lady is so far from being attractive, that she is generally dreaded as a *bore*, unless she can exercise the rare prudence and self-denial of keeping her superior knowledge to herself, and resolve on being amiable. This well-known fact cannot be explained on the hypothesis of our feminine philosophers—that men are *jealous* of all intellectual excellence in women; for the very obvious reason, that there is no ground for jealousy where there can be no competition. But it is the simple dictate of that natural instinct, which looks to the sex for the higher happiness produced by the *affections;* and is alienated and offended when the female apes the masculine character, forgetful of her own. She is welcome to the exercise of every faculty, which is in harmony with her real sphere; since that is the best earthly gift which Providence has appointed, to engage the purest feelings of every manly heart. And hence she annoys us by the assumption of this learned rivalry; not because we envy the display of her intellectual power, but because she affects what does not belong to her, and sacrifices her proper influence to a weak and vain ambition.

I pass on, however, from the error which is committed by teaching the female too much, to the opposite error which invariably attends it—namely, the teaching her too little. The time and the labor which ought to be devoted to the acquisition of true and useful knowledge, are wasted on an absurd attempt to obtain what is neither useful nor true. And it results, of necessity, that she leaves the school with the name of having studied the dead languages, mathematics, and many other branches—all of no conceivable value to her future life—while she is ignorant of those solid, serviceable, and attractive attainments which would qualify her for her duties to her family and to society. Let us consider, therefore, what ought to be the extent and character of a reasonable and accomplished female education.

First, of course, the pupil should be daily trained in the principles and practice of Christian morality, and taught to understand the relative position of the sexes, according to the Word of God. Here she would learn that, while it is the allotted sphere of man to govern, to labor, and to toil in the business of the world; it is the far more blessed sphere of woman to pursue the peaceful and unostentatious path of domestic duty, relieved from the struggle for gain or honor, and occupied in promoting the comfort and happiness of those around her. To this end, she should be warned against the indulgence of temper, the display of vanity, the assumption of pride, the temptation of indolence, the love of distinction, and the weak idolatry of dress and fashion. She should be thoroughly instructed in the virtues of truth, modesty, gentleness, benevolence, and filial duty. She should learn to guard her tongue against the common faults of exaggeration, scandal, and censoriousness; and to respect the rights, the character, and feelings of others, as she would have them respect her own. She should be led, practically, to the Saviour, and seek His favor, by watchfulness over her own heart, and by prayer for His help and blessing.

And she should be taught to understand that the attainment of these personal habits of thought and action is of infinitely more importance to the happiness of herself and those connected with her, both here and hereafter, than all the other learning and accomplishments in the world.

This is the most difficult, the most delicate, and by far the most essential branch of female education; and therefore to it, every thing else should be subordinate. With respect to the various branches of secular learning, the pupil should be thoroughly instructed in her mother tongue, to read with grace and propriety, to write with perfect correctness, and to be familiar with the ordinary course of arithmetic, so far as it is useful in the common business of life. She should have a fair knowledge of geography, and the manners and customs of nations; and be well grounded in history, from the earliest ages to her own day. To these she might profitably add some work on the plan of Goldsmith's Animated Nature, and a course of botany, which would tend to cherish and develop her taste for plants and flowers, in connection with drawing in pencil, crayons, and water-colors. But I should disapprove, decidedly, of her learning oil-painting at school, because this can only be useful to the artist; and crayons and water-colors are better suited, in every way, to the health, the neatness, and the convenience of the private female amateur.

Along with these, however, I should attach considerable importance to music, which is one of the most appropriate embellishments of social and domestic life, and harmonizes admirably with the great design of making home attractive to the family. But, in this, it is not desirable to aim at the performance of the most difficult and scientific compositions, which excite astonishment far more than pleasure, in all except the professional musician. Simple airs and melodies are enough, especially when the instrument accompanies a voice of truth and expression. Singing should form, in my opinion, the main object, as a general rule; because it is this which gives to music its greatest charm. And where the girl is so deficient in ear or voice that she cannot be taught to sing, I would excuse her from the useless drudgery of learning the piano, as likely, with few exceptions, to prove a mere waste of time and money.

If, after all this, the pupil has some hours to spare, she should go over a well-selected course of English poetry, in connection with Johnson's Lives of the Poets, and other later biographies. Portions of the old standard essayists, Bacon, Addison, Steele, Hawksworth, with Goldsmith's Citizen of the World, and the Vicar of Wakefield; discourses chosen from the eminent divines, South, Tillotson, Taylor, Barrow, Sherlock, etc., for Sunday reading; and, lastly, our own distinguished American authors, so far as a judicious instructor would deem them profitable, might finish the work of ordinary female education; and produce a far more satisfactory result, for all the objects of solid principle, correct taste, sound judgment, and social intercourse, than could possibly be attained by the masculine studies of a college course, or the shallow and, for the most part, useless smattering of French, German, and Italian.

But there is another element which ought never to be omitted, in consideration for the sober utilities of family life and domestic economy. One day in every week should be systematically devoted to the needle, the art of making the ordinary garments, and the operations of housekeeping and cookery. And this I would recommend, not merely for the sake of the actual skill acquired, but especially in order to form the true principle and habit of association; which can alone protect the educated female from a total dependence upon hired servants, and from a foolish disgust towards the labors which will, in most cases, be required for the future comfort and good order of her home. This course is the more important in a country like our own, where so many young people are constantly emigrating to the new States and settlements, and are obliged to help themselves, if they would be helped at all. But it should be regarded as indispensable for every female, whatever may be her rank or her position. The knowledge of these things is easily acquired, if it be commenced in time. It operates beneficially in the wealthiest as well as the poorest households. It aids most powerfully in facilitating the work of benevolence and charity. It protects the wife and mother from constant imposition and mortifying disappointments. It secures the satisfaction of the husband, in the regularity of her inspection over his garments and his table; and cuts off the most frequent occasions of domestic trouble and alienation. And thus this sadly-neglected branch of a true female training, when it is understood as it deserves, becomes a strong security of wedded comfort; for which it is impossible to find any substitute in the whole range of fashionable learning or accomplishment.

Finally, in the system of female schools, I would utterly discard the universal custom of public examinations. It seems to me a cruel ordeal for a young and sensitive girl, whose sex and modesty should shield her from such an infliction. It is well, doubtless, for the college youth, who expects to stand before the people in the future duties of his business or profession, and must learn to bear the popular gaze with unshrinking fortitude. But why should such an exhibition be demanded of the gentle maiden, who is never called upon to endure it again? The only reasons which I can imagine for such a custom, are furnished by the threefold argument, that it gratifies the love of display, on the part of the parents; that it raises the importance of the school in the popular esteem; and that it stimulates the pupils by its resemblance to the impressive close of the college course, since it gives to the female, as well as to the male, the same stamp of public interest and approbation. But none of these reasons seem to me sufficient to countervail the objections, which rest upon the constitutional difference of the sexes, already explained, and the violence offered to the laws of truth and nature. Let us consider their validity in detail; and then, although I have no hope of converting the reader to my opinion, while the current of fashion runs so strong in the contrary direction, I shall at least have discharged what I hold to be my duty.

The first reason in support of public examinations in the female school, is "the gratification of the parents' love for display." I doubt not that this love of display exists, for it is forced upon us continually in a hundred varieties of form. Neither do I question that it is natural for mothers, especially, to desire that their daughters' merits should be exhibited to all possible advantage, in the eyes of their acquaintances and friends. But I deny that this love of display deserves to be encouraged; because it is not a virtue, but a weakness, springing directly from pride, and seeking to be gratified, on the same selfish principle as emulation. It is the professed object of education to inculcate what is good, and discourage what is evil, with reference to the great duties of the future life. And therefore, although we may regard this love of display with a benevolent spirit of excuse, as a pardonable maternal infirmity, yet it is no apology for a practice which is at variance with the whole design of systematic Christian training. The most direct proof of its inconsistency with true principle is afforded by the fact, that hardly any mother would be willing to acknowledge it openly, or even confess it to herself, as her real motive of action.

The second proposition, namely, "that these public examinations raise the importance of the schools in the popular esteem," may be also true. But even if so, it is, like the other, no ground of justification, because the highest interest of the pupils should be the measure of the popular esteem, and these exhibitions afford no just standard of improvement or of character. The popular esteem is therefore founded upon a popular mistake. And it is the duty of those who undertake the task of education, to discountenance, instead of encouraging, the error. They should consider that the real success of female training cannot be brought to the test of any public ordeal; but must be known in the purity of principle, the love of duty, the regulated temper, and the general amount of useful knowledge, which can only be properly appreciated in the intercourse of private life. And instead of inviting the public to sit in judgment upon themselves as well as on their pupils, under the name of an examination, they should inform that public better, and honestly tell them the truth, that the notion is a mere delusion.

The third reason, however, is even worse than either of the others. It may be true that "it stimulates the pupils to make the examination resemble the impressive close of the college course, and thus give to the female, as well as to the male, the same stamp of public interest and approbation." But the very fact alleged constitutes, in my opinion, a strong ground of objection. For I maintain that the pupils of a female school ought not to be stimulated by the vanity of ostentation, but by far higher principles. Nor ought they to be thrust into a false position by a competition with the other sex, for public interest and approbation. And the reason has been already given: that the young man, as an American citizen, is educated with express regard to *public* life, whereas the appropriate sphere of the young woman is in the circle of *private and domestic duty.* And hence the custom of public examinations in her case should be discarded altogether, as an open and direct inconsistency with the radical laws of true female education.

When we look more deeply into the practical working of this prevalent mistake, there will be found much to condemn, and nothing to recommend it. To the few girls who are superior to their companions in personal beauty, or in showy accomplishments, the day of examination is doubtless full of interest, because it is an occasion of display. Yet even with these, it can hardly fail to be a painful trial to the modesty and sensibility which most become their sex. And it must be a temptation, operating on their feelings for a long while before, to the excitement of contest, envy, and selfishness, which are all hostile to the proper design of female training. The successful candidates for the prizes are apt to be puffed up by the distinction, although they may be far inferior to many of the rest, as examples of Christian duty. For the character and habits which should be the great and controlling objects of all real education, are never mentioned at all on such occasions. And hence it may often happen, and I doubt not usually happens, that the distinguished favorites of the public applause are by no means the most deserving, with respect to those genuine but retiring virtues, which form the highest claim of every female to confidence and affection.

But this is not the worst: for unhappily the exhibition is too frequently an inducement to a kind of fraud, which is entirely irreconcilable with strict moral principle. The pupils are sometimes drilled beforehand, so as to appear to know a vast deal more than they have really attained, in languages, mathematics, &c. They exhibit paintings which have been finished by the professor, and these are splendidly framed, and displayed as their own work, when the poor girls are perfectly aware that they could not produce them alone, if their lives depended on it. They perform pieces of music on which they have labored assiduously for the occasion, and gain credit accordingly; notwithstanding their private consciousness that they will not be able, after they have left school, to play the simplest new air by themselves; and that the piano will gradually come to be regarded as a respectable piece of parlor furniture. And thus they are tempted to practise an actual imposition on the public and their friends, without the slightest reflection on the want of moral principle involved in the deceit. But what is the result? While education itself thus patronizes and sanctions hypocrisy, by requiring its pupils to seek for applause, and accept a formal sentence of public approbation which they know is not deserved, can we wonder that the world is so full of false show and vain pretension? Is it strange that honesty and truth should be altogether out of fashion, when the wives and mothers of our land have not only been allowed, but stimulated, by the very system of their own training, to be content with the appearance instead of the reality; and learn to think themselves fortunate if they can purchase praise at so small a price, as the sacrifice of sincerity and candor?

However doubtful we may be, as to the superiority of domestic training over a public school, in the case of the male sex, I hold it to be indisputable that it is the best and safest system in the case of females. And such has always been the opinion and the practice among the higher classes in Europe, where the mother can find a competent governess, and the father can afford the expense of the numerous masters, which are supposed to be necessary; or where (which is altogether preferable) the parents are themselves sufficiently accomplished, and can afford the time and attention required. For this private system, I consider the female seminary to be only a substitute; and as a substitute, it should have as much as possible of the family character. Now the idea of a public exhibition is utterly foreign to domestic education; and the best-bred ladies of our mother country would start back from such an ordeal, as entirely inconsistent with the delicacy and modesty of their daughters' habits. Why should it not be equally inconsistent with delicacy and modesty, amongst the pupils of a female school? Are these qualities to be so much regarded in the one case, and yet altogether set at naught in the other?

But it may be said that public examinations have long been established in the female schools of England. True: and therefore our teachers are certainly free from the reproach of introducing any novelty. Yet the energy which is so marked an element in our American character, has carried the system much farther, by associating those examinations with an avowed purpose of rivalry with male education. And hence we are liable to experience much more of the natural result, when our females are taught to set aside the distinction so broadly drawn between the sexes, by the word of God and the natural faculties; and to contend with the college graduate for the prize of intellectual vigor, and the meed of public applause.

So strong, however, is the tendency in this direction, that I have no expectation of any result from the remonstrance of an humble individual. I have written frankly, under the single impulse of duty to the truth, and with a full conviction that in avowing such unpopular opinions, I shall certainly incur the censure of many, whose favorable judgment I would willingly have secured. But while I cherish a sincere admiration for the talent, the devotion, and the brilliant success, which have marked the names of some distinguished leaders in the cause of American female education, I am unable to regard the theory which is now in the ascendent, without serious apprehension; because, for the reasons already assigned, I cannot consider it as in harmony with the rules of Christian morals, with the true interests of domestic affection and peace, or with the ultimate promotion of the public welfare.

It is, after all, however, but a small minority of our females who are sent for any considerable time to the boarding-school. It is even a minority who are long continued in any school at all. To all the rest, who are obliged to grow up to mature age without such helps, I would say, if I could have access to them, "Be not discouraged or in anywise cast down, by the want of those advantages. The rudiments of knowledge are easily acquired; and if you are devoted to your duties, faithful to your Saviour, attached to your parents, and diligent to give your spare time to useful books and safe society, you may improve far more in all that is truly valuable, than the great mass of those who have passed through the public seminaries; and make much happier wives and mothers than even the distinguished 'graduates,' who have borne away their prizes with honor and applause. For, notwithstanding the zeal, the talents, and the various attractive appendages associated with those admired institutions, there are many difficulties and temptations surrounding them, from which you are comparatively free. The best school in the world is usually found in the circle of the family. The safest friends are those whom Providence has already given you. Your wisest teacher is an affectionate and pious mother. And your brightest and most lasting prizes must be earned at home."

CHAPTER XXVIII.

ON PHYSICAL EDUCATION.

The body is the instrument of the mind, and this alone should secure to it a due share of attention, from the hour when the infant enters into the world, to the last moment of dissolution. But, in truth, it is much more than the instrument; since it is also the associate and companion of our spiritual nature, and possesses a most extensive influence on the whole range of intellectual operation. Thus we know that there are certain conditions of the body in which all thought is suspended; others, in which memory fails; others again, in which the faculties are strangely exalted. Some stimulants affect the mind in such a way that the exercise of judgment is impossible; and some, on the contrary, seem to increase, for a time, at least, its vigor and sagacity. In a word, the body and the spirit are so united that each acts upon the other with a reciprocal power, which physicians are compelled to notice, but which no human science can explain. The sum of our knowledge in this is embraced in the words of the Psalmist, that "we are fearfully and wonderfully made;" and that the body, as well as the mind, must be in a healthy state, if we would perform the various functions of life with due success, and enjoy its privileges with solid satisfaction.

It is manifest, therefore, that education, to be rightly conducted, must include all that is required for the care and development of the physical frame. And this is generally admitted in theory, but yet very poorly exemplified in practice. The consequence is that a large proportion of our youth are deficient in bodily strength and vigor; that our best students in the colleges are pale, thin, and dyspeptic; and that very many of the pupils in the female seminaries become the subjects of diseases of the spine, scrofula, or consumption, with a variety of other disorders; all of which might have been avoided by a proper and regular system of air and exercise, commenced in time, and continued with perseverance. The evil, however, does not end here. For in case of marriage, the unhealthy parents propagate an unhealthy offspring; and no tongue can tell how far the sad result extends, through a wide and melancholy range of suffering and wretchedness.

Our medical writers have frequently put forth excellent rules on this important matter, and several authors on the subject of education have done the same. But as my readers may not have met with those works, I propose to devote this chapter to some of the most essential rules of physical education, together with certain suggestions concerning the best mode of carrying them into effect.

Like every thing else which belongs to the art of youthful training, this should begin at home, under the watchful eye of the mother. She should be careful, from the first, to avoid the absurd custom of swathing the infant, or confining its tender frame with any ligatures. Its clothing must be perfectly loose, and neatness or beauty of dress should never be suffered to interfere with the free development of nature. It is painful to see the prevailing violation of this important rule, amongst the great majority of mothers; who seem to treat the child as if it were a doll to be adorned with finery, instead of a living, growing mortal, whose whole future health and strength may be irreparably injured, if the members, in childhood, be deprived of their fullest liberty.

For the same reason, the infant should not be carried too much in the arms, nor rocked to sleep in a close cradle. The safest plan is to provide it with a large crib, covered with a hair mattress, and placed in a position where it can be properly ventilated, by night as well as day. On no account should it sleep in the same bed with the mother, nor be kept from fresh air through fear of its taking cold. For, the vigor of the whole system depends on the action of the lungs, through which the oxygen of the atmosphere is imparted to the blood in respiration. And if this be impeded, or if the air be impure, all the care and physic in the world will not prevent the ruinous result to the constitution.

It is a very common error, though a very gross one, to suppose that the smallest rooms in the house will answer for the sleeping apartments. On the contrary, those apartments should be the largest, the most lofty, and the best ventilated of the whole. Or, if that be impossible in the present mode of constructing our dwelling-houses, the matter should at least be so managed that the lungs may never want their proper natural supply. The windows should be let down at the top, and the door should be left open. An aperture should be made communicating, near the ceiling, either with the chimney or with the open air, in order to let the impure atmosphere of the room escape more readily. And the head of the sleeper, instead of being placed next the wall, in the usual manner, should rather be towards the middle of the apartment, so that a gentle current of air may pass over it. These little details may seem trifling to my readers, but I give them on the observation and experience of half a century. And my motive is simply that they may profit by a kind of knowledge, the want of which I believe to be the cause of more than half the diseases of civilized society.

The food of children should be pure and simple, consisting chiefly, after they are weaned, of good milk, reduced, if too rich, by water; and bread made at home, with honest yeast, and without *salœratus*. Sweetmeats, candies, and confectionery of all sorts, should be avoided, as well as spices, pickles, &c. No medicines, cordials, or nostrums of any kind should be administered, unless by the prescription of a physician. Every morning, the whole body should be washed or bathed in cold water. And early rising should be steadily maintained, as a fixed principle of health and future industry.

It is common to give young children exercise in a little carriage, drawn by the nurse or by the elder members of the family. But this should never be allowed until they are old enough to sit up; because, if they be lying down during the motion, there is danger of injury to the tender brain, and therefore the practice should be avoided, as well as the custom of rocking them to sleep in a cradle, for the same reason. The best exercise which they can take is to creep about, in a loose shirt or tunic, and in pure air, at their own pleasure. No contrivance of art can insure their proper growth and health so well as the simple course of nature.

But in due time they become large enough to run into the streets; and this is the period when those mothers who live in cities, without a large yard or garden, find the greatest trouble to provide their young people with sufficient exercise in the open air, and yet keep them out of danger. In the country, there is no difficulty; and there would be as little in the city, if there were a sufficient number of convenient parks allotted to the use of children, where, at proper hours in every day, they might be permitted to gambol at their will, under the eyes of some careful overseer. Much may be done, however, in a small yard, by a little attention and management. A few pieces of boards and wooden blocks, an old saw, hammer and nails, the jumping-rope, a swing, a rocking-horse, a small wheelbarrow, and especially the company of some trusty person, to give interest to their play by conversation and suggestions, will secure them exercise enough, if the mother be willing to give some time and take some trouble in the matter. And she would be well repaid for this in the end, by their health, their safety, and their increased affection. Nor would she fail, during the process, to do a most useful work in the gradual formation of their character. For the temper and the selfishness of children are most apt to show themselves in the hours of play; and she would then have an opportunity to teach them their best lessons in mutual regard for each other's feelings, in generosity, and in self-denial; which would greatly facilitate their subsequent course, in all their social relations, and tend powerfully to make them just, considerate, and amiable, to the end of life.

But now we come to the period when, at the age of eight years, after acquiring the rudiments of learning and the principles of religion under her own instruction, the children may be sent to school: and at this point begins the systematic provision which should be made for their physical training.

The school-house should be large, lofty, and thoroughly ventilated. It should stand in an open plot of ground, with space sufficient to allow of room for exercise in the open air. The scholars should never be allowed to sit at their lessons more than an hour at a time; and should then be sent out to take a race round the building for some ten minutes, to set their blood in lively motion, and prevent all risk of dullness and stupidity. If the weather be such that this cannot be done, the same period should be occupied in marching round the room, during which they should join the teacher in singing. There is no exercise better adapted to give play to the lungs, and to strengthen the pectoral muscles; and it should be universally retained in all our primary schools, for these and other purposes; for it banishes effectually the drowsiness and inattention of the pupils, invigorates them for the next hour's work of study, and spreads a most useful and pleasant spirit of cheerfulness over all the work of juvenile education.

An hour after school should be faithfully given to bodily exercise in the open air, in the grounds allotted to the school-house, and under the eye of the teacher, or some trusty assistant; and nothing can be more admirably fitted to this object, in our large cities, than the German system of Gymnastics. In the country, the same end may be accomplished by useful occupation in the garden, if the parents or other members of the family will work along with the children; since, without this, it will be very apt to amount to mere idle sauntering, which is good for neither the body nor the mind. But besides gymnastic exercises in the open air, there should be attached to all our public schools, a large hall protected from the weather; where the same amount of bodily recreation may be taken in winter, or at such other times as comfort may require. For girls, the exercises so well known by the name of Calisthenics should be substituted; the same principles belonging to both, and being only modified, in the latter case, by an ingenious adaptation to the female system. Thus two hours each day would be given to physical training, and this is none too much for the vast advantages which must result in bodily health, development, and vigor. The same plan should be continued in the high-schools, the colleges, and the seminaries, up to the very close of the period allotted to education; subject, of course, to such exceptions as might arise from necessity, in which case, on the application of the parents, the pupil would be excused.

Now, all this is open to the manifest objection, that it would increase the expense, and impose some additional trouble on the teacher. But I hold it to be disgraceful to our national and republican character, that our public schools should be fettered and starved by a miserable calculation of false economy. There is no duty of the Government to be compared with the importance of securing, to the mass of the rising generation, the inestimable blessings of "a sound mind in a sound body." The difference in the pecuniary cost should not be considered worthy of a moment's hesitation. It is a shame to see the utter want of attention to those principles, which lie at the very root of all our private welfare, and all our public prosperity. Suppose our common-schools, erected on a liberal plot of ground, planted with trees, and filled with groups of healthy, happy, and dutiful children; instead of being cooped up in close neighborhood with other houses, excluded from the free air of heaven, and rendering all healthy exercise impossible. Suppose our high-schools, colleges, and seminaries, in like manner, well built, well ventilated, and surrounded with a wholesome atmosphere; and all of them exhibiting, at regular hours of every day, the judicious, safe, and invigorating exercises of youth; cheered by the melody of well-chosen songs, exempt from all violence and disorder, and exhibiting a spectacle at which the heart of true humanity must rejoice with hope and thankfulness. And then imagine the contrast which such a spectacle would exhibit, when compared with any thing elsewhere to be found in the wide world! It is impossible to exaggerate the importance of the results to the highest and best interests of our beloved country. Foreigners from every land would gaze in admiration at our system of public training. And if the entire circle of national education were thus raised to its proper height, the superiority of these favored United States—instead of being limited to the theory of our Constitution, the cheapness of land, and the better price of labor—would be seen and felt in the moral character, the intellectual progress, and the bodily vigor and beauty of our whole community.

In order that the controlling power of Government may

be brought to bear, in the most practical manner, on the whole of this extensive subject, I shall close this chapter by suggesting a measure which would furnish, in my humble judgment, an available instrumentality for commencing and carrying forward the great work of improvement and reform.

I would respectfully recommend, then, 1st, that the Legislature in every State should establish by law a permanent body to be called "The Board of Education," to consist of men of high intelligence and established moral character, elected by the Senate on the nomination of the Governor, holding their office during good behavior, and supported by a liberal salary, so as to enable them to give their whole time and attention to their duties. Their numbers might be three, five, or seven, according to the population of the State, and the extent of their supervision.

2. That this Board should have power to inspect, as legal visitors, every school, seminary, college, and university established by the authority of the law, or by a legislative charter, once a year, at least; and that they should examine their course of instruction, their moral standing, their discipline, their buildings and their grounds, their provisions for air and exercise, and the health of their pupils and students; making a regular record of the whole.

3. That an abstract from this record should be prepared by the Board, presented to the Governor one month before the regular meeting of the Legislature, and laid before that body at the commencement of their session, accompanied by such suggestions of improvement and reform as the Board may deem advisable.

4. That the Governor be requested to notice this Report of the Board in his Annual Message; that a Joint Committee

on Education be the first appointed by the votes of the two Houses, to take the said Report into consideration; and that the Report of this Committee should have the precedence over all other business, as involving the most important topic of legislative duty.

5. That the Report of the Board of Education be printed in full, and sent by mail to every teacher, inspector, professor, and president of a college or seminary throughout the State, together with the recommendations of the Governor, the Report of the Committee, and the action of the Legislature on the same.

6. That an appropriation be annually made to be expended by the said Board, in the work of building, enlarging, and improving the public schools, according to their best judgment; beginning with one, as a general model, and bringing the rest to the same standard, as soon as the time and the means supplied from year to year may allow.

7. And finally, that the said Board should have the power to fix the salaries of teachers in the public schools, to appoint them to their office, and to dismiss them on due proof of neglect or incapacity.

The object of these provisions would be to create a standing body who should be constantly devoted to the practical advancement of public education. At present, there is no proportion whatever between the magnitude of the interests involved, and the systematic attention bestowed upon them. A vast amount of watchfulness, of examination, and of practical wisdom is required, to elevate this most important class of subjects to its true level, and make the future citizens of this great republic worthy, in all respects, of their own professed principles, and of their lofty position in the eyes of the world. And hence the work demands a fixed department to itself, and the labors of such a Board should be regarded as one of the most essential parts of our internal policy.

It must be manifest, as I presume, to every intelligent and thoughtful mind, that this fundamental duty, on which the individual happiness and the public welfare so largely depend, is now very imperfectly performed, and needs a thorough reformation. In order to make this evident, I have endeavored to fulfil a very ungracious and thankless task, by pointing out, without fear or favor, the manifold defects which require an effectual remedy. But in this I have only sought to promote, to the extent of my humble ability, the highest welfare of our beloved country. To me—drawing, as I am, towards the close of life, and without any personal interest in the question—it is a matter of small importance; since the improvements which I propose, even if they were acceptable, could hardly be accomplished before I shall have passed away. Yet it is some satisfaction to hope that I may aid in leading the thoughts of abler and more influential men to an examination of the subject; and thus contribute somewhat to the desired result, under a wiser scheme of regulation.

The rights and duties of the American citizen, with regard to the whole of this extended subject, are sufficiently obvious. He has a RIGHT to the best education for his family which the State can bestow, in Christian morals, in useful knowledge, in the vigor of health, in all the range of the social relations. And it is his DUTY to secure that right, by making himself thoroughly acquainted with the principles which should govern his own course, as a husband, a father, and a "partner in the republic;" by a faithful exhibition of those principles in his own example, and by endeavoring to interest his friends and neighbors in those measures which may lead to legislative action.

For with us, happily, the people are sovereign. And, therefore, every individual amongst the people has a special right to commence a salutary movement on any subject which involves the general interests of the whole. A single intelligent man may talk to a few like-minded individuals. This may lead to a private meeting. This again may be followed by a public one. Speakers of known ability may be enlisted for the occasion. A memorial to the Legislature may be extensively circulated by a common effort. Prominent members of either House may be interested to bring this memorial forward, and advocate its claims. And thus the result may be so far accomplished, in the appointment of a Board of Education; by whose labors the good work would go on, year after year, with growing success and prosperity. For in such an enterprise we are entitled to anticipate the favor of Providence. We know how much that benign Providence has already done for the welfare and greatness of our nation; but we may well fear that the Almighty will abandon us to all the evils of licentiousness and anarchy, if we will not use the necessary means of training our youth to intelligence and virtue.

The best and most available of those means, as I have endeavored to show, is found in the family relation; when the circle of home is in all respects as it should be. But on the broad and comprehensive scale of the general good, the Government can operate with the largest power and the greatest efficiency. To this, therefore, the American citizen should have recourse, because it is the highest duty and interest of our Legislatures to perfect the public system. In proportion as that system rises, all the private schools and seminaries will also rise of necessity; since their only hope of support must rest on the general opinion that they are superior to the public institutions of the country. And thus the whole work of education would attain, in due time, the utmost limit of practicable excellence, and our glorious Union would stand forth, in this most essential and happy enterprise, as an example to the world.

CHAPTER XXIX.

ON SOCIAL LIFE.

I HAVE led my kind readers over an extensive series of topics, with the view of illustrating the rights and duties of the American citizen, on the multifarious subjects embraced by religion, politics, business, and the domestic relations, the last including the all-important interests of education. It only remains that I add some practical considerations on social life, which will conclude my humble labor.

And this is no trifling theme, because it embraces a very wide field of human action and solicitude. Connected as we all are with society, and each living in a little world of our own, whose favor and good-will we are bound to propitiate; the pleasures, the hospitalities, and the friendly intercourse of those around us become invested with a large measure of importance. No opulence can raise us so high as to be independent of the sympathies of others. No poverty can sink us so low that we are entirely cut off from the regard of our fellows in misfortune. We are social beings by nature and by habit; and we cannot cast aside the kindly chains which bind us to our companions, unless we are tempted to abjure our race, in the melancholy madness of misanthropy.

The disposition which fits us for general intercourse is therefore happily expressed by the term *sociability*, and the man or woman who is esteemed *sociable*, is always a favorite in the circle, whether small or great, which constitutes their world. True it is that this sociability cannot be strictly numbered among the virtues. But it is no less true that it is very difficult to secure a character for virtue without it. Indeed, so great is its influence in the intercourse of life, that a sociable man will often gain more favor without virtue, than a virtuous man can gain without sociability. For, it is an amiable quality, which enters readily into all the feelings of others, with a certain amount of sympathy. It is accessible, conversable, genial, and kindly. It suits itself readily to the feeling of the hour, and reflects, without an effort, the expression of sorrow, or the animation of joy. It goes to the funeral with the language of condolement. It goes to the wedding with the words of congratulation. It gives a willing sigh to the house of mourning, and a ready smile to the house of feasting. In a word, it seems to be the friend of every one, and every one is its friend in turn. So that if sociability be not actually a virtue, it is assuredly the best substitute for virtue in the general estimation of mankind.

But in all this, there is nothing at war with the spirit of Christianity. On the contrary, so far as it goes, sociability is in entire harmony with the precepts of the Gospel. For the Saviour commands us to weep with those that weep, and to rejoice with those who rejoice. And the Apostle directs us to be kindly affectioned one towards another. Thus our Lord himself was a guest at the Marriage Supper, and gave his countenance to the innocent festivity of the occasion. Thus He wept at the grave of Lazarus, and consoled the mourners, Martha and Mary. Thus He passed his daily life amongst the multitudes of Judea, and manifested his deep interest in all the sorrows of humanity; repelling no one who sought his aid, receiving all, and comforting all with more than the words—the deeds of genuine sympathy.

Yet no one would dare to say that the blessed Redeemer was an example of sociability; although, to a certain extent, this quality may seem to be in accordance with His sacred character. For His sublime benevolence was the result of an infinitely higher principle—divine LOVE. And therefore the sympathy of His followers is a *virtue*, because it has its source in the spirit of Christ, and its motive power is in the soul. But the sympathy of the social instinct goes no deeper than the bodily temperament. It belongs to the natural disposition, and is often most active in those who know least of the real power of love. And hence it is nothing more than a pleasant representative of affection; always ready enough to display a limited amount of kind consideration, but never, of itself, to be relied on for any act of friendship, which involves the sacrifice of interest, or the labor of self-denial.

Nevertheless, in a world like ours, this quality of social sympathy is by no means to be despised, nor its value underrated. It is a gift of God to our bodily nature, and like every thing else belonging to the body, it bears the marks of His benevolence and wisdom. We should lose much, and could gain nothing, therefore, by quarrelling with sociability. It rather becomes us to accept it for as much as it is worth; and to acknowledge its salutary influence, under the defect of a higher principle, in promoting the amiable courtesies of good neighborhood, smoothing down the asperities of ordinary life, and diffusing a genial air over the general aspect of the community.

This distinction between the social instincts of our animal sympathies and the loftier range of spiritual and moral virtue, may help to teach us the true idea of happiness; which is two-fold of necessity, because humanity is two-fold, consisting of the body united to the soul. Perfect happiness demands that both should be constantly supplied with their appropriate enjoyment. But, since the fall of man, there is no perfection upon earth; and happiness only comes by glimpses, like gleams of sunshine through a stormy sky. And such is the disorder which sin has introduced into our double being, that the soul may be happy while the body is stretched on the bed of sickness, and the body may be happy while the soul is sinking into ruin. The spiritual nature therefore, when it is awakened to a full consciousness of its wants, "seeks those things which are above," and takes small interest in the pleasures of social life on its own account, because they never rise to the sphere of its higher aspirations. And yet it accepts them thankfully, so far as they are lawful and consistent with the divine will; and is ready to encourage them as a gift of that wondrous beneficence, which provides alike for the body and the soul. But the animal nature makes those pleasures its chief object of desire, and follows them without regard to the far superior enjoyments of the spirit, or to the rules of religious government and subordination. And hence it is, that as the spiritual life is developed only in the few, while the animal life is developed in all, mankind at large know nothing of happiness, beyond the gratification of the senses and of the social sympathies. Yet still they seek to be happy, because this is the natural law of every living being; and therefore they are impelled to those pleasures which they are able to understand. And thus the world is filled with such innumerable forms of social enjoyment, some of which are consistent with our spiritual welfare, if rightly guarded and restrained; while others are hostile to wisdom and piety, and not a few are full of danger to the body itself, by weakening its powers, undermining its health, and dooming it full often to painful sufferings, and untimely dissolution.

By this phrase, *social enjoyment*, it will of course be understood that I do not mean any of those simple and natural pleasures which are appropriate to the family and the home. Neither does it apply to the enjoyment derived from the contemplation of the beauties of nature, from the practice of the arts, or the pursuits of science. Nor does it embrace, in any sense, the higher and purer delight derived from acts of benevolence and charity, the duties of the patriot, the success of noble plans of enterprise, or the self-denying labors of piety and virtue. Distinct from all of these, social enjoyment signifies precisely the enjoyment of society; which seeks pleasure in the kind of intercourse so well understood by the term *society*, and is therefore dependent on the co-operation of those who form the little world of each individual.

The clearest method which I can pursue in the discussion of my subject, will probably be to consider, first, those kinds of social pleasure which are consistent and useful, and then pass on to those which are dangerous and objectionable.

1. Ordinary visiting may be taken as the lowest degree in the scale of social enjoyment, because it necessarily

precedes the rest, until we come to the special topic of public amusements; and it devolves chiefly on the females, as the men, for the most part, are too busy to keep it up with systematic regularity. In itself, there is certainly nothing to be censured in this universal custom. On the contrary, it affords an opportunity of great usefulness. Suppose the visitor to find the party at home, to enter with cordial kindness into the various matters which concern her feelings and her interests, and to carry on the conversation with a sincere desire to make it not only agreeable, but serviceable to the good resolutions and principles of both; and it is manifest that a visit like this would be not simply a social enjoyment, but a mutual benefit. At such a time, the heart of a wise and benevolent female may often find occasions for deep and genuine sympathy. She will hear many an affecting relation of family griefs and trials—many a secret confession of doubts and ignorance of duty—many a revelation of inward suffering, under an outward appearance of comfort and of ease. And she may confer an inestimable benefit by her kind encouragement and prudent counsel, if she have enough of gentle tact and experience to improve the opportunity. In such an aspect of the matter, visiting becomes an arrangement of peculiar value, since it gives access to the practical influence of goodness and of virtue.

But there is another side to the picture. Visiting may be an excuse for leaving neglected the paramount claims of home and children. The visitor may go from house to house, merely to kill the time, to spread the idle gossip of scandal, to indulge her censorious temper on absent persons, to pry into the concerns of other families, or at best to discuss the fashions, prattle about the weather, and interrupt her neighbor's occupations with so little discretion, that it is a positive relief to see her rise and go away. Yet even so, the visit may not be quite useless. The display of faults frequently teaches by way of contrast. The party visited may learn a lesson of caution, that she do not commit the same errors herself which she has found so disagreeable in another. Or if she be of a superior character, she may find occasion to rectify her visitor's notions, by some judicious and kind suggestions or advice. At all events, the visit helps to keep up that friendly intercourse, which, if it do no good now, may be the means of good hereafter. And therefore, although this ordinary visiting is liable, like every thing else, to great abuse, yet it deserves a reasonable encouragement, as a valuable social institution.

Some general rules, however, may be laid down upon the subject, to which the American citizen may perhaps find it not altogether unprofitable to direct his wife's attention.

1. She should never suffer her visiting to interfere with her domestic duties, because the care of her family and home stands before all other social obligations. To manage the matter systematically, she may keep a book with the names of her friends arranged either alphabetically, or according to the places of their residence. And then, by subdividing them into weekly portions, and marking the time, she may readily dispose of the whole ; without falling into arrears and being thought neglectful on the one hand, or interfering with the order of her family upon the other.

2. She should always set out on her visits with a desire to do whatever good she can, by seeking useful information from those who are older and wiser than herself, by imparting it to those who have less knowledge, and by showing to

all an amiable, unassuming, discreet, and cordial disposition.

3. She should be careful not to make her calls too long. When conversation flags, it is usually time to be going. Far better is it that the parties should desire to have more of her society, than that they should find her visits tiresome and fatiguing. Of course, however, the application of this rule will depend entirely on circumstances. It is usually good in the case of mere *acquaintances*, but not always proper with those who are really *friends.*

4. She should guard most diligently against the feminine habit of exaggeration, and always speak the exact truth. Nothing, in time, will so insure the perfect confidence of those who know her. Never should she talk of the absent in any terms, except those which she is willing to have them hear. And in all matters where others are concerned, she should be careful to judge charitably, and put upon their motives and their conduct the best construction; or else not speak of them at all except in confidence to her husband.

5. And lastly, she should always return to her home, in due season, and not run the risk of wasting his time and putting him out of humor, by finding his house out of sorts and his meals delayed, without knowing why or wherefore. It is true, indeed, that a wise and kindly tempered man will take such trials patiently; but it is also true that he will be very apt to think lightly of his wife's affection and consideration for his comfort. And she will hardly be excusable if she gives him any needless cause for an impression like this.

These rules may suffice for the general course of the visitor. I have said nothing of those occasions where the visit is of a higher character, either paid to "the widow or the orphans in their affliction," or designed for the succor of the sick or the poor. For these belong to the sacred sphere of religion and benevolence, and I take it for granted that every true woman's heart will sympathize with the objects of pity and compassion. My present topic belongs to the inferior circle of ordinary social intercourse, in which mistakes are much more likely to occur. The female who knows how to pay such visits wisely and well, can never be deficient in the other. Nor can she fail, in due time, to be respected and beloved, as a treasure in the community.

The next branch of social life which comes to be considered, is the dinner or the evening party. This is a duty to society which men are usually expected to pay, when it accords with their means and their position; and the mode in which they discharge it has great influence on the general estimation of their associates. For it is a well-known fact, that there is no way so open to the favor of the majority as the way of feasting. The most enlightened class in the nation—even senators and representatives in Congress—are said to be more accessible through this channel than any other; and those *lobby members*, as they are called, who go to the seat of government with some special object to accomplish, are usually supposed to place far less reliance on facts and arguments, than on good dinners and champagne.

It would doubtless be interesting, and perhaps useful, if I could precisely state the *rationale* of this influence. But this is no easy matter. I am by no means satisfied that it can be explained by the near neighborhood of the stomach to the heart. Still less would I account for it by supposing that the brain of senatorial wisdom can be so affected by wine or other stimulants, at night, as to govern the legislative judgment of the parties in the morning. I rather incline to the opinion that the remarkable result is to be attributed to the excitement of the social principle in human nature, of which the feast is not so much the *cause* as the *occasion.* For suppose the entertainer to prepare the most luxurious table and the richest liquors that ever tempted the appetite of an epicure, while he receives his guests with a cold and repulsive air. Would he succeed in inspiring the slightest cordial feeling? Assuredly not. His stiff and chilling manners would deprive the banquet of all its genial influence, and the labor and expense would be entirely thrown away. This, as it seems to me, relieves our legislators of the gross imputation, that the attractiveness of the feast consists in the mere gratification of the appetites. On the contrary, it is the beaming smile of welcome, the warmth of friendly attention, the animating power of sympathy, which bind the chain of fraternity around the feelings, and make it hard to disappoint the wishes of the man who has shown his solicitude to make them happy, though it were but for an evening. With these social qualities, a very moderate entertainment will suffice. Without them, the most costly would lose all its genial pleasure.

The most plausible theory of this familiar fact which I can frame, may therefore be thus stated. Men are created for society, and social sympathy is a law of nature which the divine benevolence has implanted, in order to draw them together in the bonds of kind fraternity. And the advantages of the feast lie in this: that they meet under the most favorable circumstances for the operation of this law; because there are fewer obstacles to counteract it, when the sole object of their meeting is to enjoy each other's company. It is true, indeed, that they come together perpetually at other times, yet never in the same way. On the commercial exchange they assemble to bargain and make money, and the social principle is mastered by the love of gain. In the army they come together, under rules of discipline even in times of peace, and, in time of war, to battle with the enemy. In the courts of justice they come together, to settle the rights of opposing litigants. In the hall of legislation they come together, to contend for party supremacy. In theatres they come together, to enjoy the music and the play. In Church they come together, to listen to the preacher. Even in the gay assemblage of the ball-room, they come together under the restraints of etiquette and the formalities of artificial decorum. In all of these, therefore, the social sympathies are fettered and kept down, by more or less of opposing obstacles. It is only at the feast that they can be regarded as free from every counteracting influence, since they come together there to "eat, drink, and be merry." Hence there is nothing now to hinder the genial force of the social law. Their entertainer invites them all as friends, and as friends they accept the invitation. His ostensible object is to make them as happy as he can for a few hours; and nature responds to his kindness, by the spontaneous warmth of social sympathy. The feast itself only serves as an agreeable accompaniment to the same social element, which rises to the ascendant in words and looks of kindliness, in the harmless jest, the lively sally, and the laugh of good humor. All cares, troubles, and contests are laid aside and forgotten for a season. And they part, through the unchecked operation of natural hilarity, with an increase of friendly feeling towards each other; and especially towards their host, who has spent so cheerfully his money and his time, to procure for them this pleasant gratification.

This giving of parties, therefore, may be regarded as the most effective mode of bringing the social sympathies into exercise; and it is currently accepted as a branch of that hospitality which has always been honored as a virtue amongst mankind. The principles of Christianity do not condemn, but rather encourage it. All great occasions of gratulation in the Old Testament were marked with a feast. Abraham made a feast, when Isaac was weaned. Jacob made a feast, on his reconciliation with Laban. The men of Israel were commanded to assemble at a public feast, three times in every year. Our Lord represents the rejoicing father as marking the return of the prodigal son with a feast, followed with music and dancing. And in the Church, the old feast of the Passover was succeeded by the feast of love—the Eucharist. It would be happy for the world if every other part of its ordinary practice were as easily justified by the word of God as this, so far as the mere allowance of feasting is concerned. The error does not lie in that; but in so conducting the feast as to separate it from all religious principle, and making it an occasion for the enjoyment of the lower bodily and social sympathies, without any regard to Him who is the divine Giver of these, as well as of every other blessing.

Let me proceed, however, to state the rules which properly belong to this branch of social life, with a view to consistency, propriety, and useful influence, on the part of the American citizen.

1. In the first place, then, the circumstances and position of the individual should be carefully considered. For, the majority of men are not able to give parties, in the ordinary sense of the phrase; although there are very few who cannot dispense, to some extent, the simpler duties of hospitality,

in which the acquaintance, the friend, or even the stranger is made welcome, without show or special preparation, to the daily board; and thus treated for the time as one of the family. It is this, in my humble judgment, which is presented to us as a Christian duty. We are told by the apostle to use hospitality one towards another, "without grudging." "Be not forgetful," saith he elsewhere, "to entertain strangers, for by so doing, some have entertained angels unawares." Beyond this we are not required, as a general rule, to go. The giving of parties, therefore, is not so much a Christian as a *social* duty, and must be regulated by the position of the individual, on the social scale. Hence it is altogether essential that his friends consider him *able to afford it;* since, if they have any doubts on that point, he will be much more likely to attract censure for his pretension and extravagance, than praise for his generous profusion.

2. Secondly, he must be careful to conduct the occasion so as to show that his design is to promote the pleasure of his guests, and by no means to make an ostentatious display of his own wealth or importance. It was a saying of the ancients, that a private feast should not consist of less than the number of the Graces, nor of more than the number of the Muses. And the modern dinner-party is considered full, when twelve persons sit down to table; so that a thirteenth is even absurdly regarded by some as "unlucky." The evening party, of course, admits of a larger company, because refreshments are partaken without fixed order, and they are not expected to gather at once around the same board. But the rule of common sense in both cases is the same,—that the main object of the occasion should be to promote the enjoyment of true social intercourse, which is

hardly possible in a crowd. And therefore the guests should never be so numerous as to incommode each other, or hinder the genial sympathy of friendly converse, by the positive annoyances of heat, noise, and confusion.

Nevertheless, though I am no admirer of large evening parties, I am far from condemning them as entirely useless for all social purposes. They doubtless possess the recommendation of enabling the opulent to gratify the whole list of their acquaintances by one grand display; while they keep the smaller and more select occasions for their special friends, or for strangers to whom they desire to pay particular attention. Those splendid *routs*, as they have been aptly called, are also attractive to many who love noise and confusion, if they be attended by lively excitement and gayety; because their object is not "the feast of reason and the flow of soul," but the feast of fun, and the flow of fashionable folly. Hence they are popular amongst the wealthier classes; and doubtless will continue so, notwithstanding their poor adaptation to all intercourse which is truly rational and refined.

3. But to return to those select parties which are limited to a small number, I would next enter a protest against our American custom of excluding females from the dinner table, and confining it to men alone. Our English friends have set us a better example, and one which we should do well to follow. No truly social enjoyment should be regarded as attainable without the presence of that sex, which forms the purest and the safest element in all society. The restraints which it may impose are good and salutary, especially to those who are most ready to complain of them. The subject of politics, or other matters in which females cannot feel an interest, may be taken up when they retire. And with regard to the rest, it should be remembered that

the jest or the story which is not fit for the ear of woman, must be still less fit for the ear of God, and had far better remain unspoken.

4. The fourth rule which I would recommend respects the feast itself, which is often a matter of considerable trouble and solicitude, in order that it may be as choice and delicate as possible. But I hold this to be a great mistake. The best maxim is to be content with respectability and moderation. The fare should be abundant and good enough to need no apology. And it ought not to be so exquisite as to lead the guests to suppose, either that their host is an epicure himself, or that he imagines any of them to be so.

5. The selection of the company is usually a point of still greater difficulty, and really demands a large share of tact and observation. In general, persons ought not to be brought together who are known to dislike each other, who are leaders of opposite parties in politics or science, or rivals in business; because the result would probably destroy, or at least seriously diminish, the cordial harmony of the occasion. For the same reason, two professed wits ought not to be invited, nor two notorious talkers, nor two remarkable beauties or musicians, nor two eminent authors, unless they be men of good common sense and amiable dispositions. The safer rule, for the most part, is either to select the guests from different walks in society—but all possessing a fair average of urbanity and intelligence,—or else to take the opposite course, by having a considerable number from the same. In either case, the danger of rivalry is avoided, which is the greatest bane of social enjoyment. By the first plan, there will be no two of the same class, and thus the risk is shunned. And by the second, there will be so many of the same class that rivalry is impossible.

Such rules, however, are seldom of much use, because these parties usually consist, mainly, of those who are familiarly known to their host and to each other. Their social qualities, therefore, are already ascertained, apart from their particular class in the community; and these qualities form the best guide in the selection. Yet it is always difficult to calculate, beforehand, upon the result. It is by no means common even for wise and good men to hit the precise point, between talking too much in company, and talking too little. Nor is it easy at all times to argue with pleasantry, and to take opposition with good humor,—to be frank without offence, and courteous without servility. And it is often a task of rare tact and delicacy for the entertainer to exert such a friendly guardianship over his guests, that the conversation shall flow on in a cheerful and lively strain;—and never sink into dulness on the one hand, nor rise into dispute and altercation on the other.

The great barons in old time had a resource in this respect, which doubtless aided to keep their feasts in tolerable order. Each one had his jester or his fool who made the guests laugh, and his minstrel who sang to the harp the adventures of romance and heroism. The ancient Greeks did still better, by making it a part of every liberal education to accompany the voice upon the lyre. And at their banquets, the instrument was handed from one guest to another; and each, in his turn, was expected to do his share, in this pleasing and social way, for the entertainment of the company. In Europe, at the present day, vocal music is much more cultivated than with us; and it is not uncommon to fill up the pauses in the feast by singing. And here, every one who is in the habit of giving dinners knows how convenient a resource it is, when he can have some ready individual amongst his guests, to enliven the rest with a pleasant ballad, or with amusing anecdotes. The scarcity of these accomplishments, however, is such, that the man who is thus gifted is very apt to find his notoriety lead him into danger. He dines out so often, in accommodation to his supposed friends, that his business is neglected, his habits injured, his home forsaken, and his health and character destroyed. And those *friends* who only cared for his social talents, will usually abandon him to misery and starvation in the end, with this cheap tribute of sympathy: "Poor fellow! I remember him well. He used to sing an excellent song, and tell a capital story!"

In all these varieties of social enjoyment, nevertheless, though lawful and even useful in themselves, there is no small need of caution. As an occasional indulgence, to be taken in safe and good society, and never carried beyond the limits of prudent moderation, such parties are not only innocent, but are capable of yielding an acceptable service to the individual man, and to the general interests of the community. But when they interfere, as they are very apt to do, with the regularity and comfort of home, with the happiness of the wife and children, with the claims of business, with the maxims of contentment, with the habits of strict temperance, and the preservation of health, there is nothing of which the American citizen has greater reason to beware, lest they beguile him to destruction. The path is so gentle in its declivity, so easy to tread, and so covered with flowers, that he goes on without suspicion of the abyss to which it leads him. At first, he is only a partaker of a pleasant and harmless indulgence. In the end, he may find himself a confirmed lover of dissipation. Alas! it would be hard to estimate the multitude of unhappy victims, in our cities especially, who have thus blasted all their cherished hopes in life; and, from being once respected and beloved, have become things "for scorn to point its slow unmoving finger at." Doubtless there are many individuals, of ample means and of high virtue and intelligence, who dispense a noble hospitality without ever descending from their elevated position, or sullying their own pure example with a single moral stain. And the Christian philanthropist may look at such as these, presiding over the generous feast of social enjoyment, not only with allowance, but with cordial admiration. But after all, he is the wisest and the happiest man, who, while he surveys the ordinary amusements of the community in a kindly spirit, and without the slightest feeling of sour censoriousness, yet, for himself, desires no recreation separate from his family, seeks all his delights in the path of usefulness and duty, and cares little for any atmosphere of pleasure except what he finds within the circle of his home.

CHAPTER XXX.

ON OTHER FORMS OF SOCIAL LIFE.

Next to visiting, and dinner or evening parties, the musical soirée, the conversation party, the exhibition of tableaux, the ball or dancing-party, and the card-party, present their claims for consideration, as established parts of our modern system of social enjoyment. The American citizen may learn little or nothing from me on any of these subjects; but it will do him no harm to read a few remarks upon them all, which may possibly aid him in forming his own opinions.

1. With respect to the first, viz. the *musical soirée*, I regard it as one of the most innocent, safe, and pleasing modes of passing a social evening; provided, always, that the music selected be of a proper character, and free from every unchristian or immoral tendency. Instrumental music, of course, is clear of all exception on this score. But vocal music is often taken from the Opera, and is frequently connected with words which no modest and Christian tongue would choose to utter. These words, indeed, are usually in Italian, and are regarded as of no importance. Even in the case of English songs, many are heard to say that the music is all, and that the words are nothing. I confess myself quite unable, however, to understand the meaning of this assertion. Words are *things*, and things of the greatest importance, because they are the medium of thought, and principle, and action. The rule of Scripture is strong, and not to be evaded: "By thy words thou shalt be justified, and by thy words thou shalt be condemned." "For every idle word that men shall speak, they shall give an account thereof in the day of judgment." Hence the impossibility of Christians singing, with good conscience, words which their conscience cannot approve. And, therefore, in order that the musical soirée may be really unobjectionable, and even improving, I should be obliged to require, that the words which accompany the melody be fitted to the lips of the performer. There are songs enough which are pure in sentiment, if the singers will take a little pains in looking for them.

2. The next variety is the *conversation party*, which is fairly entitled to all reasonable encouragement, since it seems quite exempt from every risk of abuse or dissipation. As introduced by the eminent Dr. Wistar in Philadelphia,

nearly half a century ago, it was confined to men, without any admixture of females; and no refreshment was admitted, except lemonade or sugar-water. It has since been modified, however, in this respect, by the addition of an informal supper; but remains, otherwise, as before. For myself, I must say that I doubt the wisdom of excluding the gentler sex from this or any other social enjoyment. Their conversational powers, when properly cultivated, are at least equal to those of men; and their presence, with due regard to a judicious selection, would add largely, in my humble judgment, to the interest of the occasion.

My reasons for this opinion are founded on the very design of the assembly. It is a *conversation* party, because its object is this, and nothing more. But what is conversation? It is something very different from argument, from discussion, from a pedantic show of learning, from all professional egotism, and from every obtrusion of individual vanity and self-importance, which is designed to cast others in the shade. It requires, therefore, a pleasant flow of thought and language, in which all may take a share, while no one shall be too prominent. There should be a good fund of general information as its basis; but it allows freely of harmless wit, short anecdotes, lively remarks, genial humor, elevated sentiment, literary criticism, and ingenious illustration. The main rule is that each shall talk with a friendly desire to bring out his neighbor, rather than to exhibit himself; and to promote the general cheerfulness and spirit of the company, instead of confining attention too long to any individual display. And hence, well-educated and intelligent women are often better fitted for conversation, than the correspondent class amongst the men; because they are less likely to run into discussion and argument, and are more accustomed to the *impromptu* style of thought and utterance, which are especially adapted to this unexceptionable sort of social party.

3. Very opposite to this is the third variety, which consists in the exhibition of *tableaux vivans*, or living pictures. Here, the company are invited to the spectacle of persons dressed in appropriate costumes, and assuming the attitude and expression of some scene, which the pencil of the artist, or the imagination of the poet or the novelist, may have embellished. The room chosen for the display must of course be arranged somewhat after the manner of a little theatre, having a curtain to divide the performers from the audience, which is raised when the *tableau* is ready, and dropped again in a very few minutes; lest they become too tired to sustain their respective positions, and so spoil the picture by moving. And the enjoyment is derived from the accuracy, and faithfulness to dramatic and artistic effect, with which the characters are represented.

For this very modern addition to the circle of social amusements, we are indebted to the French; and *tableaux vivans* were all the rage, as the phrase is, for a few years after their introduction. I believe they are still a favorite with sentimental young ladies, and it may seem very harsh to regard them with disapprobation. I must honestly confess, however, notwithstanding a sincere disposition to make the largest allowance for all innocent recreation, that I can see nothing in this thing to recommend, but somewhat to censure. It belongs to the same species as private theatricals. The scenes represented are, of necessity, such as would form a striking picture; and, therefore, are often of a character which it is not well to have the young imagination dwell upon, much less personate; being compounded of romantic love, revenge, or other excitement of the passions. The time devoted to the preparation of costume, to say nothing of the expense, is quite too great for the transient nature of the exhibition. The impressions left upon the thoughts of the actors are altogether unlikely to be good or salutary. And there is no conceivable improvement to be derived from it, unless it be of that sort which properly belongs to the private *studio* of the artist, or the preparations of the stage. On the whole, therefore, I cannot count this novelty among the legitimate objects of social life; although it may, doubtless, be practised by persons of great moral worth, and without the slightest consciousness of impropriety.

4. The next variety is one of a more general interest, viz.: the *ball*, or *dancing-party*, which has existed for centuries, and possesses a most extensive popularity. And it demands some reflection and care, to determine its true value; because it is not only an established favorite in social life, but even forms an important element, according to the common judgment, in the work of a finished education. In order to deal as fairly with it as I can, I shall consider, first, the arguments in its favor; next, the objections which are urged against it on the ground of health and Christian morals; and lastly, the result, as it appears to my own judgment.

1. Its propriety may first be sustained on the score of universality. The ancient Hebrews had their dances. So had the Greeks and Romans. So have the Chinese and the Turks. So have the barbarian Africans. So have our American Indians. In fine, so has every nation in the world.

2. Its lawfulness, in the eyes of Christians, may next be shown by the facts, that after the overthrow of Pharaoh and

his host in the Red Sea, Miriam, the prophetess, led the women of Israel with timbrels and dances—that king David danced before the Lord—that the Psalms command men to praise the Lord in the dance; and that the Saviour introduced music and dancing into His parable of the prodigal son, with seeming approbation.

3. Its usefulness may be demonstrated by the fact that in itself it is an innocent and healthy exercise, admirably adapted to give grace to the person, freedom to the carriage, and ease to the manners. Hence, it is rightly encouraged as an excellent branch of education, and a favorite element in the enjoyments of social life; tending to exclude scandal, and many other hurtful practices, and passing the time in harmless and becoming hilarity.

I believe that this is a fair statement of the argument in favor of dancing, and I grant that it deserves a full and candid answer.

1. With respect to the universality of the custom, there is no dispute. All nations have adopted dancing. But with the ancient Hebrews, it was a *religious act*, as I shall show under the second head of the discussion. So the old Greeks and Romans had their dances, in connection with their religion; which, as my readers know, was filled with idolatry. There was the dance of war, in honor of Mars; the dance of the Bacchantes, in honor of the god of wine, &c. Terpsichore was the muse of dancing; and hence, with them, as well as with the Hebrews, dancing was directly associated with religious worship. Doubtless this may have beeen one reason why it was held entirely inconsistent with the true faith, by the primitive Christians.

The Chinese and the Turks do not associate dancing with their religion, but allow it in the class of their dancing girls, who exhibit themselves at their feasts for money, and whose character is never of the best description. The same observation applies to the Hindoos, although there is also a religious dance retained by the dervishes, as an act of devotion. The dances of the Africans are likewise connected with their idolatry. And the men amongst our American Indians dance on certain great occasions, as in the war-dance, the dog-dance, &c. It is plain, therefore, that none of these have any bearing upon the question under discussion, since dancing, as a religious or a public exercise, is one thing, and dancing, as an element of ordinary social life, is another. The Shaking Quakers, as they are commonly called, are the only people amongst us who have a religious dance ; and no one contends that society at large should copy their example.

2. We come, then, next, to the second argument, which is intended to prove that dancing should be lawful in the eyes of Christians, because Miriam danced, and David danced, and the Psalmist commands dancing, and our Saviour introduced music and dancing into the parable of the prodigal son. But all this was the *religious dance*, of which I have already spoken. The proof that it was so is manifest from the statement of Scripture in the three first cases, because Miriam sung a noble hymn as the accompaniment of her dancing: "Sing ye to the Lord, for he hath triumphed gloriously. The horse and his rider hath he thrown into the sea." So David "danced before the Lord," in company with the priests, on the solemn occasion of bringing the ark to Jerusalem. So the Psalmist saith, "Praise the Lord in the dance." Dancing, accordingly, was the established accompaniment of pious joy and thanksgiving, amongst the ancient people of God. And therefore, when the Redeemer of the world, who was faith-

ful in all things to the Mosaic law, speaks of music and dancing in His parable, we are bound to suppose that He referred to the familiar dance of religious thanksgiving. The only instance where we find any other mentioned in the New Testament, is in the case of the daughter of the infamous Herodias, who appeared as a dancing girl at the feast of the king by her mother's orders; in the hope, as it would seem, of inducing the monarch to reward her by the death of John the Baptist. But that exhibition was evidently of the same sort which is still practised in the East, and had no relation whatever to the social dancing of our day. It is plain, therefore, that the Scriptures, fairly understood, yield no support to the advocates of the present custom; which has nothing in common with religious dancing on the one hand, nor with the dancing girls of the Eastern type upon the other.

3. The third branch of the argument in favor of our modern practice remains to be considered; and as this includes all the real strength of its claims, I shall examine it in detail.

First, it is said that dancing is an innocent and healthy exercise. And I grant, most willingly, that it is so, in itself; but I do not grant that it is more innocent and healthy than walking, running, leaping, or any other active motion of the body. We all know, however, that it is not practised for the sake of the exercise; for this exercise would be far more healthy, and certainly quite as innocent, if it were performed by daylight, in the open air. But when it is done at late hours in the night, and in heated rooms, as is the constant custom; every physician knows that it becomes the prolific parent of disease, and often brings consumption in its train, to its most lovely votaries.

Secondly, it is urged that dancing is admirably adapted to give grace to the person, freedom to the carriage, and ease to the manners. This, however, I hold to be a popular mistake. Grace to the person and freedom to the carriage are much better secured by military and gymnastic exercises for the male, and calisthenics for the female, and horsemanship for both. But to prove the error of the argument on the other side, I appeal to the well-known fact that dancing-masters—who, on the common theory, ought to be models of personal grace and noble carriage—are seldom possessed of either. As to the third supposed advantage, viz., ease of manner, I have no hesitation in saying that the ball-room is one of the worst schools for its acquirement. But here, perhaps, a definition of the phrase may be necessary. By ease of manner, I do not understand boldness or effrontery, but a certain polished self-possession, which conducts itself with courtesy and propriety in the social circle. And all experience proves that only by *long familiarity with refined society*, can this last finish of good-breeding be acquired at all. So far, indeed, as youthful modesty is to be considered an obstacle to this ease of manner, I grant that dancing-parties are well adapted to get rid of it. But I have an old-fashioned partiality for modesty in youth, especially in females. There was a time when it was reckoned among the virtues; and I doubt the benefit conferred, either on the manners or the character, by driving it altogether away.

My chief objections, however, to this fashionable accomplishment, are found in conflict with the next proposition—that dancing is rightly encouraged as a useful branch of education; since I believe, on the contrary, that it is a dangerous enemy, in the great majority of cases, to the improvement of the mind in useful knowledge, and the improvement of the heart in the principles of religion and virtue. This, I am aware, is a very grave accusation; and I hold myself bound to assign my reasons, with frankness and candor.

According to the ordinary custom at the present day, dancing begins at the age of eight or ten years, and forthwith absorbs the chief attention of the pupils; because it brings the sexes together, and draws the thoughts to dress, to vanity, and to premature notions of flirtation. It is this, in fact, which invests it with such powerful influence. And it is this which makes it the active foe of all that should occupy the mind of youth, at that delicate, sensitive, and important period. For it is a fact well known to experienced teachers, that every other study loses its interest, except in the few who are happily destitute of personal attraction. The lessons drag through their formal course, but the scholars' brains are filled with more interesting cogitations, and the efforts of the instructor are spent in vain. The improvement of the feet gains the victory over all the improvement of the head. The practising ball inspires far more zeal than the day of examination. And that most unwise and mischievous indulgence called the *children's party*, concentrates all the solicitude of those young hearts, in feelings of rival vanity and feverish impatience, which are not only entirely unsuited to their age, but perfectly hostile to the real work of education. The result too often is, that the dancing-school co-operates with all other causes to make our boys and girls fancy themselves men and women before the time—that the love of personal display is so prominent a fault amongst our females—that the passions, excited prematurely, suffer a premature decay—that dissipation, commenced in childhood, stunts the growth of mind and body—

and that the later years of life are made to pay a fearful penalty for the folly which thus sacrifices, to the phantom of juvenile enjoyment, the true interests of health, prudence, and utility.

I do not by any means suppose, however, that these results are always found to follow; because, happily, other influences may interpose to give a better direction to the character. Many of our youth, of both sexes, become soon weary of the dancing-school, when they find themselves eclipsed by others. Many are withheld from the dissipation to which it leads, through the want of means to support the heavy tax imposed by a frequent indulgence in its pleasures. Many meet with a wholesome mortification in the outset, which gives them a disgust towards the whole of its fascination. But I have rarely known a zealous and constant devotion to this accomplishment, which did not seem to injure, more or less, the constitution both of the body and the mind. And I have met with no superior dancers, of either sex, who became at all distinguished for intelligence or virtue, until the ball-room had lost its charms, and, in the expressive phrase of the world, "their dancing days were over."

It is not possible to form a correct judgment on this question, therefore, by looking merely at dancing itself, as a simple bodily exercise. We must take it as it is presented by the ordinary customs of society, in connection with its vanity of personal display, with its extravagant love of dress, with its premature aping of men and women, with its youthful flirtation, with its attendant dislike of sober industry and improvement, with its late and unwholesome hours, with its waste of time and thought, and with its strong tendency to dissipation. These are the appendages which constitute, at once, its attractions and its danger, considered as a branch of education. Its value as a social enjoyment in the ball or dancing-party of mature life, whatever it may be, is quite too dearly purchased by the risks of its attainment. And its incongruity with the fundamental principle of Christian morals fully justifies its ordinary exclusion from the pale of religious sympathy.

This branch of the question is easily understood, when we remember that the first and great rule of Christian morality is to follow Christ, as the high and perfect model of social life and duty. But who can associate the following of Christ with the dancing-party or the ball-room? Who can reconcile the appropriate style of dress with the apostle's precept, that women should be "soberly apparelled?" Who would be willing to see even an ordinary minister of the Gospel take his place in the dance, notwithstanding there may be some who fancy it all right enough in his family?

But it may be said that such reasoning proves too much. There is a difference universally acknowledged between the clergy and the laity, so that many things are allowed in the one which would be totally inadmissible in the other. To this, however, I answer, Not so, in the moral principle of the Gospel, which makes Christ the example of us all. That principle is enjoined in Scripture on the people as well as on the ministry. "Be ye followers of me," saith St. Paul, "as I also am of Christ." And it is the familiar ground set forth in the Baptismal Office for Children, in the Church of England and in the Protestant Episcopal Church of the United States, that "Baptism representeth unto us our profession, which is to *follow Christ and be made like unto Him;* that as He died and rose again for us, so *we who are baptized* should die unto sin and rise again unto righteousness, continually mortifying all our evil and corrupt affections, and daily proceeding in all virtue and godliness of living." Here the rule that we must *follow Christ and be made like unto Him*, is plainly laid down, not for the ministry, but for *all who are baptized in infancy, without exception.* The parents and sponsors are bound to train up the child so that he shall "renounce the vain pomp and glory of the world," of which the favorite pleasures of the world certainly form an important part. They are also bound to "teach him all things necessary to his soul's health," that he may lead "a godly and a Christian life;" and assuredly, there is nothing stronger than this in the moral duty of the clergy. For although it is their office not only to preach the Gospel and to administer the sacraments, but also to set a good example to their people, as leaders in the path to heaven, yet the path itself is the same to all; and it is manifestly absurd to expect the minister to *lead*, if the flock be under no obligation to *follow.*

The Church of Rome, indeed, for many ages, has patronized this popular though perfectly baseless distinction, between the priests, the monks, and nuns on the one side, and the laity on the other. And therefore, within her pale, there is no inconsistency whatever between the unrestrained enjoyment of worldly pleasure, and the character of a regular communicant, so far as laymen or women are concerned. In justice to her accommodating system, however, it ought to be remembered, that she has invented a Purgatory, in which satisfaction must be rendered for the earthly punishment of sin by years and even centuries of fiery torment, unless the friends of the departed soul can shorten the term, by the purchase of masses or indulgences. It is strange enough to see the course which many Protestants adopt, in relation to this subject. On the one hand, they approve the Roman system, which allows the people to enjoy the largest license in worldly pleasure. On the other hand, they condemn the notion of Purgatory, and the costly superstition of masses and indulgences for the dead, on the just ground that the Scriptures give no warrant to support the doctrine. But they do not pause to consider that they are bound to take the Scriptures as their guide on both parts of the question. The Bible is full, express, and positive against Rome on the first point, while it is chiefly negative on the second. And hence they are chargeable with the grossest kind of inconsistency, since they play fast and loose with the only authority which they profess to venerate; take Rome against the Scriptures for the sake of worldly pleasure; take the Scriptures against Rome in order to get rid of Purgatory, and thus live on as if there were no real standard of duty, content if they can follow the fashion and please themselves, without any fear of the final consequences.

The only remaining argument which is sometimes heard in defence of the dancing-party is, that it tends to exclude scandal, and enables the parties concerned to pass the time in harmless hilarity. To this I would simply reply by denying the fact. Dancing can only be said to exclude scandal, so far as it checks the license of the tongue during the time when the feet are busy. But there is abundant opportunity for talking, during the intervals of each measure; and if there be no scandal spoken in those intervals at the present day, the lovers of dancing must have become marvellously improved since I was one of them. On the contrary, I am persuaded that the ball-room produces a large amount of the rivalry, envy, dislike, and ridicule, in which scandal finds its most powerful stimulus. The appearance and deportment of each individual are sure to be inspected with the sharpest scrutiny, and the most unsparing criticism. And therefore I am confident that he who expects to find the spirit of kind allowance and charity displayed in the dancing-party, will find himself egregiously disappointed, if he will only submit the question to experience and observation.

Hence I am obliged to conclude, on the whole, that the hilarity of the ball-room cannot be truly harmless, because it stands associated, of necessity, with all the evils which I have enumerated. In the period of youthful education I have shown that dancing is chargeable with the waste of time, the interruption to useful study, the indulgence of personal vanity and display, and the premature incitement of the passions. At the age of maturity, it adds to these no small danger to health, by late hours, flimsy dress, heated rooms, and exposed persons: while its incongruity with strict Christian sobriety and principle, and its tendency to the love of dissipation, are so manifest, that no ingenuity can make it consistent with the covenant of Baptism. It would give me sincere pleasure to have expressed a very different opinion, because I am well aware that few of my readers will relish my unaccommodating sentiments on such a theme. But candor and honesty forbid, and I may not sacrifice what I believe to be the truth, in the service of worldly expediency.

The last subject which belongs to the list of private social enjoyments, is the *card-party;* and this will also need a full discussion, because, to do it justice, I must consider the principle which ought to govern the judgment, with respect to games in general.

A game may be largely defined as an artificial contrivance, devised with more or less ingenuity, in order to pass away the time agreeably, where the parties are so circumstanced, by the rules laid down, that the success of one must be attended by the failure or defeat of the other. The idea of *contest*, therefore, is inseparable from every game, properly so called. And hence it may be doubted whether any game is in true harmony with the morals of Christianity. For these command us to be followers of Christ, to love our neighbor as ourselves, and in honor to prefer one another. Contention for a personal victory, therefore, seems quite inconsistent with the true spirit of the Gospel, because we are not authorized, without necessity, to derive our pleasure from that which gives another pain.

But this, to most men, would be a rule of great severity. What are we to do with the innocent and healthy games of children? What with the athletic sports of youth? What with the favorite pastimes of manhood? What with the solace of old age? If all games are to be excluded, the whole theory of lawful amusement must become changed, and the world must be deprived of the most agreeable and harmless resources of society.

Such, I take for granted, would be the general and indignant remonstrance against so sweeping a principle. And yet, there is nothing in the Christian rule which militates against human happiness, since there are thousands who are ready to testify that they are happier without games than they ever were with them. For after all, these games are only a *pastime*, at the best. And if we would accustom ourselves to *pass our time* in a more interesting as well as useful manner, the introduction of a game would be no addition to our enjoyment, but the contrary.

And this, I assert, on my own experience, aided and confirmed by many years of observation. I have known some who were brought up in the usual mode of the world, adepts in all the ordinary games of society, and practising them to the age of manhood, when they cast the whole away in compliance with the strictest rule of Christian consistency. But they could not find, when they looked back upon their youthful days, that their games had ever given them any happiness. They were occasions of excitement, doubtless, to the animal spirits. They were sometimes followed by a certain pleasure in victory. But they were just as likely to be attended by the mortification of defeat, and there was no real enjoyment in the strenuous energies of contest. On the other hand, they had consumed a vast amount of time, which could not be recalled. These games had often interfered with the duty of improvement. They had sometimes brought them into evil company. And in no instance, that they could remember, had they done them any good. They had frequently seen these games give rise to quarrels, to bad tempers, to swearing, and profanity. They had known them convert friends into enemies, but had never found that they converted an enemy into a friend. They had witnessed their influence in degrading many a promising character, but had never met with an instance where they strengthened the principles of virtue, honor, or integrity. And therefore they were perfectly convinced that they had gained much and lost nothing of true enjoyment, in laying them aside; and contenting themselves, through the rest of their lives, with the safe social pleasures of rational visits, music, and conversation.

Those persons, however, spake only of *games*, and not of *gambling*, which is a most serious aggravation of the evil. From this, they had always abstained, and therefore their experience bore only on the best form which belongs to the subject. And I shall confine my own remarks to this, because gambling can never be fairly considered in the light of a social enjoyment; but is generally condemned as a most perilous and destructive abuse, by those who maintain the propriety of games, conducted for amusement only.

With respect to the necessity of allowing the usual games in the education of children, I am perfectly aware that almost all the world consider them quite indispensable. But I have known one example where a large family, consisting chiefly of boys, were educated without the knowledge of a single game; and the result was that they were the happiest, the healthiest, the best improved, the most energetic, and the most industrious, on the whole, that it was ever my lot to meet with. Here was a practical demonstration that there is no real need of games, even in that period of life when most men suppose it impossible to live without them.

Nor was there any mystery in this. The principle was laid down in that family that every employment should be connected, as far as possible, with the improvement of time; and that no portion of life should be willingly wasted in such a way, that they could not give, to their heavenly Judge, a good account of it. In-doors, therefore, the leisure hours, in the intervals of study, were occupied with amusing and yet instructive books, pictures, music, drawing, and the use of tools. The out-door recreations were varied, according to circumstances, with gardening, boating, fishing, excursions to collect plants and minerals, and swimming, in the summer;—in winter, skating, sliding, coasting with the sled, making snow-houses, and experiments in chemistry, optics, and electricity. In this way, there was no want of useful and agreeable occupation, and the whole system of games was entirely unnecessary. But the end was a far greater variety of serviceable knowledge, a much better practical habit of industry, a truer estimation of the value of time, and a more constant sense of the great principle that happiness can only be secured in connection with duty and utility.

In the progress of this peculiar system, however, one game was introduced, and one only. The eldest son, having finished his collegiate course, went abroad, and there learned the game of chess,—the philosopher's game, as it has been called, for distinction. His health became impaired, and he returned to his home, bringing his chessmen with him. His father had learned the game in his youth; and in order to help the invalid to pass his wearisome hours, he took it up again, after a cessation of nearly thirty years, and permitted the younger members of the family to acquire it. He thought it well, from that time, to consider this game as an exception; on the ground of its remarkable adaptation to the improvement of the reasoning powers, in which it stands alone and unlike any other. It is true, however, that it involved the principle of contest, which rendered it obnoxious to the law of Christian love. But this he endeavored to obviate, by teaching his children that they should conduct the game in a proper spirit; and should rebuke themselves when they found that they were either elated by victory, or mortified by defeat. After a while, they all learned not merely to play it with considerable skill, but to do it with an amiable temper; bearing the triumphs of their adversary in patient good humor, and gaining their own without any manifestation of self-complacency. And thus the game was converted into a sort of moral test, as well as a means of intellectual culture.

I do not say that he was altogether consistent in this, although I incline to the opinion that the game of chess really deserves to be adopted as a useful branch of education. The tract of Dr. Franklin, called "The Morals of Chess," presents a very just argument in its favor. And it certainly stands on peculiar ground, being quiet, retired, and thoughtful in its tendency, taxing the understanding by the closest calculation, and never leading to the objectionable consequences which may be justly charged on almost every other. So different, indeed, is its character, that it is extensively patronized by religious and philosophical men, who reject all the rest. It is never played for money. It is not capable of being pressed into the service of the social company, because it needs abstraction and silence. It is entirely a game of skill, and chance has no part in it. Its arrangement affords an ingenious analogy to human life and government. Such is the intellectual interest attached to it that many books have been written on this single subject. And it is the only game in which an eminent degree of ability confers a large amount of respect and consideration.

With these remarks on the general subject of games, I proceed to the special topic of the card-party. And here, the objections lie not only against the principle involved in the thing itself, but against the fact that this is a game of chance, at which men rarely play without betting money; and thus it becomes the direct road to the habit which leads thousands into ruin. It is a grave question how far we are at liberty to place our pleasure in any practice, which puts temptation in the way of others. On the ground of strict morality, this can hardly be justified, unless by the argument of some reasonable necessity, or serious advantage to ourselves. But no form of mere social amusement can amount to necessity or serious advantage. And hence, the card-party is generally chargeable with a certain breach of manifest obligation, in which not only the immediate parties, but their families, their friends, their domestics, and the community at large, are directly interested.

With respect to the parties themselves, I am willing to suppose that the stakes for which they play are very small; only enough, as they usually say, to give interest to the game, and never more than they can afford to lose, without any inconvenience. But this excuse cannot change the principle. In the first place, it is an acknowledgment that the game itself has not interest enough to amuse them, unless some money be involved with the occupation. In the next place, it is an acknowledgment that the winning of this money gives pleasure on the one side, and of course gives at least as much pain to the losers on the other. In the third place, no man can certainly know whether the losing party, if he has what is termed "a run of ill-luck," can really afford it. But mainly, the whole thing is an introduction to the habit of gaming, which every one admits to be the road to destruction.

For when our youth are thus led to sanction and approve the excitement of playing for a *little* money, by the established fashions of society, who can protect them from the temptation to play for a *little more?* It is but a question of degrees, and they are started upon an inclined plane, on which there is no fixed stopping-place. Once accustomed to the most prudent kind of card-party, they are likely to play on every other opportunity, as the readiest contrivance for passing the time. The stakes become higher. The debts incurred are "debts of honor," because they cannot be enforced by law. By and by, they are led to those horrible places of brilliant abomination, which are set up in all our cities for the sole purpose of gambling; and which even the world itself calls "hells," on account of the iniquity and misery with which they stand associated. The wretched hope of retrieving their losses by some "lucky hit," lures them on, till their own funds are exhausted. Then they are tempted to raise money, by embezzlement or forgery; but still in the expectation that fortune will favor them, and they can make it all right at last. Until finally, they are betrayed into infamy, their whole prospect for life is blasted without redress, and the hearts of their friends and families are wrung with grief and anguish, at the dreadful consummation. Such, in the case of thousands, is the melancholy end of the course commencing at the card-party. That many excellent persons may be seen at that sort of party, who escape the fate of the gambler, and close their days in respectability and credit, is certainly true; since otherwise the fashion could not be tolerated for an hour, in good society. But that multitudes are led downwards by the temptation is equally true; and no thoughtful and conscientious man can feel satisfied with the reflection that his example may have been the instrumental cause of those habits, which seduced them to their ruin.

On the whole, therefore, I should have no hesitation in recommending to the American citizen a total abstinence from all games of chance, all games of mere contest, and especially all games which are played for money. Childhood has safe and healthy exercises enough, without those perilous amusements. Youth has sports enough, connected with the promotion of improvement either to the body or the mind. Manhood has pastimes enough, which are safe from all moral danger. Old age can occupy its social leisure far more wisely and happily, in visits, in the innocent banquet of its friends, in music and conversation, without that waste of time which places, in the path of so many, a manifest temptation. And if the principle could be laid down in early life, and steadfastly maintained, that no enjoyment should be tolerated which contradicts the rules of Christian morals, which gives pain or loss to others, or can be likely to injure either the character of individuals or the best interests of society at large, there is no question that the result would be a vast increase of security, comfort and true happiness, to every member of the community.

CHAPTER XXXI.

ON PUBLIC AMUSEMENTS.

Enough has been said, I trust, with respect to the social enjoyments which belong to the private circles of intercourse; and therefore I proceed to consider those to which the public are invited, on the mere condition that they pay a stipulated price for entrance, and conduct themselves with order and decorum. Of these there are a great variety; some good and allowable, some at least questionable, and some of a dangerous and immoral tendency. I shall present a few remarks on the several classes, according to this order.

Of those public enjoyments which are good and allowable, *lectures* on improving and scientific subjects deserve the highest place; and our United States have the credit of being the first amongst the nations to introduce them, as a general and popular institution. There are now very few places of any note throughout our country, in which the winter season is not marked by a course of these lectures. Men of distinction for intelligence and talents are invited from distant parts, to instruct and entertain mixed audiences, by their learning, their wisdom, or their wit. And, with few exceptions, the result is doubtless beneficial and satisfactory.

Another variety is presented by the *concert-room*, where the performance consists of vocal and instrumental music. To this there would seem to be no reasonable objection. It is less intellectual than the preceding, but its tendencies are usually to refine the taste and elevate the general tone of feeling; unless it be degraded to an association with words, sentiments, or exhibitions which are immoral and impure.

A third sort of allowable and useful exhibition is the *gallery of the Fine Arts*, where the best productions of painting and sculpture are displayed to the spectator. These, indeed, like music, are sometimes debased by a connection with grossness and sensuality. For the most part, however, they are calculated to increase the general interest in the beauties of nature, as in landscape scenery; in the facts of history, as when the important scenes of past times are depicted by the pencil; in the perils of vice, as when the rake's progress is delineated by the genius of Hogarth; in the honors of virtue, as when the busts and statues of the great and the good, bear testimony to the public veneration; and in the power of religious faith, as when the narratives of Scripture, the persons of the apostles, or the heroic constancy of the martyrs, are the subjects of the artist's skill. And therefore, on the whole, including the varieties of the diorama, the panorama, &c., they deserve to be encouraged as a laudable and improving resort for the community.

Collections of natural history, museums, models displaying the manners and customs of nations, antiquities, and, in a word, all that may contribute in any way to the safe enlargement of the mind and the increase of true knowledge, are of course to be approved, as useful and desirable resources to lawful curiosity. In this view, public libraries stand in the first rank; but they do not come so fairly within the scope of my present topic, because they are designed not so much for general resort, as for the spread of individual information amongst the more intellectual classes of society.

I come next to another, and exceedingly important kind of social enjoyment, which I should be glad to praise, if I could do so with truth and honesty—namely, the *theatre* and the *opera*. These may be both included in the general name of the theatre, the only difference being in the much larger proportion of the musical element which constitutes the opera, while the substantial qualities of the two are precisely the same; and in the results to the morals, the habits, and the sober interests of the community, there is scarcely any difference between them, although the one may be more aristocratic, and the other more popular. In discussing this interesting subject, however, I shall be obliged to treat it at large, and must therefore invoke my reader's patient attention.

The design of the theatre consists in the *acting of a story*, in which the performers enter, for the time, into the characters prepared by the art of the poet; and represent them, to the extent of their powers, with the likeness of reality and nature. Its attraction depends on the strong interest which all mortals take in a faithful delineation of human events and feelings, assisted by the potent aid of actual personation, together with the dress, the language, the gestures, and the scenery which are most appropriate. And hence the excitement produced in the assembled spectators must be of the liveliest kind, and make the deepest impression, when the actors perform their part with superior skill.

It would seem, however, that the *literature* of the drama is not necessarily dependent on the theatre. The plays on the Passions, written by the late Joanna Bailly, were intended to be read and not acted. In like manner, the pleasure which the scholar enjoys in the tragedies of the old Greeks, Euripides and Sophocles, or in the comedies of Aristophanes, or in the plays of that far more wonderful writer, Shakspeare, is in no respect derived from seeing them performed. On the contrary, to a mind of thorough training, the reading gives a higher pleasure than the spectacle; because it is quite impossible to command the services of a company who are all perfectly skilful in their parts, and the miserable acting of the majority offends the critical judgment, and excites disgust instead of satisfaction. Moreover, the scenery, and the paltry attempt to imitate nature in many parts of those exquisite plays, fall so far below the truth, that it is a relief to be rid of them, and left to the suggestions of the fancy.

Thus, in the Tempest, and the Midsummer Night's Dream, what can the actors do with Ariel, Oberon, and Titania? In Macbeth, how far beneath the poet's conception of the witches is the personation! In the ghosts of Richard III. and Hamlet, how inadequate, and often ludicrous, are the representations of the spectres, which appear upon the Stage! In King Lear, how utterly contemptible are the rolling of the barrels and the pyrotechnic blaze, intended to imitate a thunder-storm! And in the numerous scenes of warlike conflict, how perfectly absurd is the incongruity of the smooth boards for the battle-field, and the footlights for the open day; with the opposing combatants, fencing so carefully that they may not hurt each other, and clad in the gay habiliments which they wore in the beginning of the Play, but altogether unsuited to the time and the occasion! To the reader, however, if he has a mind capable of relishing the genius of Shakspeare, these defects are at once supplied without an effort; and there is nothing to disturb the picture presented, with such marvellous skill, to the imagination. And hence, it is easy to perceive that the literature of the drama may remain, and even be greatly augmented by future accessions to the end of time, without the slightest necessity for any attempt at theatrical display, which, in so many cases, can be little better than a mere abortion.

I am desirous to mark this distinction plainly, because I should be very reluctant to lose the higher and the better class of dramatic authors. The drama is a poem or story, thrown into a certain form, and possessing, in that form, a peculiar life and animation. In itself, it is nothing more than an extension of the dialogue, adapted to a variety of characters and a certain course of supposed events. And although I shall not undertake to prove that such a form would ever have been adopted, if there had been no Stage, yet now that it is introduced, and applied, in several instances, to compositions not intended for the theatre, it is obvious that the preservation and production of dramatic literature may be perfectly secured, without the adjunct of scenic representation. The reader will at once call to his recollection, doubtless, the Faust of Goëthe, the Wallenstein of Schiller, the Ion of Talfourd, the Festus of Mr. Bailey, and other works; which serve, as well as the Plays upon the Passions, to illustrate my meaning.

This being understood, I recur to the statement already given, viz., that the proper object of the theatre is the *personal acting of a story.* To this I will now add that the actors include not only men, but women; that the moral character of the profession is usually loose and disreputable; that the hours of exhibition are in the night; that the audience includes a regular supply of the worst class in the community; and that the habit of frequently attending the performances is too often found to lead to dissipation and licentiousness. Hence, there is nothing more dreaded than this habit, by all prudent fathers, on account of their sons, and by all careful merchants, on account of their clerks or apprentices. An occasional visit, indeed, is allowed to youth, by most persons, at rare intervals, in society with judicious friends; but an intimate acquaintance with the theatre is generally held to be one of the surest paths to ruin.

Yet the advocates of the Stage consider it as a school of virtue. It is said, very truly, that some examples have now and then been found, of actors and actresses who stood well in society, as Garrick, Mrs. Siddons, and her brother Kemble. Men of known religious principles have written for the theatre, as Dr. Johnson, the author of Irene; Addison, the writer of Cato, and other plays; and Thomson, the son of a Scotch clergyman. Even ministers of the Gospel have done the same thing, as Hoadley, the younger son of the Bishop of that name, and author of several comedies; Dr. Young, the writer of the Revenge, and Busiris; and Home, a Presbyterian divine, who wrote the tragedy of Douglas, with others. How are we to account for this striking discrepancy of sentiment and action?

I answer, Just as we account for a hundred other discrepancies in the opinions of mankind, namely, by the strong influence of custom and fashion. The world, in our day, although it is by no means partial to piety, is at least so far improved that few could now be found to justify any Christian minister in writing for the Stage, or even in being personally present at the performance of a Play. Still, however, there are many who contend that the Stage is a useful and even a moral institution. And therefore it may be proper for me to show why, in my humble judgment, it cannot justly be considered as entitled to such a character, from the very nature of the actor's occupation, and the materials out of which the drama is usually composed.

1. We have seen, repeatedly, in the progress of the present work, that morality rests upon the precepts of the Gospel. Those precepts constantly inculcate *truth* in speech and action. But the whole business of the Stage consists in the effort to play a *fictitious part*, to appear what the actor is not, and to wear an artificial mask with as much natural grace as possible. Here, in the very object of the profession, is a manifest contrariety.

It may be said, however, that, in reality, there is no contrariety to truth in the matter; since the actor neither deceives, nor intends to deceive any one. He professes to be acting a part, and nothing more; and it is precisely on the skill with which he does what he professes, that he depends for the public approbation. Clearly, then, there is no lack of truth, because there is no lack of sincerity.

This is plausible, undoubtedly; but it does not remove the difficulty. For, in order to attain the truth in speech and action, we are commanded to look to the example of Christ, and endeavor to follow that, to the utmost of our ability. He is the Truth, and we are expressly told that there can be no concord between Christ and Belial. But how can the actor be thinking of imitating this divine Guide, when he makes it his very business to be imitating the conduct, and repeating the words, of fools and villains? Not one of the various characters which he undertakes to personate is like that which his moral duty requires him to study. On the contrary, he is using his utmost efforts to present a faithful image of knaves, dupes, cut-throats, robbers, spendthrifts, misers, rebellious sons, cruel fathers, romantic lovers, jealous husbands, false friends, revengeful enemies, or something else, which is equally foreign to the principles of Christian morality. Such being his very business, it must, of necessity, occupy his thoughts, and affect his whole mental constitution. He cannot act naturally, without throwing himself, for the time, into the character which he represents, and feeling as like it as he can. And hence the result would seem to follow, that as, by the laws of association, the constant effort to imitate any *one* character would make him like it, in due time; so the constant effort to imitate many different and opposite characters would not only prevent his adopting any of them, but especially make it impossible to adopt the character of Him who was totally unlike them all, being the great model of perfect Truth, in word and action.

2. The second reason which may be assigned why the theatre cannot be a moral institution, is fairly deduced from the total antagonism of the false virtues which it inculcates, to the true virtues of the Christian character. For its object is not to instruct, but to amuse. The sober happiness of practical life, passed in the regular routine of industry, of domestic affection, of kind neighborhood, of benevolence to the poor, of public duty, and official fidelity—all resting on the basis of Christian obligation—would afford nothing to interest the curiosity, or excite the feeling of the audience. Hence, the plot of the Play must be out of the track of ordinary experience. The characters must be skilfully exaggerated. The lights and shadows must be strongly colored. The events must be romantic, or horrible, or laughable. A dash of superstition, a stroke of ingenious villainy, passionate love, reckless courage, bold stratagem, and, above all, broad humor and amusing extravagance, must be mixed together in judicious proportions, in order to make a successful Play. But where is the place for moral principle? Doubtless there is a kind of morality to be found in many of those productions, making vice to be disappointed, and virtue triumphant in the end. But the vice is usually associated with meanness; and the virtue is of that gay, wild, reckless, and worldly kind, which is always attractive to the young, the thoughtless, and the dissipated, and has the least possible connection with wisdom, meekness, or discretion. Honor and pride are put into the place of religion, as the motives to action. Fortune and fate are set forth instead of Providence. Parents are represented as sordid, cruel, and unreasonable; and so it is no sin for the daughter to deceive them, and elope. Servants take bribes to cheat their employers; but it is all right, if the lovers are

made happy. Intrigue and artifice are preferred before honest candor. Straight-forward simplicity is usually associated with the character of a fool. And if there be any reference to conscience at all, it is apt to be placed in the mouth of a hypocrite.

I do not mean to complain of this, as if I regarded it possible that the theatre might become the teacher of religion. It might be of a false religion, doubtless, because it began by representing the lies of heathenism, and after a long interval, it revived in connection with the superstitions of the dark ages. But I have already endeavored to show why it is to be considered as the enemy of religious truth. And I have added this sketch of the usual ingredients of the modern drama, to prove how little it can be esteemed as a school of real morality. Indeed, I doubt whether any man who understands the principles of Christian morals, will undertake, seriously, to prove the validity of such a claim. And hence, the practical result is in precise accordance with what might be fairly expected. The theatre has led thousands into temptation and vice, but the world has yet to learn when and where it has ever converted one wicked man to virtue. Its object is not instruction but entertainment. Its patronage depends on its power, not to reform, but to amuse society. And such is the temper of humanity, as a general rule, that the attempt to reform the Stage, by making it a school of morals, would be fatal to its popularity.

3. This natural influence of the theatre, therefore, appears in the fact, that the moral character of the profession is usually loose and disreputable. The few examples of the contrary are so rare, that they are acknowledged to be exceptions. Who expects Christian morals from an actor or

an actress? Who would not be surprised to find them at Church, or amongst the better classes of the community? What respectable family is willing to see a son or a daughter devoted to the Stage? And, notwithstanding the persevering determination of some individuals, in every age, to patronize the professors of the drama, how perfectly unavailing have their efforts been, to counteract this deep-seated and universal judgment of society! Hence, in every instance where the actor or the actress has sought for an honorable position in the community, the renunciation of their profession has been an essential prerequisite to their success. And the reason has not been because the world denied their claims to talent, genius, or wealth. Nor was it because they were thought deficient in the amiable qualities of generosity, benevolence, and natural kindliness of disposition. Neither was it because they lacked education, taste, or the power of pleasing. But it was because they were generally understood to hold in light esteem the rules of strict morality, and to be friendly towards the illicit intercourse of the sexes, libertinism, intemperance, gaming, profanity, and dissipation. And therefore the fact is indisputable, that the profession has been regarded as a degraded *caste*, to which no one can descend without a total forfeiture of his general social standing.

4. When we add to this the other circumstances to which I have alluded, the moral danger of a frequent attendance on the Stage becomes still more unquestionable. For the performances are held at night, and the theatre is not only well supplied with female actresses, but it is haunted besides by that wretched class of women, who spread their toils for the young and the inexperienced. Along with these may be seen many of their associates in iniquity, who strive to

keep up their character in the eyes of the world, while they privately indulge in the worst excesses of profligate corruption. It is all true enough, indeed, that these circumstances are not united to the Stage by any necessary connection; and I acknowledge it, willingly. The ancient Greeks and Romans did not permit women to appear as actresses, but gave the female characters to boys and eunuchs, whose face and voice were suited to the representation. Moreover, they performed their dramas altogether by daylight, as is still the custom of the Chinese, and other Eastern nations. And yet, notwithstanding their exemption from some of the attendant evils of our age, there was a certain infamy attached to the profession of an actor amongst these heathen Romans, which even the extraordinary celebrity of Roscius himself could not overcome.

Granting, however, that the introduction of female actresses, the performance of plays at night, and the special temptations arising from the arts of lewdness and systematic profligacy, were not connected with the Stage in former ages, and are not *necessarily* connected with it now; yet these things have been a part of the system, in Europe and the United States, for so long a time, that the notion of going back to the ancient custom would be regarded as absurd and impossible. And therefore we must take the matter as it is, and reckon these appendages to the theatre as forming another element of serious peril to the morality of our cities; however we may be disposed to distinguish between the Stage in theory, and the Stage in practice.

5. The last ground of objection to the theatre which I shall notice is its manifest tendency to produce an unwholesome excitement of the passions; even if we take the most favorable view of the ordinary results, without any

direct temptation to immorality. For how can its love-scenes, exhibited with the usual extravagance of romance and intrigue, fail to occupy the mind of the youthful spectator with thoughts of a corresponding character? Take, for example, the highest class of Plays—those of the pre-eminent Shakspeare—and let us reflect on the natural effect, according to the fixed principles of association and sympathy.

Thus, the lesson inculcated by that fascinating tragedy of Romeo and Juliet is manifestly hostile to all morality. The hero and the heroine proceed in the very face of filial duty. The youth, although already in love with another, becomes violently enamored of Juliet. The maiden, not quite fourteen, accepts his addresses without hesitation, under the same influence of sudden passion. She consents to a private marriage without delay, and her husband gains access to her chamber by a rope-ladder. Her father commands her to wed Count Paris, and in order to evade this, the priest suggests the contrivance of her pretended death, instead of an honest avowal of the truth. Romeo seeks her tomb, unwillingly kills the Count, who endeavored to apprehend him, and then deliberately swallows poison. Juliet awakes from her death-like trance, rejects the counsel of the friar, and stabs herself to the heart. The parents, crushed down with sorrow, deplore too late their family feud. And thus, the audience is dismissed, partly with feelings of compassion towards the pair of undutiful children, dying for love, but in absolute defiance of all moral principle; and partly with resentment against the two fathers, whose pride and mutual hatred are presented as the true causes of the whole catastrophe. What is the too probable influence of such a Play, on all the young and susceptible portion of the spectators? Is it not perfectly manifest that it must encourage them to pursue their own wild inclinations against the authority of their parents—to cast off all the wholesome duties of filial affection, confidence, and truth towards their best friends and their natural protectors —to seek the indulgence of their desires by intrigue, falsehood, and disguise—to trample under foot all regard to conscience and religion, and even to count suicide itself allowable, as a refuge from the disappointment of their inordinate and selfish passions? And can such a result be risked by any reflecting parent, for the sake of an evening's amusement, without incurring a very serious responsibility?

It is painful to pronounce such an opinion, against a performance which abounds so much in the most exquisite beauty of dramatic delineation; every character being drawn with such artistic skill, and the whole forming such an extraordinary union of natural humor, playful wit, and strong appeals to human sympathy. But in spite of the highest admiration of Shakspeare's unrivalled genius, it is impossible to justify the public representation of this Play, without a total disregard to the essential maxims of morality. To say nothing of the various allusions which are positively immodest, and therefore unfit for any youthful ear—especially of females—the conduct of the heroine is totally at war with principle. Even at the tender age of fourteen, she is capable not only of the wildest force of passion, but also of deceit, hypocrisy, and artful management, with the ready help of a "godly" friar, and her nurse. Filial disobedience is nothing—falsehood is nothing—the happiness of her parents is nothing—duty to God is nothing—the modesty and delicacy of her sex are nothing—the awful crime of suicide is nothing, when weighed in the balance with the one devouring appetite of love for a youth who has not spent, as yet, a single day in her company. Romeo, on his side, presents a fair counterpart to Juliet—equally regardless of every thing but the indulgence of his passion. And friar Lawrence, instead of using his best influence to lead them to religion and duty, lends himself to their reckless desires, and becomes a willing tool to accomplish them; as if he, too—in sympathy with those headlong appetites which he had been compelled to abjure—had forgotten all the laws of moral obligation. Yet the whole is so skilfully wrought up by the marvellous genius of the poet, that the audience are carried away by their feelings; and there is not a sentence to remind them of the lesson which might have been so easily engrafted on the tale—that the love of the sexes, when it seeks to be gratified by the violation of filial principle, honesty, and truth, is sure to lead its victims, even in this life, to misery and ruin.

That no such lesson was in the mind of Shakspeare, when he wrote this exquisite but dangerous Play, is sufficiently evident from the tendency of the far greater part of his other productions. Thus, in his famous drama of the Merchant of Venice, the sin of Jessica, in eloping from her parent Shylock, and stealing his property, to join her lover Lorenzo, is treated as if it were a meritorious act; and is even rewarded by a compulsory endowment of her father's fortune. In the tragedy of Othello, likewise, the "fair and gentle Desdemona," who is represented as a paragon of excellence, elopes with the Moor, and expresses no consciousness of her transgression against her widowed sire; although she was his only child, and he was a wealthy Senator of Venice, who had shown her all kind care and indulgence.

Neither does Othello himself regard it as a matter requiring apology, that he had "ta'en away this old man's daughter," so long as he had done it without any magical arts, and merely by the force of human affection. In many other parts of his wonderful productions, this unequalled dramatist manifests the same favor towards that passion which requires, above all others, the strong restraints of religion and morality. And yet, Shakspeare is the best established writer for the theatre, in the approbation of the wisest and most intelligent classes of society. If the Stage, in his hands, be likely to lend fuel to the passions of youth, and prostrate the peace of family government and the claims of filial duty beneath the tyranny of natural appetite, how vain must be the pretence that it is an innocent and safe resource! How much more vain the notion that it should be esteemed a school of virtue!

It may be thought, indeed, quite inconsistent with all this, to recommend, as I have done, that our highest class of dramatic literature should be preserved, although the theatre should be forsaken. The difference, however, is immense, between the limitation of these writings to books, where few, and those of the best-educated minds, would be likely to find them; and the spreading them abroad, by actors and actresses, in the most enticing forms of public display; thus bringing them continually before all ranks in the community, with every appendage of music, dress, decoration, and scenic allurement, and with no small amount of other temptations, which lie in wait for the young, the inexperienced, and the ignorant. Take away the Stage, and the literature of the drama could produce but a very trifling effect upon the moral sense of the world. The great mass of this literature would never pay the cost of publication. Those portions of it only would survive which, like the plays of Shakspeare, possess so much that is admirable and true. And the volumes thus remaining would be chiefly read by such as could make a proper use of them.

These arguments may suffice, to justify the conclusion which I am compelled to adopt, that the theatre, in all its varieties, is an unsafe resort for the American citizen, if he would guard aright the morals of his family, or his own. As a profession, it has always been, and must always be disreputable, in the judgment even of those who patronize it. As a popular amusement, its tendencies are hostile to purity, sobriety, and virtue. The real enjoyment which it affords, in its relations to the Fine Arts and to literature, can be much better secured in other ways, without its attendant dangers. And hence I have no hesitation in excluding it from the list of social recreations, which may be indulged with a prudent regard to the welfare of the individual man, and the true interests of the community.

CHAPTER XXXII.

ANALYSIS OF PRINCIPLES.

Having now gone over the series of topics proposed in the introductory chapter, it may be well to present a general summary of the objects which I have endeavored to pursue throughout the whole.

My first and leading design has been to prove, that the rights and duties of the American citizen are inseparably bound up with the moral system of Christianity, as it is laid down in the Bible. For, this is not only the religion of TRUTH, but it is also the *religion of the land;* and we cannot, for a moment, admit the possibility of any other. Hence, it is the sole foundation for the oath of allegiance, the oath of office, the oath of justice, the relations of the marriage covenant, and the whole range of social virtue; without which there can be no security for government, for law and order in the State, or for the peace, the confidence, and the welfare of private life, in the course of each individual. If religion be ignored, there is no power upon earth which appeals to the personal conscience. All these oaths sink down at once into an unmeaning form, or rather, a disgraceful mockery, which no sophistry can reconcile with manly honesty and truth. And the result is manifest, that a due and consistent reverence for Christianity stands in the highest rank of the citizen's obligations, as the indispensable guardian and protector of all his rights and duties.

My next object has been so to exhibit this principle, as to show that it was perfectly clear of any thing like a union of Church and State. For this union can never exist without an establishment of some one Church, as the Church of the whole nation; which is altogether hostile to the perfect toleration secured to every form of Christianity, known at the time when the Constitution was adopted. The American citizen, therefore, is bound to maintain the equal rights of all the Christian Churches and sects, which existed at that day, and to oppose the union of Church and State, which would give to any one a supremacy over the others; while he is also bound to maintain, in full force and vigor, that common standard of Christian principle, the Bible, to which they all appeal, although, in some respects, they differ in its interpretation.

It was my further aim to prove, that there is a plain distinction between the degrees of Christianity required for the

Church and for the State, in this: that the Church demands the conversion of the heart, while the State is satisfied with the measure of faith which binds the conscience. A true belief in what may be termed the general system of Christianity is essential to the validity of all official oaths, and all moral obligations; and hence, without that belief, no man can properly be entitled to the name of an American citizen. But this is not enough to qualify him for that higher spiritual union with Christ, which gives him a claim to the promise of salvation. I have confined myself, mainly, however, to the lower relations of the subject, throughout the whole argument; because my design was to exhibit the essential connection of religion with the government, prosperity, and order of the present life; independently of the far more sublime and important interests of the life to come. Yet, although the service of the State requires no more, it is obvious that each individual citizen owes it to consistency to follow up the convictions of his conscience, until he is led to the conversion of his heart. For, the first step should be regarded only as a preparation for the second. And as he is unable to take the oath of a citizen conscientiously, unless he believes in the certainty of the divine judgment; so he should never be satisfied to forego the complete and effectual measure of faith, by which alone he can anticipate that judgment, with full confidence in the mercy of his Redeemer.

But inasmuch as the State itself demands this first degree of intellectual Christian conviction, which binds the conscience and gives validity to the oath, and to every other moral obligation; it manifestly results that the government should employ its proper powers in securing the general knowledge and belief of the citizens to that extent, by the most effectual and extensive instrumentality, namely, public education. And therefore I have gone largely into that important subject, and suggested those improvements which seemed, in my humble judgment, best adapted to remedy the existing defects, in every department. I have shown that, in the *morals* of the Gospel, there is no difference among Christians, and that all are perfectly agreed in taking for their standard the life of Christ; that in such teaching there is no interference with the questions of doctrine, worship, and discipline, which divide the various Churches and sects throughout the land; and that, thus far, as an essential element of civic duty, the instruction of the citizens in the moral precepts of the Bible ought to be enjoined by the authority of the Legislature.

On the same principle, I have examined a large variety of topics, under the heads of politics, business, the domestic relations, and social life; so as to leave no subject altogether untouched, which is of interest to the American citizen. That all my opinions should be in harmony with those of my readers, is not to be expected. On the contrary, I am quite aware that they may often be disposed to dissent from my argument, and reject my conclusion. But at least I can aver that I have written nothing without much thought and careful examination. I have spoken with honesty and candor what I believe to be the truth, as becomes a freeman addressing the free; while I trust that I have nowhere overstepped the line of fair and frank discussion. My sole desire is to lead the minds of my fellow-citizens to that track of principle and action, which must produce the safest and the best results, for the public good and for their individual welfare. And whatever may be the amount of favor accorded to my humble work, I have the comfort of my own conviction, that its tendency can only be in favor of righteousness, patriotism, and virtue.

Before I take leave of my readers, however, I must ask their indulgence to a few suggestions on the true theory of happiness, in order to show more clearly its perfect agreement with the constitution of humanity. To these I shall only add some brief reflections on the dangers and the hopes of the republic, and thus bring the volume to its close.

CHAPTER XXXIII.

CONCLUDING OBSERVATIONS.

THAT all men seek for happiness, is a truth which is controverted by no one. It is the universal law of humanity. Every rule of duty and of interest must be reducible to this principle, and if it cannot stand the test, it may be safely rejected. But in the use of this acknowledged standard, we are compelled to take the future into view. For here lies one great distinction between the constitution of the man and of the brute—that *we* are obliged to live with reference to the future, while the *animal* cares only for the present. HOPE is therefore an essential element of human happiness; and the enjoyment which is purely sensual and content with the present, without regard to the future, is the enjoyment of the brute, and belongs only to the animal part of our nature.

It is also universally admitted that, in the present life, happiness consists much more in hope, than in possession; and hence hope is the strongest and most constant motive to action. If there be nothing to hope for, the spirit of man sinks down, either into the listlessness of stupid vacuity, or into the misery of despair. And the result is manifest, that the measure of our hope is the measure of our happiness, and the measure of our efforts. The lower our hope, the lower our happiness, and the lower our character. The higher our hope, the higher our happiness, and the higher our character. If we hope for nothing beyond the imperfect enjoyments of this world, our happiness is limited to these, and all is lost when death destroys them. But if we hope for the perfect felicity of an endless life, our happiness is exalted in proportion to our hope, and death itself is welcomed, as the period of its fruition.

We may proceed, however, a little farther, in this track of simple reason. The hope of happiness, being thus universal, as the very law of our nature, implanted by the hand of the Creator, proves that some mode must be provided by which happiness may be *certainly attained;* because we cannot suppose that God would establish such a hope in the human heart, if He had not prepared a way in which it could be fulfilled. And since all experience shows that it cannot be fulfilled in this imperfect and transitory life, it results of necessity that its attainment must be realized in the life to come.

It is on this plain and rational basis that the Gospel presents such an harmonious union between our highest duty and our highest happiness. For it is the plan established by the goodness of the Creator, through which this hope of happiness may be fully and perfectly attained. God is Love. It is His gracious will to provide for the perfect happiness of His creatures. All His laws are directed to that single end, and He commands us to obey them, not for His sake, but for our own. The living power to obey is bestowed by Himself, through faith in Christ, which is a spiritual principle. The practical model of obedience is the example of the Saviour. And just in proportion to our consistency with this, must be our hope of happiness here, and our enjoyment of happiness hereafter.

But the majority of mankind are apt to confine their hopes to the little span of mortal life, and hence their idea of happiness is delusive and untrue. Their animal spirits may be excited for the moment. The lower social sympathies may be called into active exercise. The senses and the appetites may be indulged. The ambition of fame and honor may be gratified. And they may labor for these, under the stimulus of hope, and anticipate happiness in their possession. Yet if they would listen to the wisdom of heaven, they could not fail to learn that all this is a delusive hope, sure to lead to bitter disappointment. The mercy of God has given us the Gospel, to warn us before it is too late. For here we learn the doctrine of truth and the rules of duty. We find ourselves destined to an endless existence of happiness or misery. We are told to connect the present with the future in the most extended sense, because the true future is not confined to the little round of mortality, but embraces the vast sphere of being which lies beyond the grave. We are taught that real happiness consists in securing the permanent bliss of an eternal life, and that we must never seek to indulge the body at the peril of the soul. And finally, we are led to submit ourselves in all things to that divine Redeemer, whom the love of God has sent to be the Saviour of the world; repenting of our sins, believing in His word, trusting in His promise, depending on His power, and rejecting all that would draw us aside from His unerring guidance and direction. Now then, we can rejoice in the hope of true and permanent felicity. Now we are freed from every danger of disappointment, and safe from all illusion. Now we are confident that our happiness will prove to be, not like the transient meteor which dazzles for a little while, and then goes out in darkness, but "like the shining light, which shineth more and more, unto the perfect day."

To this true theory of happiness, therefore, I have endeavored to conform my views, on the rights and duties of the American citizen, because it is the only one which is worthy of reliance. It is the same Creator who has implanted in every heart the desire and hope of happiness, and has also provided the means by which alone they can be fulfilled. Would it be consistent with His benevolence to bestow the hope, if He did not likewise bestow the power to accomplish it? Do we not see how graciously His wisdom has adapted their appropriate enjoyments to all the senses of the body; and would He fail to adapt, with yet more marvellous skill, the means of happiness to the spiritual faculties of the soul? Surely not. The very supposition is a pure absurdity, and involves a foul reproach against the goodness and the justice of the Almighty.

It is true, however, that some men suppose it possible to secure the hope of happiness, by what they are pleased to call, the religion of nature, or reason, *without a divine Revelation.* The Christian, on the contrary, relies on reason, TAUGHT BY REVELATION. For the Gospel system does not dispense with reason, much less is it opposed to reason, as the unhappy infidel would fain believe. The Creator would not have endowed us with intellectual power, if He did not require us to use it. His appeals are therefore all addressed to our reason. His very language is, "Come now, and let us reason together."* Hence, the revelation of the Scriptures is in perfect harmony with enlightened reason; and does not present a single principle of faith or conduct, which that admirable faculty cannot fully approve, as soon as it is rightly apprehended.

The practical question at issue between the unbeliever and the Christian may easily be tested by experience. If reason, without revelation, can make men happy, let us find some examples of the fact. Where is the solitary instance of a human being, who has tried this plan successfully? We may search throughout the world, from its princes, its nobles, its statesmen, its opulent merchants, its proud possessors of all that wealth and fashion can bestow, down to its lowest classes of the laborers and the poor; and we shall not be able to point out a single mortal who has attained happiness, independent of revealed religion. It is impossible. The gayest heart amongst them is often shrouded in gloom. The liveliest mind amongst them is often filled with secret discontent and repining. The man may deceive himself for a while, in the excitement of social mirth and artificial pleasure. He may be surrounded by every aid of earthly luxury. He may have gained the topmost pinnacle of fame and reputation. Every object of human hope may seem to have been reached, and the cup of his prosperity may be filled to overflowing. But in the midst of it all, there is a dark void within. His spiritual nature yearns after happiness, and yearns in vain. His pleasures cloy by repetition. Society grows wearisome. Solitude brings no relief. Friendship and love pass away with every

* Isaiah, i. 18.

other youthful illusion. In due time, the body itself gives tokens of decay. The senses lose their keenness. Weakness and pain force him to think of the hour of dissolution. What can his untaught reason tell him of the conditions on which he may look for happiness beyond the grave? What promise can it give, that the future shall be less wretched than the past? What security can it afford against the peril of the divine judgment, upon his life of sin and selfish sensuality? What SAVIOUR can it set forth, from the sentence of condemnation? Reason, uninstructed by revelation, has no light to shed upon the darkness of the grave. And hence, the miserable man sits face to face with death, deserted by all human aid, beyond the reach of human consolation, in doubt, in distraction, or in sullen despair,—a melancholy proof that there is no real happiness in the widest range of earthly wealth, honor, and enjoyment, without the hope of true religion in the soul.

Let us next turn to the other class, who seek for happiness in reason, guided by divine revelation—namely, the class of sincere and consistent Christians. What is their experience? With one voice they declare that they have found the prize of life; that religion has given them what the whole world could not bestow. And this acknowledgment is the same, under all the variety of outward circumstances. Whether rich or poor, learned or ignorant, healthy or diseased, young or old, honored or unregarded, they all repeat the same evidence of the power of divine truth to make them happy. For, the dark void, which lies within the depths of the unbeliever's soul, is illuminated by the Christian's faith with the sure hope of immortality. Worldly prosperity cannot dazzle, nor worldly pleasure delude, nor worldly fame intoxicate; because he looks beyond them all to the enjoyment of life eternal. Disappointments, trials, losses, bereavements, may spread gloom over his earthly lot; but he knows that this gloom is only for a season; and the light within shines yet more brightly, like the rainbow in the storm-cloud which is soon to pass away. And when the end of his mortal course approaches, and he, too, sits face to face with death, his happiness is brought nearer to its consummation; for it is his blessed privilege to say, "Even so, Lord Jesus, come quickly. Though my flesh and my heart fail, yet God is the strength of my heart, and my portion forever." And thus he is able to rejoice in the sure felicity which awaits him; and to welcome the last conflict, which the love of his divine Redeemer has converted into victory.

This, therefore, is the way of real happiness, and there is no other. For God is the only source of happiness, as He is the only source of life. In the beginning He formed the body of man, and made it capable of a certain range of enjoyment, and supplied it with the means by which this enjoyment might be lawfully secured, in the objects of the senses. He also formed the soul in His own likeness, and made it capable of reflecting His attributes, and of holding communion with Himself, in which communion consisted its appropriate felicity. Thus the happiness of man was complete; because the body and the soul were in possession of all which was designed for their respective constitutions. But sin and rebellion provoked the divine sentence, which cast down our race from its high original estate, and doomed it to wretchedness and death, though not without a promise of mercy. Hence the Son of God became incarnate, that He might atone for our guilt, raise up the soul from its misery and degradation, and restore to it the happiness for which it was created. If it will not accept that happiness, there is no other possible. The body may use it as its slave. The delights of sensual gratification may surround it. The soul may drudge through life to invest those pleasures with all its intellectual powers, and give the highest dignity to the honor, pride, and luxury of this lower world; but it never can be happy in things like these, because, by the very constitution of its being, they are wholly incapable of supplying the wants and satisfying the desires of its own spiritual nature. And, even were it otherwise, death is at hand to sweep them all away.

The manifestation of this essential truth, however, although it can be fully demonstrated by the general experience of our race, may, perhaps, be better impressed on some minds by recent individual examples. Let us look, then, at the late Duke of Wellington, who combined all the elements of earthly felicity beyond any other personage of his day, in rank, honor, and wealth—in a fame which filled the world, and a popularity with all classes which has rarely been equalled. Yet this eminent man, for many years before his death, was distinguished as a constant Christian. I have seen him among the earliest to enter the Royal Chapel of St. James in London; and counted it a privilege to behold such an illustrious example of simple, devout, and, to all appearance, humble piety.

A similar instance was displayed by our own President Jackson, the hero of New Orleans, the favorite of the nation, distinguished for those qualities of intellectual force and commanding superiority, which were little likely to become associated, in public opinion, with a religious profession. Yet he, too, after his retirement from office, paid open homage to the great truth, that real happiness could only be found in the immortal hope of the Gospel.

Another example was given by that most eminent statesman, orator, and patriot, Henry Clay; who, in the midst of universal honor, won by a long career of extraordinary success and popularity, applied for the privilege of Christian Baptism, and gave his testimony to the same essential principle.

A volume might be filled with proofs of a similar kind, but I forbear, because it is unnecessary. Suffice it to say, that as this is the only foundation on which we can rest the *hope of happiness*, even so it is the only true basis for the *claims of right*, or the *rules of duty*. No other system but that of CHRISTIAN TRUTH can embrace the whole interests of man, in every office, condition, and relation of humanity. No other can secure the prosperity of the nation, the permanency of the Union, the safety of each separate Government, the peace of the community, and the welfare of the individual. No other can provide for the best privileges of the present life, in connection with the infinite felicity of the life to come.

Yet there is no aspect of our age and country so painfully and alarmingly forced on every thoughtful observer, as the careless and callous indifference of men, in general, towards this essential knowledge. There is no peril to which the American citizen and the American nation stand exposed, which threatens them with such serious and even fatal results, as the increasing spirit of religious infidelity. The fruits of the growing pestilence are already sadly manifest, in the progress of internal strife and fierce opposition—in the violent disruption of the old parties, and the hasty formation of the new—in the shameless irreverence displayed towards the Constitution—in the growing contempt for law and order—in the disposition to spurn the counsels of age and experience, and thrust the young, the forward, and the rash, into the highest ranks of office and of honor; and in the reckless energy which rushes on to its proposed end, without pausing to reflect upon the probable consequences. In natural connection with all these public evils, we see the corresponding indulgence of passionate resentments in private life. The word and the blow, followed by the dirk and the revolver, are more and more frequent in society. Self-will and proud insubordination are more and more abundant, in the family and the school. Authority of every kind, whether parental, official, or magisterial, is more and more despised. And the whole tendency of the times seems downward, to anarchy and confusion.

But still, notwithstanding these strong grounds of discouragement, I look to the future in the spirit of hope. I cannot consent to despair of the Union. The sun in the heavens never shone upon a nobler territory, since the fall of man, than the hand of Providence has given us for our heritage. The intellect of mortals never framed a nobler Constitution than the Almighty Governor of the Universe has committed to our care. And the qualities of our native population are so admirably adapted for the highest grade of excellence and influence amongst the nations of the earth, that they afford the best material for the predictions of patriotism and the zeal of philanthropy. With a people so privileged, it would seem that truth could never fail to find some favorable auditors; and that no labor honestly designed to raise the standard of principle, and the motives of action, could be altogether in vain.

For here, we have united, under the same free Government, the various races of the world, with few exceptions; while the Anglo-Saxon blood and temperament largely predominate, and must, eventually, impart a certain harmony to the whole; derived not only from the power of hereditary descent, but from the prevalence of the English language, laws, literature, and forms of religion. The peculiar circumstances which mark our institutions and our advancement, give an impulse and an energy to individual action, which are well adapted to the fullest development of character; since there is less to check, and more to stimulate, than can be found in any other nation on the globe. We are pledged to work out the most important problem of humanity, by a triumphant demonstration of the superior privileges which the great body of the people can attain, when they are obliged to govern themselves. The experiment has never been tried on so vast a field, with a Constitution of such singular wisdom, and under such conditions of unequalled prosperity. The hopes and best wishes of the masses are on our side, throughout all the civilized world; and the fears and interests of kings, nobles, and hereditary aristocrats are naturally and necessarily against us. Nor can we blame them for this, because they have no faith in the possibility of our success. Their own education, their experience, their habits, all concur with the voice of history to prove, as they suppose, that our republican system must fall to pieces, and perish. They anticipate the inevitable certainty of our disunion. They believe that the broken fragments of our grand confederation will cast aside the Utopian theory of equal rights, and assume the old, established, and only practicable form of monarchy. And hence, these two great parties—the people and their rulers—are looking to our country, from every quarter of

Europe, with such intense solicitude, that I doubt whether any empire, of ancient or modern times, has ever enlisted the same extent of influence upon the sympathies and the interests of mankind.

For these reasons, I cannot but regard the position of the American citizen as pre-eminent in responsibility. The title of citizen is invested with great importance under every government; but under ours, it rises to a height of estimation which was never known before. Every man, therefore, who bears that title, and has intelligence enough to understand its relations, should give himself thoughtfully and earnestly to the study of his RIGHTS AND DUTIES; in order that he may perform his share of the vast work which the nation is bound to accomplish, not only for itself, but for the world. He should remember that, in this nation, he is *a sovereign amongst sovereigns*, since there is no human power above the people. He should reverence the laws, because they are the appointed instrument of the government which the people have established. He should venerate the Constitution as the *supreme law* of the land, which binds together all the parts of the mighty whole. He should do open homage to RELIGION, without which neither the Constitution nor the laws can have any practical efficiency; and he should take Christianity into his heart as the only hope of his personal happiness. He should guard the UNION with his utmost vigilance, and frown upon every attempt, under whatever pretext, to weaken that only foundation of honest patriotism. He should faithfully fulfil the various relations of his business, and of domestic and social life; and inculcate the same course of consistent obligation on all around him. And thus he will be an example of the civic character, demanded by the true theory of our noble republic; and do his part towards the grand result which shall not only convince the nations in due time of its excellence and its stability, but raise the title of AMERICAN CITIZEN, under the favor of divine Providence, to the loftiest rank of universal confidence and honor.

As a faithful contribution to that glorious end, I lay my humble volume before the candid and the thoughtful; aspiring to no praise, but that of sober usefulness. I can only say, that it has been written without regard to party, or popular prejudice—conscientiously, as becomes a Christian—frankly, as becomes a freeman; and with an honest desire to strengthen, by the simple force of truth, the best and highest interests of our Country. The work is done. May it be accepted, under the divine favor, as an auxiliary, in promoting the spirit of unity and peace throughout the land, and in advancing the sacred principles of sound morality, public patriotism, and private virtue.

THE END.

www.ingramcontent.com/pod-product-compliance
Lightning Source LLC
LaVergne TN
LVHW021124110826
845150LV00005B/942